Contemporary British Television Crime Drama

Contemporary British Television Crime Drama examines one of the medium's most popular genres and places it within its historical and industrial context. The television crime drama has proved itself capable of numerous generic reinventions and continues to enjoy some of the highest viewing figures. Crime drama offers audiences stories of right and wrong, moral authority asserted and resisted, and professionals and criminals, doing so in ways that are often highly entertaining, innovative, and thought provoking. In examining the appeal of this highly dynamic genre, this volume explores how it responds not only to changing social debates on crime and policing, but also to processes of hybridization within the television industry itself. Contributors, many of whom are leading figures in UK television studies, analyse popular series such as *Broadchurch*, *Between the Lines*, *Foyle's War*, *Poirot*, *Prime Suspect*, *Sherlock* and *Wallander*. Chapters examine the main characteristics of television crime drama production, including the nature of trans-Atlantic franchises and literary and transnational adaptations. Adopting a range of feminist, historical, aesthetic and industrial approaches, they offer incisive interrogations that provide readers with a rich understanding of the allure of crime drama to both viewers and commissioners.

Ruth McElroy is a Reader in Media and Cultural Studies at the University of South Wales, United Kingdom. She is editor, with Stephen Lacey, of *Life on Mars: From Manchester to New York*, (2012), University of Wales Press. She currently leads an Arts and Humanities Research Council funded international network on Television in Small Nations.

Routledge Advances in Television Studies

Contemporary British Television Crime Drama

Cops on the Box

Edited by Ruth McElroy

Routledge
Taylor & Francis Group
LONDON AND NEW YORK

First published 2017 by Routledge

2 Park Square, Milton Park, Abingdon, Oxfordshire OX14 4RN
52 Vanderbilt Avenue, New York, NY 10017

Routledge is an imprint of the Taylor & Francis Group, an informa business

First issued in paperback 2019

British Library Cataloguing-in-Publication Data
A catalogue record for this book is available from the British Library

Library of Congress Cataloging-in-Publication Data
Names: McElroy, Ruth editor.
Title: Contemporary British television crime drama: cops on the box / edited by Ruth McElroy.
Description: New York; London: Routledge, 2016. | Series: Routledge advances in television studies; 7 | Includes bibliographical references and index.
Identifiers: LCCN 2016025061
Subjects: LCSH: Detective and mystery television programs—Great Britain—History and criticism. | Television cop shows—Great Britain—History and criticism. | Crime on television.
Classification: LCC PN1992.8.D48 C66 2016 | DDC 791.45/6556—dc23
LC record available at https://lccn.loc.gov/2016025061

ISBN: 978-1-4724-5493-5 (hbk)
ISBN: 978-0-367-88101-6 (pbk)

Typeset in Sabon
by codeMantra

Contents

PART III
Exporting and Adapting Crime

Foreword

Jonathan Nichols-Pethick

The crime drama has been a staple of television across the globe for about as long as there has been television. The reason is obvious: stories about crime and detection are natural fits for a medium that requires a constant supply of drama. The police (like doctors and lawyers) make life and death decisions and the movement from crime to punishment – from order to disorder and back again – is tailor-made for the narrative needs of any medium.

And yet, the television crime drama hasn't always enjoyed the kind of critical reflection and attention that such a tradition might warrant. Writing about the police drama, for instance, has been, over the years, reserved largely for either proclamations of 'quality' (read as 'realism' or a certain 'novelistic' or 'cinematic' aesthetic), or critical considerations of ideological power working in one direction: the hegemonic pull of consensus and a law-and-order status quo. At their worst, crime series have been seen as ultimately condoning conservative social policies and offering pernicious views of marginalized citizens. In this view, representations of the daily work of policing and detection, enacted by a beleaguered force of men and women charged with maintaining some semblance of social order in the face of constant transgression, offers temporary (and troubling) solace for a society under threat. At their best, some of these series have simply been seen as aesthetic accomplishments, well-meaning if ultimately too tied to the genre's preoccupations with justice to really do anything but hint at the possibilities of a critically progressive text. These early approaches to the crime series, while resulting in a great deal of excellent work, imposed a somewhat rigid critical apparatus on the genre.

One particular exception to this trend is Julie D'Acci's groundbreaking 1994 book, *Defining Women: Television and the Case of Cagney and Lacey.* Bringing together astute textual analysis, with grounded institutional analysis and audience research, D'Acci set the stage for understanding how the crime series could be understood as a complex product of political ambition tempered by social and institutional pressures. And these products change over time under different sets of pressures. Writing in 1998, Charlotte Brunsdon pointed to a 'structure of anxiety' that set British police series of the 1980s and 1990s apart from their predecessors of the 1960s and 1970s. This critical perspective highlighted the ways in which the police series as a generic concern could be seen as what Jason Mittell would later call a 'cultural category'. Cultural categories are flexible and necessarily accommodate changes in structure and meaning. They are categories that are forged (always temporarily) under pressure. D'Acci's, Brunsdon's and Mittell's work (as just three among many examples from this time) underscored the discursive structures of genres rather than purely textual issues – the idea that our understanding of a genre is tied more to larger social and institutional relationships than to anything necessarily inherent in the text. Of course, there are textual features (police series need police, though the degree to which they are central to the narrative might be a point of differentiation among series), but a discursive approach highlights contextual determinants of textual meanings.

The current volume takes up this discursive approach and applies it to the contemporary British crime drama. Ruth McElroy and her excellent contributors do important cultural work, expanding our understanding of the genre, illustrating its ability to accommodate a wide range of perspectives in tension with one another. McElroy has put together a collection of essays that, taken together, provide an excellent example of what Jonathan Gray and Amanda Lotz (2012) argue constitute television studies: work that understands television as a whole – and, in this case, the crime series in particular – as a complex set of cultural, social, political, industrial and aesthetic practices that 'conceives television as a repository for meanings and a site where cultural values are articulated' (p. 22). This collection brings together questions of text, industry, audience, and social context to delve deeply – and deftly – into the elements that currently animate the genre and provide a way for readers to move past the simple and limiting question of quality, whether aesthetic or ideological.

Contemporary British Television Crime Drama is an important addition to the growing literature on the television crime series. Not only does it fill a hole in the literature on British television crime series, it serves as a lively and useful primer on the range of critical possibilities for studying contemporary television drama. The contributors here comprise a conceptually and methodologically diverse array of critical approaches that highlight and compliment the array of aesthetic, narrative and political possibilities of the British television crime drama. I sincerely hope and strongly suspect that Ruth McElroy's collection will inspire a great deal more excellent work like this in the future.

References

Brunsdon, C., 1998. Structure of anxiety: recent British television crime fiction. *Screen*, 39 (3), pp. 223–43.

D'Acci, J., 1994. *Defining Women: Television and the Case of Cagney and Lacey.* Chapel Hill, NC: University of North Carolina Press.

Gray, J. and Lotz, A., 2012. *Television Studies.* Malden, MA: Polity Press.

Mittell, J., 2004. *Genre and Television: From Cops Shows to Cartoons in American Culture.* New York, NY: Routledge.

Acknowledgements

My main thanks are due to the contributors who have worked patiently and carefully to produce their chapters. It's been a treat to share our enthusiasm for television crime drama. The idea for this collection emerged partly from a conference, Cops on the Box, held at the University of South Wales (formerly the University of Glamorgan) in March 2013. I would like to extend my sincere thanks to everyone who took part in that day's discussions. Thanks to Rebecca Spear for her editorial assistance in preparing the manuscript and to Ann Donahue at Ashgate for her early support of the proposal. I would also like to record my appreciation of the helpful comments made by the peer reviewers of both the proposal and final manuscript. I gratefully acknowledge the small grant from the Creative Industries Research Institute at the University of South Wales, which helped provide time to undertake editorial work.

Television remains for most of us a social activity so I would like to acknowledge all those with whom I regularly watch and discuss television: my first year students on Contemporary Popular Television, my expert television colleagues at the University of South Wales, Martin Willis for persuading me to buy a new TV during the writing of this collection, and my late mother, Hazel McElroy, who amongst other things taught me how to enjoy taking television drama seriously.

Introduction

Ruth McElroy

In contemporary Britain, it is a rare thing indeed for a week's television schedule not to include several crime dramas in prime time. Cops, and other criminal investigators, seem always to be on the box. This collection makes a claim for the significance and distinctiveness of British television crime drama, offering original and insightful essays that reveal the sheer breadth of this popular genre on British screens. Crime dramas are some of the most viewed programmes in UK television, regularly appearing in the British Audience Research Board (BARB) Top 20 programmes. The genre's contribution to the UK industry is also evident from the number of crime drama nominations in the 2015 British Academy of Film and Television Arts (BAFTA) awards including under the categories of Best Leading Actor, Best Leading Actress, Best Supporting Actor, Best Supporting Actress and Best Television Drama Series, Best Director (Fiction), Best Editing (Fiction), and Best Writer. Crime drama is one of British television's longest-lasting, most popular forms, and one that has proved itself capable of numerous generic reinventions. It merits critical attention because it is one of the most important places where ideas of justice, transgression, retribution and civic life are represented and contested. Crime drama offers audiences stories of right and wrong, moral authority asserted and resisted, professionals and criminals, and does so in ways that are often highly entertaining, innovative and thought-provoking. For many television scholars (Corner, 1999; Ellis, 1999; Henderson, 2007; Newcomb and Hirsch, 1983), it is the medium's responsiveness to the social world – its ability to bring the anxieties of public debate into the private realm of the home through *both* factual *and* fictional forms – that marks television's unique purchase on the social world. The fictional narratives of television crime drama are not only entertaining, they also provide our culture with a place to explore social anxieties, new social relations and often deeply troubling instances of social breakdown and violence. Crime drama is a highly dynamic genre, responsive not only to changing social debates on crime and policing, but also to processes of hybridisation within the television industry itself. The rise of forensic crime dramas, ranging from home-grown series such as *Silent Witness* (1996–) and *Waking the Dead* (2000–11) to popular US imports such as *CSI: Crime Scene Investigation* (2000–15) and *Bones* (2005–), is testament to crime drama's capacity to adopt and adapt elements of the medical drama to its own generic concerns. In the United Kingdom, historical crime drama also holds considerable popular appeal, both as adaptations of literary classics such as Agatha Christie's *Poirot* (1989–2013) and *Miss Marple* (1984–92), and as fictionalised accounts of detection set in the past such as *Foyle's War* (2002–15), *Inspector George Gently* (2007–) and *Grantchester* (2014–). Nonetheless, a great deal of contemporary crime drama is based on the police procedural, a distinct form that aims to offer viewers a privileged insight into the daily workings of the police force. This subgenre allows for significant character development as we, the audience, get to know the police officers and their domestic as well as professional lives. However, the allure of the police procedural rests on its claim to authenticity delivered via the detailed procedures which emerge through the police investigation; the police procedural appeals through its seemingly democratic offer to take us, as viewers, inside a policing world that is largely remote and unknown to members of the public so that we too can get to know the system and how it works. It is simultaneously transgressive – crossing the thresholds of professional insider knowledge – and conservative, as it reinforces the privileged insights and authority of the police force. It is this tension which has been developed and exploited in many recent instances of the subgenre, such as *Broadchurch* (2013–), *The Killing* (2011–12) and *Line of Duty* (2012–).

Understanding the appeal of the crime drama genre – to viewers, commissioners, producers, and critics – is an important part of this collection's concern. The collection rejects a limited understanding of genre as solely the textual components of a fictional form in order, instead, to attend to the broad discursive relationships which shape the genre's production and reception. Of particular note here, is an emerging discourse of value surrounding British crime drama, with talk of a new 'golden age' of crime appearing in both scholarly and popular media analyses. This collection is very much in dialogue with other recent scholarly interventions in the genre's analysis including Jonathan Nichols-Pethick's *TV Cops: The Contemporary American Television Police Drama* (2012), Helen Piper's *The TV Detective* (2015) and Sue Turnbull's *The Television Crime Drama* (2014). Having traditionally been regarded as a rather plodding, conservative and predictable genre that pulls in the viewers, crime drama is enjoying something of a critical renaissance with much more cultural value now being attached to the genre's capacity for original storytelling. In a piece on 'a new golden age of crime' on BBC Radio 4's *Today* programme in March 2013, for example, Ben Stephenson, then BBC Drama Controller reflected on the genre saying that:

> [In the] classic British formula someone dies and you find out in the end who did it. Agatha Christie is a mistress of that and crime is a fantastic way of telling gripping stories. But that then allows you to go into any world and, of course, the thing about all those dramas that we love, whether it's *Broadchurch*, *Homeland*, *Line of Duty*, or *Top*

of the Lake is they take you into an extraordinary world. So the police corruption in a way is obviously more vital than to *Line of Duty* than the whodunit element. The backdrop in *Broadchurch* or *Top of the Lake* it's about community. So I think it is a modern reinvention of a fantastically traditional way of telling stories … And in terms of influences? I think it's about classic BBC 2 shows like *Edge of Darkness, Boys from the Blackstuff* and I hope that shows like *Line of Duty* and *Top of the Lake* will be remembered in the future.

At least two elements of this critical discourse stand out. The first is the way in which contemporary crime drama is seen to marry narrative power with social revelation, exemplified here by the 'extraordinary world' and 'community' which the fiction uncovers before our very eyes. The second is the discourse of tradition being used here. Contemporary British television crime drama both enjoys the kudos of Christie and is aligned with some now canonical instances of television history, exemplified here by the comparison with the classic 1980s BBC series *Edge of Darkness* (1985) and *Boys from the Blackstuff* (1982). In this way, crime drama can be seen *simultaneously* as edgy and original on the one hand, and traditional and critically respectable on the other. This book's principal aim, then, is to examine the particular nature, appeal and status of crime drama in contemporary British television. In doing so, it provides the reader with engaging resources for thinking critically about this hugely diverse and dynamic genre at a moment in its history when it is enjoying considerable popular and critical attention.

Media and Crime

The academic study of both media and culture has long been concerned with how the media reports and represents crime and how, in turn, this may shape our perceptions of criminality, punishment and the judicial system. One very striking example of this concern is nonetheless to be found in the media itself in the reports of what came to be termed, 'the CSI effect.' As Dowler et al. (2006) explain:

> the expression 'the CSI Effect' has been bandied about by such media outlets as CNN, *National Geographic, USA Today,* CBS News, and *US News and World Report*. Simply put, the CSI Effect relates to the popularity of *CSI, Criminal Minds, Crossing Jordan*, and other programs that portray scientific and forensic evidence-gathering procedures to catch criminals; the 'effect' is the rise in expectations of real-life crime victims and jury members. Prosecutors lament the fact that they have to supply more forensic evidence because jurors expect this type of evidence, having seen it on television. Of course, academic studies have yet to reveal the extent of this effect; at the time of this writing, there are no studies that show it to be genuine.

For those of us interested in television crime drama, the assumption that cop shows should directly reflect reality in a purely informational mode is missing the point. This popular but academically limited approach to assessing the relationship between media and crime rests on a too easy correlation between media representation and social reality. Fiction is a lot richer than a mirror; much more is going on than mere reflection when we watch crime drama. A more sophisticated approach to thinking about this relationship can be found in an older literature which emerged in the 1970s, and which has had an enormous impact on shaping the discourse on media and crime since. Key publications here are Stanley Cohen and Jock Young's *The Manufacture of News: Deviance, Social Problems and the Mass Media* (1973) and Stuart Hall, Chas Critcher, Tony Jefferson, John N. Clarke and Brian Roberts' landmark *Policing the Crisis: Mugging, the State, and Law and Order* (1978).

Hall et al.'s project began with an attempt to understand how a specific crime – mugging – came into existence during the 1970s. Violent robbery on the streets was not new; records of such criminal behaviour date back to at least the eighteenth century. However, during the early 1970s, there was a proliferation of discourse and imagery in both the media and Parliament about 'muggings', with reports of a huge increase in this crime eliciting fear and panic. Importantly, mugging came to be associated with young black men in Britain, many of whom reported being stopped by police seemingly without cause. The mugger, a figure largely imported from the United States, became a kind of folk devil at whose door a whole host of diverse social ills could be placed. Yet even as mugging was being talked about widely in these spheres, the crime of mugging did not exist; it was not a crime as defined by the legal system. The discourse of mugging could not, then, be understood as simply a reflection of a crime on the increase; instead, it seemed to be linked to much wider fears in society. For Hall et al. these fears characterised a crisis of late capitalism in which the police force came, ideologically, to appear as the guardians of social order at a time of social fragmentation. Behind the powerful imagery of 'violent hoodlums' (the precursors, perhaps, of today's hoodie), lay complex social, economic and political conflicts in post-industrial and post-imperial British society. The representation of the black mugger as a transgressive embodiment of social disorder itself revealed the racial tensions at play in British society at the time. Why, almost 40 years on, does this book still hold such significance for the study of media and crime? The answer rests partly on Hall et al.'s concern to untangle the complex ways in which the language and imagery of crime – its mediation – works ideologically to construct social crises. The moral panic elicited by the mediation of mugging as a crime, forged not in law but in popular discourse, reveals the power of representations of crime in popular culture and the complex ways in which they work to affirm the authority of institutions such as the police force, the judicial system, and the state itself.

Crime then has a history of providing fruitful material for the media, and our fascination with crime in popular culture is long standing. Indeed, the history of the novel has been closely tied to evolving narrative structures that probe the lives of criminals, the underworld and those detectives who seek to unmask them. Sex sells, as Daniel Defoe knew when writing *Moll Flanders*, the tale of a female criminal and miscreant who titillates and appals the reader in equal, ironic measure. The lovability of the criminal rogue, the arousal and deferral of readerly desires, and the re-establishment of moral and social order can all be seen in this early crime narrative. Moreover, it was precisely the proximity of the novel to the dark, transgressive world of crime, which led early critics to regard the novel form as itself dangerous – threatening to corrupt not just the moral values of social order, but the good nature of readers themselves.

Crime stories are narratives of transgression; they are important to the social imaginary and to the role narrative and imagination play in human life. However, certain kinds of crime – most especially violent and sexual crime – have long been more prominent in popular culture than others which seem to hold less visceral appeal. The enduring mythology surrounding Jack the Ripper is perhaps one of the best examples of this phenomenon. As Darren Oldridge has argued, 'the Whitechapel murders of 1888 were, above all, a media event' (2007, p. 46) and their enduring legacy has been the prolific continuation of what we might term Ripperology, of which ITV's crime drama *Whitechapel* (2009–13), discussed by Rebecca Williams in this collection, is but one instance. That Jack the Ripper – an unknown, unidentified criminal who was never caught, and who may or may not have committed one, or many, crimes in London's East End in the late 1880s – can still fascinate audiences today rests largely on the cultural power of narrative and the inventive storytelling of both the press and television industries. Jack the Ripper's story laid the groundwork for subsequent narratives of serial murder (Warwick, 2007) and exemplified how the reporting techniques of the press could transform a diffuse, and quite possibly unrelated, set of actual crimes into a coherent, frightening and gripping story of urban detection and transgression.

Mediated Crime: Fact and Fiction

Whilst much can be gleaned from analyses of news media's crime reporting, there are important differences between understanding the production, narrative construction and meanings of crime in the news as opposed to crime drama. Perhaps the most obvious difference is that between factual and fictional narrative. Here, I want to reflect on this distinction both to uphold it as a valuable organisational and interpretative tool and, at the same time, to suggest that absolute distinctions between fact and fiction do not hold good when reading television crime drama in its historical and cultural contexts. The desire to inform and to entertain are not polar opposites but coexistent imperatives that work centrifugally and centripetally, sometimes drawing together, sometimes pulling apart. Historically, much factual news reporting of crime drew on narrative devices that deliberately aimed to increase the entertaining appeal of news stories. The new journalism of the late nineteenth century developed sensational headlines, narrated attention-grabbing scenes and thereby sold newspapers. As Karen Roggenkamp has argued, 'urban newspapers felt pressure to create prose that entertained, and the urge to spin attractive and popular tales sometimes came at the expense of factual information. Indeed, most editors and reporters believed, as they still do today, that one could be both entertaining and factual' (2005, p. xii).

Like crime news reporting, television crime drama relies upon the appeal of crime narratives to audiences. Television crime drama now shows us crime news reporting a good deal; the press conference has itself become a staple of the crime drama genre. In a highly mediated society, the police find themselves interrogated and surveyed by the press to such a regular degree that they have specialist press officers to handle their corporate communications (see Cooke and Sturges, 2009; Mawby, 2010). Televisually, this provides us with scenes of conflict as the power of the press is managed and controlled (often unsuccessfully) by the police and their press officers. The fourth estate in action provides a bankable source of drama in contemporary police series. Older amateur sleuths and unofficial detectives, such as Christie's Miss Marple or Hercule Poirot, may not be held publicly or politically accountable via the press, but in the bureaucratic audit cultures of modern society, where politics and policing are often vividly intertwined, the demand that the police themselves be answerable to another, higher authority is an imperative that shapes both factual and fictional account of crime. So what do such press conferences achieve dramatically in the police series?

Firstly, press conferences and the subsequent encounters between investigating teams and journalists show the authority of the police under pressure, as the forces of law and order are probed and questioned by a counter-authority that has an alternative, moral and social sanction. Whilst the police generally retain the upper hand overall, the absolute nature of their authority is repeatedly tested in these scenes and the limits of both their knowledge and their power are revealed. Secondly, the will to know which underscores the investigation is often delayed and complicated through such scenes. For example, alternative suspects may be offered, and misdirections in the plotting provoked, through the questioning of police by journalists. The information gathered by journalists themselves may also be revealed with the effect of countering or complicating what the police know – or think they know – of the crime and its perpetrators. Thirdly, press conferences provide police officers with the opportunity to use the media for their own investigative purposes in ways that draw on both factual and fictional tactics for inspiration (Innes, 1999). For example, they may issue requests for further information on suspects, often accompanied by tearful families who act in ways that directly recall actual press conferences, as seen in television news reporting. Alternatively, the police may release selective information about a crime in which very precise details – the colour of a man's jacket or the exact timing of a sequence of events – are nonetheless concealed. As a plotting device, this is often used to ensnare the guilty culprit who accidentally reveals too much knowledge of the crime and who helplessly tries to defend himself by saying he 'read it in the papers.' Here, the porousness of mediated information and first-hand knowledge is offered, but swiftly resolved in the moment of self-incrimination. Fourthly, the largely conflictual encounters between press and police provide an alluring mode of address to viewers at home who are invited to draw upon their own media literacy – their familiarity with the storytelling power of the press in contemporary society – as part of the professional detection process. Fact and fiction are deliberately blurred here, as we are asked to believe that what we are witnessing is a credible reflection of actual professional practice, both on the part of the police and the press. They are, in other words, mediations of professional practice that seem both to inform us of a professional world few of us will know first-hand and, at the same time, fictional devices in the entertaining narratives of detection.

The agency of the viewer as the detective on the couch is integral to crime drama's generic pleasure and the tantalising possibility it offers that we will work out whodunnit. Like the police, we may find the interruptions and questions of journalists a distraction from this prime narrative drive and, certainly for scriptwriters and directors, they provide a challenge to keep the viewer hooked. Executed well, however, it is precisely the sharing of the press experience between detective and viewer that enriches the drama of the investigation. One of the most elegant examples of this process can be found in the BBC's *Sherlock* (2010–), a series which opened with Conan Doyle's police detective, Inspector Lestrade, fielding questions from a clamorous press corps. Flanked by the authority of the police as embodied by uniformed officers, Lestrade is nonetheless unable to satisfy the journalists' probing. Into this faltering scene of police power comes another voice, unknown yet brutally confident and controlling. To the sound of multiple SMS alerts in the press hall comes a series of texts on-screen, each decrying 'live' the statements being made by the police officers. This innovative rendering of modern life offers viewers a dramatic, transgressive scene in which the power of the police is playfully undone not only by Sherlock Holmes, as the counter-authority to the official police force, but also by the media itself; the very liveness of digital communications explodes the facade of corporate communications control. Thus, Mark Gatiss and Steven Moffat (co-creators of the BBC's *Sherlock*) offer a stylish, amusing, and deeply self-conscious update to Conan Doyle's original text, demonstrating just how the genre's representations of crime and detection respond to changing technological, as well as social, forces.

The Effects and Affects of Crime Drama

In his 1992 monograph, *Television and the Drama of Crime: Moral Tales and the Place of Crime in Public Life*, Richard Sparks concentrates on the 'long and contentious debate (in both academic and 'lay' circles) on the possibility of relations between watching television of this sort and the extent and intensity of public fear and alarm about crime' (1992, p. 1). Sparks' main interest lies in the relationship between cop shows and audiences' own sense of fear and anxiety. In this he was following but also critiquing a long tradition of media audience research going back to George Gerbner's cultivation theory of media influence. Two points stand out despite Sparks' very different starting points. The first is his early insistence on revealing his own uneasy enjoyment of cop shows: 'I have never been a straightforward fan. My pleasure and excitement have long been tinged with unease at what the conditions of my involvement might be and a sense of uncertainty as to the roots of the appeal they held for myself and others' (1992, p. 2).

It is *through* his experience as a viewer that Sparks reveals the complex *emotional* (as opposed to purely rational) response to fictional crime on screen. In so doing, he also reveals something of the sociability and social anxiety of watching television – the uncertainty of how others are viewing and interpreting the same text.

Secondly, as a sociologist of crime and punishment, Sparks argues for the need to reclaim punishment as an 'expressive institution' in which 'passions and social sentiment' are central to the 'public representation of crime and law enforcement' in 'television entertainment.' Here, both emotional and social values come to the fore in the analysis of crime drama as an inherently moral narrative, one that may provoke fear, anxiety and outrage in its viewers. So, whilst Sparks retains an ideological concern with crime fiction's tendency for narrative closure and restoration of order, his approach allows us to understand it as a cultural form that gives voice to a society's stories of passion and sentiment. Thus, he argues that 'crime fiction presupposes an inherent tension between anxiety and reassurance' and it is this which 'constitutes a significant source of its appeal to the viewer' (1992, p. 120).

More recently, Deidre Pribram (2011) has made emotion central to her analysis of film and television fictions of justice, law and order. Emotion, she argues, is central to how popular culture works; how its texts generate and communicate meanings, and why in fact cultural theorists have 'moved toward the analysis of popular culture precisely because it has mass emotional appeal and resonance' (2011, p. 1). Rather than root the analysis of emotion in biology or psychology, Pribram takes a cultural approach that considers: 'emotions as socially shared and historically developed. Borrowing from Raymond Williams, this is to understand emotions as structures of feeling. In this perspective, emotions are not solely individual or inner phenomena but, equally, collective cultural experiences' (2011, p. 2).

Pribram is concerned with how emotion helps frame and maintain ideas of law, justice and injustice and the value of her approach lies in tracing how the representation of the justice system works 'to produce and maintain popular constructions of emotions' so that 'a structure of feeling is constituted through its specific uses.' So, for example, she compares the hit US crime dramas, *CSI* and *The Wire* (HBO, 2002–08). While both series share a narrative concern with the work of law enforcement officers in detecting crime, they differ in the narrative structures of feeling which each evokes; '*CSI* offers the reassuring high gloss of science and technology while a feeling of frustration permeates *The Wire*' (2011, p. 5). Rather than see emotion as the 'problem' with TV crime drama, this approach evidences how emotion is actually central to the genre's meanings and popular appeal, a theme which is taken up in my own chapter in this collection.

Socio-Cultural Readings of TV Crime Drama

Anxiety also looms large in socio-cultural readings of television crime drama and this is clearly exemplified by Charlotte Brunsdon's landmark essay, 'Structure of anxiety: recent British television crime fiction' (1998). It examines how significant police series in the 1980s and 1990s, such as *Inspector Morse* (1987–2000), *Prime Suspect* (1991–2006) and *Between the Lines* (1992–94), came to speak 'very directly to the concerns of a Great Britain in decline under a radical Conservative government with a strong rhetoric of law and order' (1998, p. 223). Brunsdon's analysis is avowedly national and historical in focus, demonstrating how important it is to consider the specific contexts from which individual crime series emerge. This materialist approach has been integral to British cultural studies and accounts for why its analyses of television texts have been undertaken with questions of power and ideology kept firmly in mind. It is worth pausing a moment here to reflect that, whilst one of the most important figures of British cultural studies, Raymond Williams, was indeed the author of the 'structure of feeling' concept, as Pribram above acknowledges, his work was always concerned with understanding feeling as historically produced and situated. Brunsdon's claim that 'the police series in its various mutations ... has been a privileged site for the staging of the trauma of the breakup of the postwar settlement' (1998, p. 223) exemplifies this tradition and its enduring value for understanding the ideological significance of television crime drama as narratives able to engage with, and not merely reflect, the concerns of British society at moments of profound change. This nuance makes a tremendous difference because it helps us retain a clear sense of the dynamism of mediated narratives as cultural texts. As Brunsdon argues, the concern is not with making television crime drama into a literal representation of society, but rather in understanding its cultural value. This means attending to how it

> works over and worries at the anxieties and exclusions of contemporary citizenship, of being British and living here, now. This genre ... has proved so resonant with both producers and audiences because it repeatedly, even obsessively, stages the drama of the responsible citizen caught in the embrace of what increasingly seems an irresponsible State. (1998, p. 225)

It is the very political contemporaneity of television crime drama that is, for Brunsdon, core to its audience appeal.

This kind of thematic, ideological analysis is not the only route into examining the socio-cultural meanings of television crime drama. Another important approach lies in feminist scholars' concerns with detection as a gendered process, one in which the sexual politics of both the police force and the television industry may be discerned. One of the most influential of such studies has been Julie D'Acci's *Defining Women: Television and the Case of Cagney and Lacey* (1994). This was one of the first works to examine the police series' social construction of gender and its representation of both women and competing discourses of femininity in the police procedural. D'Acci's methodology was distinctive in combining textual analysis with detailed observations of the show's production and reception. *Cagney and Lacey* (1981–88) was a US television cop show (transmitted by the BBC in the United Kingdom) set in New York which featured Christine Cagney and Mary Beth Lacey as the titular detectives. Where Cagney was a single woman focussed on her police career and raised in an Irish-American family that had a history of policing New York's streets, Lacey was a wife and mother who often struggled to manage the competing demands of work and home. Today, female detectives abound on British television (McElroy, this collection) so it is all too easy to forget how radical this programme was in placing two women as police leads in prime time. At the time, however, the television industry was deeply anxious about the portrayal of two professional women undertaking traditionally male work and this contributed to CBS's decision to pull the series after its first season. If crime drama is transgressive in its narrative themes, it may also be transgressive in its representation of detectives themselves who, in the case of *Cagney and Lacey*, were seen on the one hand as the stereotypically masculine figures of a dangerous feminist movement and, on the other, as credible, engaging representations of the gendered realities of many women's daily lives. One of the most exciting aspects of television crime drama – its capacity to respond to and work through changing social mores – thus also poses a potential problem for the television industry where change can elicit anxiety in broadcasters eager to retain ratings in a fiercely competitive environment.

In the United Kingdom, *Cagney and Lacey*'s nearest British counterparts were the BBC's *Juliet Bravo* (1980–85) and ITV's *The Gentle Touch* (1980–84) who were, in turn, the precursors of one of the genre's most powerful cop characters, DCI Jane Tennison in Lynda La Plante's BAFTA-award winning, *Prime Suspect*. La Plante is one of the few British women television scriptwriters to have gained significant scholarly attention. In part this may be due to her interest in what might be considered traditionally male genres, including the heist drama, *Widows* (1983; *Widows 2*, 1985), the police procedural, *Prime Suspect*, and the prison drama, *The Governor* (1995–96). In February 2014, La Plante announced her intention to write a prequel novel to *Prime Suspect* with the screen adaptation due to be transmitted in 2016,

25 years after DCI Jane Tennison (Helen Mirren) first appeared on UK tele-vision screens. The resonance of Jane Tennison lies in the historical moment which her on-screen biography captures. The strains and accomplishments of Tennison's job are made visible to the viewer through both the sheer quality of Mirren's performance and through the locations she occupies, from the antagonistic and heated scenes set in the police station from where she runs her investigations, to her interactions with the suspects and victims who she uncovers, sometimes literally in the morgue. Crime costs not just the criminal, but also the detective whose personal life seems often to be shattered by the demands of the job. In her analysis, Deborah Jermyn argues that *Prime Suspect* engages 'critically and consciously with the politics of the "glass ceiling" and the systematic and insidious discrimination that police-women experience' (2003, p. 50). However, Jermyn also notes that it is not purely at the level of narrative that *Prime Suspect* examines the sexual poli-tics of crime, but also through the series' recurrent aesthetic devices. In par-ticular, the camerawork used in the series raises questions of visibility – who is seen, who looks and who is looked at – which brings home to the viewer the relative social invisibility of female victims of sex crimes. The 'insistence on looking, or refusal to look, at women – more specifically at Tennison and the spectacle proffered by the female corpses – is marked as a central motif in *Prime Suspect*'s gendered aesthetics and its investigation of male struc-tures of power' (2003, p. 55). Stylistically, *Prime Suspect* is a key moment in the history of British (and US) crime drama signalling, as it does, a new highly productive concern in series such as *Silent Witness*, *Waking the Dead* and *CSI*, with forensics and the sight of bodily trauma.

Style Matters: Reading the Aesthetics of Crime Drama

How television looks and sounds is a core component of our experience of it; viewers' pleasures are not reducible to social or narrative concerns alone. It is perhaps the genre's sheer ubiquity which has blinded us to the *art* of crime drama and its stylistic accomplishments. The challenge of such a task is considerable, not least because of the range of television crime dramas. These include the forensic crime dramas mentioned above, police proce-durals [e.g., *Broadchurch*; *Law and Order: UK* (2009–); *Lewis* (2007–); *Luther* (2010–15)], adaptations of literary sleuths (e.g., *Miss Marple*; *Poirot*; *Sherlock*), criminal melodrama [e.g., *Midsomer Murders* (1997–); *Death in Paradise* (2011–)], comic crime [e.g., *Babylon* (2014)] and historical crime series [e.g., *Foyle's War*; *Life on Mars* (2006–07); *Whitechapel*; *Ripper Street* (2012–)]. Slippery though the boundaries of these diverse forms are, it is their aural and visual *style* which helps mark out their differences from one another. The transition from the pretitle sequences to the opening theme tune of crime dramas can be especially revealing here, working both to hook the audience and also aurally announce the performance. In the BBC's *Death in Paradise*, for example, the pretitle sequence routinely opens with a tropical location and a group of people, often tourists, going about their business. It culminates in the shocking, yet entirely predictable, murder of one of the group members, often in a quite violent fashion, such as poisoning or stabbing. The camera shows us the corpse in situ before a loud, bright, cheery theme tune of brass and steel drums begins in a rather absurd but alluringly melodramatic clash of joyous sounds and violent death. By way of contrast, the Scandinavian drama *The Bridge* (*Bron/Broen*)'s pretitle sequence plunges us darkly into the complex plot, simultaneously reminding us of what has gone before, whilst also presenting us with new shocks and twists that give us little time for thought or recovery. Here the eerie, haunting theme tune, 'Hollow Talk', sung by Copenhagen's Choir of Young Believers, adds to the series' high-art style as it plays over a lingering and quite beautiful tracking shot of the bridge across Øresund, and the sight of one of the detectives, Saga Norén's, classic olive-green Porsche. Even the credits that appear on screen as the music plays are carefully designed, using a paired down simple font to connote a stylish, clean minimalism.

As Jonathan Bignell has argued in his analysis of style in the police series, the 'mise en scène is highly significant in its literal meaning of where and how the drama is staged' (2009, p. 7). A series' design contributes to its meanings, pleasures and distinctions. The rich, ornate mise en scène of *Poirot*'s art deco interiors, for example, contrast sharply with the functional ordinariness of *Scott and Bailey*'s police station. The pleasures they afford, the meanings they produce, and the performances which they help anchor are all deliberately distinctive in their address to the viewer. At its most dramatic, this stylistic difference may itself take centre stage, as in the closing episode of *Life on Mars* (see Lacey and McElroy, 2012) where DCI Sam Tyler (John Simm) appears to leap from the modern bureaucratic scene of a modern tower-block office and into the more (literally) colourful past of a dynamic 1970s world replete with bright red Ford Escort car and the enigmatic and nostalgic tones of David Bowie.

One of the most suggestive ways in which crime drama's style operates is in creating a sense of place. In recent years, the importance of place to crime drama seems to have grown, and a marked tendency may be discerned (or at least argued for) in both television crime made, and shown, in Britain. For example, recent US imports such as *Homicide: Life on the Street* (1993–99) and *The Wire* have made use of inner-city mise en scène to construct a gritty narrative of Baltimore crime that 'engages what we might call the sociological imagination of crime and corruption in urban America' (Nichols-Pethick, 2012, p. 173). A rather different aesthetic is visible in many of the Scandinavian series to have hit British television screens in recent years. The Nordic noir aesthetic of *The Killing*, for example, draws upon the conventions of the noir film genre and the use, by Danish television producers, of 'colours in the blue and grey end of the scale, climatic elements such as rainy cold autumn days, and bleak urban cityscapes' (Jensen and Waade, 2013). Such aesthetics, borrowed from cinema, use specific 'Nordic imagery' to evoke 'a feeling of melancholy' through the 'landscapes, architecture, colours and light, all of which in combination characterize the Scandinavian crime series as a bestseller and/or blockbuster brand' (ibid.). The distinctive otherness of these Scandinavian settings works intertextually in their reference both to cinematic aesthetics and to popular literary fiction, reminding us that television crime drama often rests on exploiting existing audience interest in crime novels, in this case by writers such as Stieg Larsson, Henning Mankell, Camilla Läckberg and Karin Fossum. The symbiosis between literary and televisual crime aesthetics is also evident closer to home in the rise of British regional crime drama. Examples include *Rebus* (2000–04), the STV series based on Ian Rankin's Edinburgh crime novels; *DCI Banks* (2010–) based on Peter Robinson's Yorkshire police detective, *Shetland,* (2013–) based on Ann Cleeves' novels and *Vera* (2011–) also based on Cleeves' novels and set in the fictional Northumberland and City Police force. The capacity of the crime genre to articulate a sense of place beyond the metropolitan centre of London reflects the distinctly regional organisation of the police forces in England and Wales. England, for example, has close to 40 different police constabularies, whilst Wales, a country of just over three million people, has four separate forces. It also reflects the organisation of the British television industry itself, particularly the regional structure of independent television (ITV) since its establishment in 1955. This is a peculiar characteristic of British broadcasting and one that scholars unfamiliar with the multinational nature of the United Kingdom (a state comprising four nations) overlook. As Johnson and Turnock demonstrate, one of the ways in which ITV was made distinctive from the BBC and its London-centric structure was by setting up ITV 'along regional lines, with licences issued by the ITA [Independent Television Authority] to regional franchises charged with the responsibility of providing programming for that specific region of Britain' (2005, p. 19). The prominence of Yorkshire crime drama is due not only to the success of a novelist like Robinson or a scriptwriter such as Sally Wainwright, but also to the long tradition of drama production by Yorkshire Television. Providing audiences with a sense of place is one way in which regional television producers can create visual distinction in the crowded marketplace of television crime drama.

Stylistically, the prominence of British landscapes in British contemporary crime drama is striking. Viewers are frequently offered lingering, photographic images of landscapes and seascapes, many of which are beautiful and meditative in their composition and editing. Series such as *Broadchurch*, *Shetland*, *Vera* and the bilingual crime drama, *Y Gwyll/Hinterland* (2013–) appear to take inspiration from other television genres, most notably geographic television as exemplified by the hugely successful BBC series, *Coast* (2005–). As Helen Wheatley (2011) has argued, the proliferation of spectacular landscapes in such programmes is made possible by technological developments such as high definition filming, which deliver substantial improvements to the quality of landscape photography on offer to viewers who, in turn, are now more likely to be watching on flat-screen digital tele-visions. When television crime drama offers us such shots it achieves three things; firstly, it invites us in to appreciate and dwell on the stylishness of its representation of a specific British place, thereby setting the scene for the criminal action and detection; secondly, it sets the tone for the series, offer-ing us a kind of photographic mood board for the series overall; and thirdly, it establishes a sense of place that can address the requirement for Public Service Broadcasters (PSBs) to represent the diversity of the UK's regions and nations on screen, while also providing a distinctive British landscape signature for export.

As Bignell (2009) argues, one objective of working on style is to help identify its function in the ideology of the police series. Bignell is concerned, not only with analysing how style contributes to the structural conventions of the genre (its movement from the enigma of the crime through its detec-tion towards resolution), but also to understand how this ideological oper-ation works in the context of television's own disposition towards linear storytelling. Television narratives need always to be realised within the con-straints of the television schedule. Attention to the style of police series thus reveals something of the industrial contexts in which they are produced:

> Thus the ideological work of solving crimes is mapped onto a tem-poral structure characterised by linear progression towards a conclu-sion, and onto an institutional structure determined by the funding of network programming by spot advertising. Style, especially its rapid definition early in a programme as a marker of the programme's dis-tinctive identity and continuity across commercial breaks, becomes a kind of glue, a differentiating marker, an ideological function and a unifying mechanism for the one-hour episodic form of television police series... (2009, p. 6)

Making Crime Drama: What Cops Do for Television

Television is an industry and the programmes it makes need to be under-stood as the products of a complex – increasingly global – production sys-tem. Bignell's concern with the industrial production of the police series is shared by Nichols-Pethick (2012) whose study of US police drama argues carefully for the need to attend to the industrial contexts of the genre's pro-duction. This entails going beyond text-based, ideological assessments of the genre and its supposedly formulaic conservatism (bluntly put, the tendency for the forces of law to triumph and restore social order as criminals are caught, exposed and punished). Instead, we might ask, what does crime drama do for the UK television industry? What scheduling, branding, and marketing opportunities does the genre afford?

We need to begin by recognising the dynamic nature of the contemporary television industry. Increasingly operating in an international marketplace,

British television has been transformed by the rise of both the multichannel and the increasingly converged landscape of digital television. Where PSBs once competed only with each other, today they compete with hundreds of channels delivered to viewers via satellite, cable, digital providers and on-demand Internet providers that are far less regulated in content. This is a step-change from the PSB environment in which the British crime drama (*Dixon of Dock Green*, BBC, 1955–76; *Z Cars*, ITV, 1962–68) has its roots. Gaining, building and maintaining an audience has become more complex and, arguably, more important for PSBs (and it *is* they who transmit the vast majority of British crime dramas) that aim to provide the public with diverse, intelligent and original material, whilst also ensuring that support for the ethic of publicly funded broadcasting for all is maintained. Crime drama – a genre that is popular, familiar, yet open to innovation – is one answer to the problem of how to maintain high audience ratings and appreciation indices (the measure of how highly a series is valued by viewers), whilst producing programmes that viewers and critics will talk about in person and online. It is the genre's elasticity – its capacity to probe the enduring social realities of law and order through diverse realist, melodramatic, historical, plot and character-driven forms – that makes it such a valuable asset to British PSBs and their schedules. Crime drama has come to play an important role in helping commissioners and channel controllers develop a distinct sense of channel identity in an ever more crowded marketplace (Garner, this collection). Original drama, more generally, has emerged as a valuable marker of quality for British PSBs at a time when audiences have had more than a decade of watching cheaper reality formats and where many channels offer low-budget content or numerous repeats. British crime drama holds the potential both to attract broad audiences familiar with the genre's existing appeal, and to innovate and develop distinct narratives and investigators who can attract viewers in search of more demanding material. In the United Kingdom, unlike the United States where the television system is more starkly divided between relatively risk-averse networks (NBC, ABC and CBS) and subscription-based services targeting affluent consumers (Showtime, HBO, etc.), it is possible for the same broadcaster to achieve both as is evident by the diversity of output from the BBC on both its mainstream channel BBC One and its niche channels, BBC Two and BBC Four (McCabe, this collection). Crime drama is a genre especially responsive to changing socio-cultural conditions, meaning that it is able to exploit television's close relationship to the present, everyday world. Although most crime dramas are not immediate fictionalisations of real life crime, they do work through changing perceptions of crime and policing. In so doing, they provide the genre with a privileged sense of realism and immediacy. Moreover, the serial nature of much crime drama also means that one of the most traditional aspects of television – its regularity – can be exploited in order to tell complex, unfolding stories over a period of several weeks. Done well, this can provide an opportunity for commissioners to laud the quality of their drama output, whilst also maintaining ratings from audiences eager to find out whodunnit. The scheduling of crime drama provides broadcasters with new opportunities to engage viewers through social media, such as Twitter, which can provide them with the space to share immediate responses to each episode as transmitted and to exchange views of the likely end result. Rather than signalling the end of live (as opposed to box-set) television, such integration of social media exemplifies how converged media tools can draw audiences into even richer discussions of law and order on screen.

The first example here (examined in detail by Ross P. Garner in this collection) is ITV. ITV is a commercially funded public service broadcaster. During the mid-2000s, it faced major financial challenges with decreasing advertising revenue and declining audience ratings. This was coupled with criticisms of some of its lower-end reality formats such as *Celebrity Love Island* (2005–06). ITV found itself being talked about in the press as appealing to the lowest common denominator or as Simon Edge, then TV critic at the *Daily Express* put it: 'Every time you think they have reached the bottom of the barrel, they scrape off a little bit more' (Edge cited in Bishop, 2005). ITV's major rebrand in the winter of 2013 made a clear strategic move to render original drama far more prominent in the story it tells its viewers, making quality popular drama central to its mainstream offering. As Jennifer Ranking and John Reynolds (2014) put it, '*Downton Abbey* and *Broadchurch* have restored a reputation for drama that had been obscured by the success of entertainment formats such as *The X Factor* and *I'm a Celebrity*.' The serial crime drama, *Broadchurch* (Kudos for ITV) was not only successful in terms of its audience ratings (the final episode gained more than nine million viewers), it also generated considerable positive press attention for the quality of its complex plot in the shocking investigation of the murder of 11-year-old Danny Latimer in the fictional Dorset seaside town of Broadchurch. The quality of the performances was also widely credited, especially that of Olivia Colman (who played DS Ellie Miller) who went on to be nominated for a BAFTA for Best Actress. The nature of the crime committed in *Broadchurch*, the twists of its plot and the gradual revelation of the dark layers of social violence beneath the picturesque scene of its coastline through strong character performances from popular actors such as Pauline Quirke, together challenged the conception that ITV was no longer capable of making high-quality, edge of the seat drama. Managing to be both mainstream and critically acclaimed, *Broadchurch* demonstrates how British crime drama can help alter the brand perception of an ailing PSB, simultaneously winning audiences and gaining critical acclaim.

By contrast, *Top of the Lake* (2013), *The Fall* (2013–) and *Line of Duty* demonstrate how crime dramas – both imported and British-made – can reinvigorate a more niche channel, such as BBC Two, at a time when it has faced competition from BBC Four (especially its Saturday night international crime series) and has suffered substantial budget cuts meaning that its daytime schedule now largely runs repeats. The first series of *Line of Duty* (World

Productions for BBC Two) delivered the channel its highest drama viewing figures for 10 years, whilst the final episode of the second series drew more than four million viewers (http://www.barb.co.uk/viewing/weekly-top-30?). *Line of Duty* is a police procedural with a difference – the main investigation is of the police themselves, conducted by the anti-corruption squad of AC12. The politics of police corruption loom large in the investigation, whilst the complexity of the plot – and the fundamental problem of who to trust – means that the viewer needs to be attentive, engaged and deeply involved in the investigation. This is demanding and thrilling viewing for the audience of a channel which offers what its former Controller, Janice Hadlow, describes as 'intelligent pleasure' (Plunkett, 2014). At the end of the first series, the then BBC Drama Controller, Ben Stephenson acclaimed it as a 'brilliant series ... that encapsulates my vision for bold, authored and utterly original drama on the channel.' At the end of the second series, *The Guardian*'s media critic, Mark Lawson, seemed to speak for many when he said that if *Broadchurch* was declared the best TV drama of 2013, 'twelve months on, it's clear that *Line of Duty* is going to take some beating to the 2014 prize' (Lawson, 2014). Again, it is the quality of both the writing (Jed Mercurio) and the acting (notably Keeley Hawes's performance as DI Denton) which seems to have garnered such loyal, excited audiences. Played out over six weekly episodes, the intricate plots are the product of a single writer, Jed Mercurio, who invests the police procedural with realist detail, emotionally engaging characters and credible legal knowledge. In turn, Hawes' performance as the anti-heroic suspect and victim forces the viewer to linger and look at her inscrutable face, unable to decide whether she is telling the truth even in the dogged interrogation scenes. What is most striking, however, is just how much time British producers are able to give to telling the story, providing the viewer with space to deliberate over the developments before the next, thrilling episode. Free from the frequent commercials which mean that US shows normally average 42 minutes in length, the BBC's own crime drama is able to vary its length and have more content per transmitted hour than its American equivalents. The profound uncertainty and confusion created by *Line of Duty*'s complex plot is central to audiences' pleasure in it; as one poster put it on Twitter, 'Line of Duty has left me emotional and unsure of anything or anyone' (Steve Taylor-Bryant_@ OpinionGeeks, 27 February 1:49am). Chris Chibnall, writer and co-creator of *Broadchurch*, himself noted in a BBC Radio 4 interview that in this new golden age of crime drama:

> ... you've got an ability to tell these long-form stories where you've got eight or ten hours to tell the story, make it a little bit novelistic and it is a shift from the more episodic series we've had in the past few years. That's very exciting for the writer.

If UK crime drama is offering renewed opportunities for serial storytelling, it is also witnessing an increased internationalisation of content by British producers and broadcasters who are selling television to a global market-place. Both series discussed above have been sold internationally. Kudos, the independent production company behind *Broadchurch* has worked with Shine International to distribute the series to over 100 territories including the United States, Australia, France, Germany, Norway, Spain, New Zealand and Russia, whilst the series was remade as *Gracepoint* in the United States by Fox. Meanwhile, *Line of Duty* has been made available in the United States via Hulu and sold at MIPTV (the annual Cannes international market in tele-vision) by Content Media. At the same event, All3Media acted as the interna-tional distributor for the English and Welsh-language crime drama *Y Gwyll/ Hinterland* (Fiction Factory for S4C) which had already been bought by DR Denmark, the makers of crime dramas such as *The Killing* and *The Bridge* (2011, transmitted by the BBC, 2012–). Crime dramas form an important element in the United Kingdom's export of finished television programming, which is the United Kingdom's largest source of TV revenue, worth £612 million in 2012 (see PACT, 2013). Perhaps the single greatest success here is ITV's long-running feature-length series, *Midsomer Murders* (Bentley Pro-ductions), one of the United Kingdom's most successful television exports, having been sold to 225 territories since its first UK transmission in 1997 (Sherwin, 2013). The 100th episode saw DCI Barnaby and DS Nelson travel to Copenhagen in a playful homage to *The Killing*. This fusion of European detection exemplifies the innovative nature and popular appeal of the crime drama genre, as Kaare Schmidt (DR Denmark series acquisitions executive), put it: '*Midsomer Murders* is a benchmark in television entertainment and Danish viewers' favourite programme for more than a decade. It's an honour and a thrill for us to be able to contribute to the series' distinguished line of murder victims and police detectives' (Schmidt in Sherwin, 2013).

A staple of many countries' television schedules, crime drama – its social and moral narratives of justice and detection – has the potential to find audiences outside the territory of its first transmission. The dominance of the English language globally means that English-language television crime drama from the United Kingdom can follow where literary precursors (such as Arthur Conan Doyle's Sherlock Holmes, and Agatha Christie's Miss Marple and Hercule Poirot) have already lead. At the same time, the increas-ing internationalisation of television means that British viewers are now exposed to a wider range of European crime dramas and to highly devel-oped franchises such as *Law and Order: UK* that have emerged from across the Atlantic. The demand for content to fill schedules means that finding new ways of acquiring and exporting crime drama is likely to remain an important tactical response to a rapidly changing televisual ecology.

Cops on the Box: Examining Television Crime Drama

This book aims to capture the breadth of aesthetic, social and industrial fac-tors shaping contemporary British crime drama so as to provide a thorough analysis of its critical and popular appeal. It adopts a range of rigorous conceptual and methodological approaches in order to reassess the genre's place in contemporary television and to argue for a discernible British approach to a popular international genre. In this way, it contributes both to the study of contemporary television and to the more specific recuperation of crime drama as a genre meriting critical attention. It is organised into three sections.

Section one begins by examining the development of the crime genre in contemporary British television, examining both its changing social and narrative preoccupations and its new, often hybrid iterations. Charlotte Brunsdon provides a characteristically ambitious periodisation of the British police series. Despite appearances to the contrary, she argues, the British police series is undergoing a moment of crisis reflective of the changed political and policing order brought about by Western government's so-called 'war on terror.' A turn to investigations of sex crimes committed against children, to narratives preoccupied by the target culture of modern policing, and to the kind of paranoia at work in antiterror legislation that actually removes many forms of law and order from police forces in favour of the intelligence services are all identified by Brunsdon as characteristic of the current period. Steve Blandford's chapter takes up this critique of the contemporary police series through his analysis of the work of Jimmy McGovern, one of the most critical British writers of television drama. McGovern resolutely refuses to allow police officers to be the main focus of his crime drama, probing instead the often ordinary, devastated lives from which criminal acts emerge. The effect in both *Common* (BBC, 2014) and *Accused* (BBC, 2010–12) is to make crime and justice, rather than policing, the central narrative focus. Martin Willis' chapter considers how a key locale of the genre – the body of the victim of crime – has become a site for forensic sousveillance that both offers greater imaginative freedoms and at the same time delimits its humanity. Willis argues that the body is both written by, and yet resistant to, medical narratives of its progress through life. In so doing, he situates forensic crime dramas, such as *Silent Witness* and *Waking the Dead*, in intertextual relationships with contemporary medical writing and medical television drama. Rebecca Williams' chapter extends the analysis of crime drama's intertextualities in her examination of the Gothic crime drama. Providing an initial genealogy of this subgenre's appearance on television screens, Williams charts how the BBC's *Ripper Street* and ITV's *Whitechapel* (both of which aired on BBC America) invoke the spectre of Jack the Ripper and enduring cultural understandings of Whitechapel's landscape as haunted, dangerous and uncanny.

Section two focusses specifically on the role of the police in British crime drama. My own chapter draws attention to the substantial discrepancy between the number of actual female Detective Inspectors in British policing and the abundance of women police officers who now lead investigations on the small screen. Placing women as detective leads in series such as *Scott and Bailey* (2011–) enables scriptwriters to examine how women perform their professional identities both in the field and in the office or station. In so doing, the crime drama manages both to explore the complex character of the police professional and to provide viewers with a space to work through the changing nature of women and men's professional lives. In his chapter, Manel Jimenez-Morales examines *Line of Duty* (BBC Two) and its exploration of the absurdities of the police bureaucratic system. Positioning it as a drama that responds to both American and British precursors, including *The Wire* (HBO), Jimenez-Morales argues that *Line of Duty* is a meta-discursive series concerned with observing the police as criminal and revealing the inoperability of the force's own attempts to clean an organisation when it is completely corrupt. By way of contrast, Stephen Lacey's chapter looks at the historical crime drama, *Foyle's War*, and its eponymous protagonist, Christopher Foyle (Michael Kitchen), who acts as a moral agent, exposing hypocrisy and subversion – sometimes committed by the British state in the name of national interest, as well as the wartime enemy. The series re-enacts the period drama's complex relationship between past and present, with a strong sense of contemporary cultural values in negotiation with those of an earlier period, embodied here by Foyle and his team. Jonathan Bignell's chapter considers how the space of policing is connected with modernity and mobility, and the use of a scopic regime to apprehend and control the real. He examines the aesthetic and narrative significance of police cars in series such as *Inspector George Gently*, *Vera*, *Z Cars*, *The Sweeney* (1975–86), *Inspector Morse*, *Life on Mars* and *Midsomer Murders*. In so doing, he helps us better to understand the commonalities and distinctions between UK and US police series as they have moved from being largely studio-set to location-based programmes.

Section three examines the industrial and global nature of television crime drama, paying detailed attention to how crime is adapted for different territories and for distinct industrial purposes. Ross P. Garner examines how discourses of 'quality' television are constructed and intertextually activated in ITV's promotion of its crime dramas. With a particular focus on *Broadchurch*, he provides close analysis of the broadcaster's rebranding strategy and the complex place of mainstream, quality crime within it. In turn, Janet McCabe focusses on the BBC, and the industrial as well as the cultural context which explains the recent rise to prominence of internationally imported crime drama. Paying detailed attention to questions of cultural value in British debates on public service broadcasting, her chapter reveals both how crime may travel, and how its adaptation and translation speaks to national specificities of the genre. One of the United Kingdom's most popular crime fiction exports, *Agatha Christie's Poirot*, is the focus of Mary F. Brewer's chapter. Drawing on audience research and adaptation analysis, Brewer reveals how the success of *Poirot* in the United States speaks to a cultural trend among conservative white Anglo-Saxon Protestant viewers for fetishizing Englishness, an act that patronises its object at the same time that it pays homage to it. This contrasts with the United Kingdom's reception of the series which, Brewer argues, evinces a nostalgic longing for a bygone England. Finally, Deborah Jermyn takes up this concern with transatlantic adaptations by examining a common, but rarely discussed aspect of the global television industry – the failed imported remake. Focussing on *Prime Suspect USA* (2011–12), Jermyn teases out the reasons for the failure of one of the most influential and highly regarded TV police series of all time to 'make it' in its transatlantic translation. In the process she raises important questions about the operation of transnational remakes and the benchmarks for success in the competitive landscape of contemporary crime TV.

References

Bignell, J., 2009. The police series. In: J. Gibbs and D. Pye, eds., 2009. *Close-Up 03*. London, England: Wallflower. pp. 1–66.

Bishop, T. 2005. Can ITV return from ratings slump? [online]. Available at: http://news.bbc.co.uk/1/hi/entertainment/4087998.stm [Accessed 31 August 2015].

Brunsdon, C., 1998. Structure of anxiety: recent British television crime fiction. *Screen*, 39 (3), pp. 223–43.

Cohen, S. and Young, J., 1973. *The Manufacture of News: Deviance, Social Problems and the Mass Media*. London, England: Sage.

Cooke, L. and Sturges, P., 2009. Police and media relations in an era of freedom of information. *Policing and Society*, 19(4), pp. 406–24.

Corner, J., 1999. *Critical Ideas in Television Studies*. Oxford, England: Oxford University Press.

D'Acci, J., 1994. *Defining Women: Television and the Case of Cagney and Lacey*. Chapel Hill, NC: University of North Carolina Press.

Dowler, K., Fleming T. and Muzzatti, S.L., 2006. Constructing crime: media, crime, and popular culture. *Canadian Journal of Criminology and Criminal Justice*, 48(6), pp. 837–50.

Ellis, J., 1999. Television as working-through. In: J. Gripsrud, ed. 1999. *Television and Common Knowledge*. London, England: Routledge. pp. 55–70.

Hall, S., Critcher, C., Jefferson, T., Clarke, J.N. and Roberts, B., 1978. *Policing the Crisis: Mugging, the State and Law and Order*. 2013. Basingstoke, England: Palgrave Macmillan.

Henderson, L., 2007. *Social Issues in Television Fiction*. Edinburgh, Scotland: Edinburgh University Press.

Innes, M., 1999. The media as an investigative resource in murder enquiries. *The British Journal of Criminology*, 39(2), pp. 269–86.

Jensen, P. M. and Waade, A. M. 2013. Nordic noir challenging the "Language of Advantage": setting, light and language as production values in Danish television series, *Journal of Popular Television*, 1(2), pp. 259–265.

Jermyn, D., 2003. Women with a mission: Lynda La Plante, DCI Jane Tennison and the reinvention of British TV crime drama. *International Journal of Cultural Studies*, 6(1), pp. 46–63.

Johnson, C. and Turnock, R., eds., 2005. *ITV Cultures: Independent Television Over Fifty Years*. Maidenhead, England: Open University Press.

Lawson, Mark, 2014. How Jed Mercurio made *Line of Duty* unmissable TV. *The Guardian*, [online] 20 March 2014. Available at: http://www.theguardian.com/tv-and-radio/tvandradioblog/2014/mar/20/line-of-duty-jed-mercurio.

Lacey, S. and McElroy, R. 2012. *Life on Mars: From Manchester to New York.* Cardiff, Wales: University of Wales Press.

Mawby, R.C., 2010. Police corporate communications, crime reporting and the shaping of policing news. *Policing and Society*, 20(1), pp. 124–39.

Newcomb, H.M. and Hirsch, P.M., 1983. Television as a cultural forum: implications for research. *Quarterly Review of Film Studies*, 8(3), pp. 45–55.

Nichols-Pethick, J., 2012. *TV Cops: The Contemporary American Television Police Drama.* New York, NY: Routledge.

Oldridge, D., 2007. Casting the spell of terror: the press and the early Whitechapel murders. In: A. Warwick and M. Willis, eds., 2007. *Jack the Ripper: Media, Culture, History.* Manchester, England: Manchester University Press. pp. 46–70.

PACT. 2013. UK Television Exports 2012.

Piper, H., 2015. *The TV Detective: Voices of Dissent in Contemporary Television.* London, England: I.B.Tauris.

Plunkett, John, 2014. BBC2 controller steps down. *The Guardian*, [online] 11 February 2014. Available at: http://www.theguardian.com/media/2014/feb/11/bbc2-controller-step-down-janice-hadlow).

Pribram, E.D., 2011. *Emotions, Genre, Justice in Film and Television: Detecting Feeling.* London, England: Routledge.

Ranking, J. and Reynolds, J. 2014. ITV seeks new acquisitions as it returns to profit and falls back in favour. *The Guardian*, [online] 26 February 2014. Available at http://www.theguardian.com/business/2014/feb/26/itv-profit-viewers-crozier-studios-downton.

Roggenkamp, K., 2005. *Narrating the News: New Journalism and Literary Genre in Late Nineteenth-Century American Newspapers and Fiction.* Kent, OH: Kent State University Press.

Sherwin, Adam, 2013. DCI Barnaby enters the land of Sarah Lund: *Midsomer Murders* travels to Copenhagen for special joint episode with Danish broadcaster of *The Killing. The Independent*, [online] 3 September 2013. Available at: http://www.independent.co.uk/arts-entertainment/tv/news/dci-barnaby-enters-the-land-of-sarah-lund-midsomer-murders-travels-to-copenhagen-for-special-joint-episode-with-danish-broadcaster-of-the-killing-8795924.html.

Sparks, R., 1992. *Television and the Drama of Crime: Moral tales and the place of crime in public life.* Maidenhead, England: Open University Press.

Stein, L.E. and Busse, K., eds., 2012. *Sherlock and Transmedia Fandom: Essays on the BBC Series.* London, England: McFarland.

Turnbull, S., 2014. *The TV Crime Drama.* Edinburgh, Scotland: Edinburgh University Press.

Warwick, A., 2007. Blood and ink: narrating the Whitechapel Murders. In: A. Warwick and M. Willis, eds., 2007. *Jack the Ripper: Media, Culture, History.* Manchester, England: Manchester University Press. pp. 71–87.

Wheatley, H. 2011. Beautiful images in spectacular clarity: spectacular television, landscape programming and the questions of (tele)visual pleasure. *Screen* 52(2). pp. 233–248.

Television Programmes Cited

Accused (RSJ Films for BBC, 2010–).
Agatha Christie's Marple (ITV, 2004–13).

Agatha Christie's Poirot (Carnival Film and Television for ITV, 1989–2013).

Babylon (Nightjack Limited for Channel 4, 2014).

Between the Lines (World Productions for BBC, 1992–94).

Blue Murder (Granada, 2003–09).

Bones (Far Field Productions, Josephson Entertainment, 26 Keys Productions, 20th Century Fox Television for Fox Network, 2005–).

Boys from the Blackstuff (BBC, 1982).

Bridge, The (DR Denmark, SVT, NRK, ZDF, 2011, transmitted BBC, 2012–).

Broadchurch (Kudos for ITV, 2013–).

Cagney and Lacey (CBS, 1981–88).

Coast (BBC Birmingham, Open University, 2005–).

Common (BBC Drama, 2014).

CSI: Crime Scene Investigation (CBS, 2000–15).

DCI Banks (Left Bank Pictures for ITV, 2010–).

Death in Paradise (Red Planet, Kudos, Atlantique, for BBC, 2011–).

Dixon of Dock Green (BBC, 1955–76).

Edge of Darkness (BBC, 1985).

Fall, The (Fables Limited, Artists Studio, BBC Northern Ireland, 2013–).

Foyle's War (Greenlit Productions for ITV, 2002–15).

Gentle Touch, The (London Weekend Television, 1980–84).

Governor, The (La Plante Productions, Samson Films, Yorkshire Television, 1995–96).

Hinterland (Fiction Factory for S4C, first transmitted by BBC Cymru Wales, 2014 –).

Homicide: Life on the Street (NBC, 1993–99).

Inspector Morse (Carlton Television, 1987–2000).

Inspector George Gently (BBC, 2007–).

Juliet Bravo (BBC, 1980–85).

Killing, The (DR Denmark, SVT, NRK, transmitted BBC, 2011–12).

Law and Order: UK (Kudos, Wolf Films, NBC Universal for ITV, 2009–).

Lewis (Granada for ITV, 2007–).

Life on Mars (Kudos for BBC Cymru Wales, 2006–07).

Line of Duty (World Productions for BBC Northern Ireland, 2012–).

Luther (BBC, 2010–15).

Midsomer Murders (Bentley Productions for ITV, 1997–).

Miss Marple (BBC, 1984–92).

Murder in Suburbia (Carlton, 2004–05).

Prime Suspect (Granada, 1991–2006).

Prime Suspect USA (ITV Studios America, Universal Media Studios for NBC, 2011–12).

Rebus (Clerkenwell Films for STV, 2000–04, STV, 2000–07).

Ripper Street (Tiger Aspect Productions for BBC, 2012–13, Amazon Prime, 2014–, transmitted BBC, 2015–).

Scott and Bailey (Red Production Company for ITV, 2011–).

Sherlock (Hartswood Films for BBC Cymru Wales, 2010–).

Shetland (ITV Studios for BBC Scotland, 2013–).

Silent Witness (BBC, 1996–).

Sweeney, The (Thames Television, 1975–78).

Top of the Lake (See Saw Films, Screen Australia, transmitted BBC, 2013).

Vera (ITV Studios, Company Productions, 2011–).

Waking the Dead (BBC, 2000–11).

Whitechapel (Carnival Films for ITV, 2009–13).
Widows (Thames Television, 1983).
Widows 2 (Thames Television, 1985).
Wire, The (Blown Deadline Productions, HBO, 2002–08).
Y *Gwyll* (Fiction Factory for S4C, 2013–).
Z *Cars* (BBC, 1962–78).

Part I

The British Crime Drama – New Adventures in an Established Genre

1 Bad Sex, Target Culture and the Anti-Terror State

New Contexts for the Twenty-First Century British Television Police Series

Charlotte Brunsdon

This chapter is concerned with the early twenty-first century police series on British television, taking the 2010 cancellation of *The Bill* (1984–2010) as a significant temporal marker. In this period, I will argue that, despite appearances, the British television police series is in difficulty. Even though there seem to be television police and crime series all over the British schedules, and some digital channels are devoted solely to the genres of crime, my argument is that the changing contexts of policing have hollowed out the necessary assumptions of the British television police world. This crisis is hiding in the light of television screens peopled by Victorian policemen, 1960s policemen, 1950s policewomen, pathologists with policing remits, serial killers, senior women police officers and even charismatic senior Black officers. Before I outline this argument – and it will be an outline, a sketch to provoke discussion – I want to set out some methodological preliminaries.

The television police series is a durable and flexible ingredient of the television schedule, one which can be transformed in a variety of ways to suit changing institutional, cultural and historical contexts. The generic constants of the police series – its narrative configuration of police officers, criminals and 'community', its historically variant crimes, its technologies of detection – are sufficiently familiar to provide ground for both innovation and imitation. The police series can answer particular demands at specific historical moments in different broadcasting contexts, while always, at the same time, at some level, articulating something about living as a citizen there and then. For example, in Britain, there is a very long tradition of the police series being used to satisfy demands that television should represent the regions of the United Kingdom. Police series such as *Heartbeat* (Yorkshire, YTV, 1992–2011), *Wycliffe* (Devon, HTV, 1994–98) and *The Chief* (East Anglia, ATV, 1990–95) have contributed significantly to the place images of their settings, and some – like *Taggart* (Glasgow, STV, 1983–2010) – have been so successful that the franchise continued after the 1994 death of Mark McManus, the actor who played DI Taggart. In a rather different way, a show like Dick Wolf's *Law and Order* (NBC, 1990–2010) can multiply its revenues by franchising the format for customised production in different national contexts, providing a 'glocal' variant, sensitive to local settings, policing and legal conventions, while also still exporting the US version.

The police series is both a reliable resource for broadcasters, and also a rewarding site for researchers, partly because of its continuing attraction for audiences. The genre is ubiquitous, but does not always do the same things and is not always interesting for the same reasons. My concern here will be mainly with the relationship between the police series and the contemporary social world, but I am not proposing that this is the only aspect which merits study, nor do I think this approach should be pursued without complementary understanding of shifting broadcasting economies and questions of style, genre and performance. Whilst I do not have much to say here about the long-running *Midsomer Murders* (ITV, 1997–), with its England of villages, vicars, blackmail and black magic (but no Black people), there are clearly analyses to be made about the persistence of this image of England, and its popularity with audiences both in Britain and abroad.[1] My aim here is to propose some ways of thinking about the changing historical contexts of the twenty-first century British police series. My interest lies in the way in which the contemporary police series, because of its traditions of headline sensitivity and realism, is in some sense a state-of-the-nation genre, while at the same time being a genre through which the state, in however etiolated a form, is figured. It works over questions of what is permitted, forbidden, feared and concealed in particular cultures; how villainy, victimhood and law enforcement are enacted; and to what extent and how the different players in these dramas – community, criminals, police – can be understood as responsive to broader social concerns. There is not space to make these arguments at length, nor to engage with some of the stimulating new scholarship on the genre, such as the recent books by Sue Turnbull (2014) and Helen Piper (2015), but I hope that a relatively unadorned presentation will make them available for others to challenge and develop.

'If We Can Do this Show in Uniforms'

Just as the police investigate crime and law-breaking, programme makers have used the genre to investigate contemporary society. I briefly want to consider two very distinguished examples of this which are separated by 40 years. Firstly, the playwright John McGrath writing retrospectively in 1975 about the way in which the police series format could be used in the innovatory 1960s series, *Z Cars* (BBC, 1962–78), which was set near Liverpool in the fictional Newtown, based on Kirkby. The aim was

> [T]o use a Highway Patrol format, but to use the cops as a key or a way of getting into a whole society … a kind of documentary about people's lives in these areas, and the cops were incidental – they were the means of finding out about people's lives.[2]

This can be contrasted with Tony Garnett, speaking much later, in 1998, about the controversial series he produced (as World Productions), *The Cops* (BBC, 1998–2001):

[W]hat I really wanted to do was a show that allowed us to go into parts of our society that are not shown on television, and which are not the experiences of the middle classes who are watching. The society we want to represent in *The Cops* is one where 'sink estates' show the result of grinding poverty through the generations: it's a society where there's no hope or expectation, and a society where all sense of community and stability has disappeared.

Now if I'd gone to the BBC or Ch4 and said 'I'd like to do a series about social workers', or a similar group of people that would naturally access this context, they'd have thrown me out of the room; but by going and saying 'I want to do a show about cops' I could be sure of an enthusiastic response. They're very interested then ... So I thought, if we can do this show in uniforms, I can get the show made and I can get an audience to watch it, but the uniforms will take us into parts of society that we usually don't enter.[3]

In each of these cases, the police series is the pretext. The interest, for both the makers of *Z Cars* and *The Cops*, was in a wider social realist/documentary project. They want to use the genre as a way of gaining access to television, a mass medium which offers unprecedented opportunities to bring the realities of excluded lives into the living rooms of its audiences. As McGrath goes on to point out, there are difficulties with this project which are manifest in the serial form, the ways in which the recurrent figures of the police develop their own autonomy: 'After the cops kept appearing week after week people began to fall in love with them, and they became stars. So the pressure was on to make them the subjects, rather than the device.'[4]

McGrath's comment illustrates the history of television through a key difference between himself and Garnett. McGrath is writing about a project, *Z Cars*, near the beginning of the development of contemporary, written-for-television serial drama in the early 1960s and he is, as a writer, learning about what happens through regular broadcasting. Garnett, in contrast, is by 1998 a very seasoned industry professional who is, in turn, using the police series itself as a strategic device 'if we can do this show in uniforms' to get a commission. In each case though, there is confidence about the suitability of the police genre for investigating contemporary culture. TV cop shows are a vehicle for a traditional social realist project, which, in Raymond Williams's terms, will be 'contemporary, secular, and socially extensive' (1977, p. 65).

New Contexts for the TV Police Series

It is this project and use of the genre which I am arguing is currently in crisis, and to make this argument, I will return to an essay I wrote about the genre 20 years ago. My argument then was that the police show at that time was a privileged and dynamic genre through which some of the difficult social transformations of the period were articulated. Writing in 1996 – before the election of the last Labour government – in what proved to be the final year of the Conservative government elected in 1979, I proposed the idea of the discursive context as a way of specifying, in the broadest terms, different material conditions, discourses and practices which could be seen to have particular resonances for the police series. I suggested that the relevant discursive contexts for this period were 'law and order', 'privatisation' and 'equal opportunities' (1998). I argued that the police series (as distinct from the crime or detective series) was proving a particularly dynamic genre because of the structural relationship between the police and the state, which was thrown into relief in a period when the post-war settlement's understanding of the relationship between the citizen and the state was under attack. This is not an argument that the people involved in making these programmes were necessarily involved in a conscious project to discuss politics of the period such as urban rioting (e.g., events in 1981, 1985 and the Poll-tax riots of 1990), the neo-liberal assault on the welfare state, the militarisation of the police and the policing of the Miners' Strike. Instead, it was an argument that the premises of the genre, and its historical headline-sensitivity, meant that it became, in roughly the 1982–94 period, an often inadvertent site through which the viewers' and the citizens' relationship with the state is imagined and worried over.

Times change, and so do genres. Here, working with an imperfect and perhaps premature periodisation, which is roughly 2002 to 2012/13, with a caesura in 2007/08 for the financial crisis, I want to revisit this methodological device of the discursive context. I am fully aware that 'discursive context' does not provide any hard evidence of the relationship between police series and the contexts in which they are produced, but it is, in its very imprecision, usefully suggestive, and will make possible an exploration of whether there are equivalent formations in the current period. In doing this, I will be putting aside the question, which I have addressed elsewhere, of the ways in which changes in the television industry and its modes of circulation make this a much trickier project in the twenty-first century (Brunsdon, 2010). Despite what Graeme Turner (2009) has accurately characterised as an attenuated relationship between television and the national, there is still some purchase, in a country which produces and exports as much television as Britain, in considering the contexts in which it is made and viewed. However, the informing and shaping context must be an international one, that of the 'War on Terror', and it is this that provides the opening periodisation. In the aftermath of the attacks on the World Trade Center, the war in Iraq, 'extraordinary rendition' and Guantanamo Bay, is 'law and order', so important for so much of the twentieth century, still a significant context for policing? Now that so many services previously provided by the local and national state have been privatised, is that privatisation still a contested and resonant category? How has 'austerity' and its associated macho posturing affected the fictional world of the police service? And what of equal opportunities in the twenty-first century?

If the first relevant discursive context in the earlier period was the persistence of 'law and order', this has been the area of most significant transformation, for instead of ideas of law and order, the dominant formation is now the apparatus of anti-terror legislation and the rhetoric and practices of the new necessities of security: the anti-terror state. The anti-terror state (which is the home-front version for a country that has been at war for much of the twenty-first century) in its very discursive constitution, trumps 'law and order' in the name of protecting a citizenry which will, in return, render up ancient rights such as *habeas corpus*, privacy, jury trials held in public and, through the introduction of prolonged legal detention without charge, pretty much the right to be considered innocent until proven guilty. Detention without charge or trial, in particular, opens up a narrative black hole in the generic rules of the police series and is one element in the current shift towards conspiracy narratives, while the ambiguity of the identity of the operatives of the anti-terror state makes another shift away from drama based on uniformed 'boys in blue.' For the iconography of the British police series, one thing is clear: the officers are either armed, female, or living and policing in remote, often picturesque non-metropolitan centres.

A related and dependent context is the rise and recognition of surveillance culture. The importance of technology to the history of the police genre is well documented, from fingerprints to radios to telephones. In this long history, surveillance culture was already having significant effects on the look of the TV crime series – the multi-screen aesthetic which incorporates CCTV footage into the narrative world; the grainy look of CCTV footage; the seemingly easy recourse to the tracking of the movements of individuals anywhere – and its narrative possibilities and pace. However, the Wikileaks affair followed by the Snowden revelations has shifted and expanded the discursive context of surveillance, and the ambivalences of constantly surveilled citizenship have become more readily apparent.

The second contemporary discursive context is target culture, the new managerialism with its imperatives of 'deliverables', 'outputs', 'impact', 'performance', 'competitive tender'; its perverse adjectives ('robust', 'challenging', 'diverse', 'vibrant'); and its TLAs (three letter acronyms[5]), infecting the whole of the former public sector. The privatisation which was a significant discursive context in the 1980s has now become more taken for granted, and it is widely accepted – at least in practice – that essential services will be outsourced to agencies and that in a competitive bidding environment, 'deliverables' must be quantified. The erosion and devaluation of ideals of public service, which had been such a core part of nineteenth and twentieth century British culture (patriarchal and patrician as it often was) has led to a pervasive cynicism and demoralisation in public life in which there is a widespread understanding of the gulf between the preposterous PR pronouncements about how much better services are being delivered and the experience 'on the ground.' While this PR driven target culture itself has been the direct object of satire in *Babylon* (Channel 4, 2013–14), what is more interesting for my purposes is its penetration into the everyday detail of the police genre.

Historically, the genre has always been hostile to 'paperwork', and one of its most familiar tropes is the opposition between the real police and those 'upstairs', the managers obsessed with procedure and filing. *The Sweeney* (ITV, 1975–78) used to provide a particularly fine instance of this in the struggles between Carter (Dennis Waterman), Regan (John Thaw) and their boss, Haskins (Garfield Morgan), but it is widespread across police fiction in television and film. The overwhelming current sense of 'service delivery' being driven by targets in ways that most strongly recall Soviet five-year plans and their fantasy statistics, gives a new pertinence to these traditional generic tropes of hostility to directives from upstairs, and there is an interesting and noticeable strand of critique present in some shows in relation to changes which do not permit proper policing. While the US series *The Wire* (HBO, 2005–08) provides, partly because of its immense duration, a very sustained critique of the effect on policing of the demand to 'juke the stats', there is nevertheless, across a number of British series, a sense of a policing project which is everywhere impeded by cost, rationalisation and targets. This was the clear topic of *Line of Duty* (BBC, 2012–), the acclaimed World Productions series for the BBC, where the charismatic officer of the year, Tony Gates (Lennie James) was investigated for 'laddering', a process whereby crime clear-up statistics are inflated, and both police and suspects are shown, at the point of charging, to understand the benefits to themselves of adding offences that can be 'Taken into Consideration' (TICS) when it comes to sentencing.[6] As an apprehended burglar puts it, when offered the opportunity to claim guilt for other unsolved crimes, 'Ah TICS – I don't want prison, I've got Benidorm booked' (*Line of Duty*, 2012, Series 1, Episode 2). While the narrative drive of *Line of Duty* explores exceptional dramatic corruption into which Gates becomes implicated through a sexual liaison, for my purposes the more interesting figure is the deeply cynical young female police officer whose response to the same burglar's injured body, lying on the ground after he jumps out of a window, is to sigh and observe: 'That is so many more forms to fill in' (*Line of Duty*, 2012, Series 1, Episode 2).

The perversion of target culture is accentuated, in the post-2008 period, by the rhetoric of austerity, which has its own paradoxes. The traditional generic conflict between officers on the street and managers can now be articulated through questions of budget, whether it be manpower for searches or DNA testing. The rebellious act of the rule-breaking, insubordinate but morally upstanding officer which is necessary to close the case may now involve not beating-up a suspect to get a confession, but disregarding budget limitations (or sometimes both, as in the case of John Luther). In this formation, we find the representation within television fiction of the marketisation of the police service and ancillary services such as forensic pathology. Since the cancellation of *The Bill* (ITV, 1984–2010), this is most noticeable in not-strictly police series, such as *Silent Witness* (BBC, 1996–), set principally in a forensic pathology lab, which have been sufficiently long running to be able to register changes in context in a manner in which comparisons can be made, or series, such as *Vera* (ITV, 2011–) and *Rebus* (STV, 2000–07), with central figures formed in earlier traditions of policing. While the frustration of the officers who actually do the policing is a traditional complaint in the police series, in the current period this 'rub' is articulated with criticism of the problems of outsourcing and the imposition of targets.

At the same time, as national television markets have become less predictable, the pressure on production companies to produce material which will export well has increased. This is not the place to discuss the impact this has had on casting, but, in relation to austerity and target culture, the heightened production values deemed necessary for export means that, in some police dramas, the resources available to individual chief investigators far exceed those of a small town, even while complaints about bureaucracy persist. DCI Banks, for example, was able to call in a helicopter, six vehicles and numerous armed police in a chase for an armed man, and the narratively motivated helicopter was also, conveniently, able to provide aerial shots of the dramatic denouement on a picturesque Yorkshire viaduct.[7] So, while target culture and austerity is a significant context in the current period, it is not one that is necessarily simply manifest through, for example, fewer police doing more work and complaining about targets.

The final contemporary discursive context, which I am labelling 'bad sex', is in some ways a perverse shadow of the discourse of equal opportunities which was discernible in the earlier period. It is the phenomenon, in an enormously sexualised culture, of attention to 'bad sex' such as incest, paedophilia and various kinds of sexual abuse. Vice and vice squads have always been popular topics for television crime fiction, and the prostitute a figure of fascination and voyeuristic pleasures (ITV directly addressed this tradition with a successful series called straightforwardly, *The Vice* 1999–2003). Essential to this narrative has often been the figure of the innocent young girl (or sometimes boy), captured or lured into a life which will destroy them but from which they may be rescued by the hero. However, I want to suggest that bad, or unbearable, sex as a discursive context is slightly different from this traditional generic preoccupation with forbidden and, in their televisual versions, often safely 'naughty' pleasures. This difference can perhaps be introduced through the change of scale introduced by late twentieth-century storylines about mass trafficking of illegal immigrants and, particularly, increased news coverage of trafficked women. This version, in which truckloads of foreign girls are imported for sex, has proved popular across series and continents. However, this is only one aspect of 'bad sex', which is more significantly, in Britain, involving a compulsive and horrified engagement with the histories of widespread, concealed, systematic sexual abuse across a range of national institutions and involving former pop cultural figure-heads such as Jimmy Savile, Gary Glitter and Rolf Harris. The implication of senior political figures, members of the judiciary and the police themselves, as well as the central role of the care system, are currently being contested, and there is an undeniable 'explosion of discourse' about these matters. This is of many different types, from the testimony of victims and attempted whistleblowers to 'robust denials' and salacious tabloid outrage. What is significant here is that the television police series is one of the sites on which 'bad sex' is repeatedly imagined and represented. The particular consequence for the genre is that the tumult of testimony and denial about 'bad sex' creates a context in which the narrative route of bad individuals ('perverts' and 'paedos'), so much easier to identify and punish, is once again preferred to the more difficult, troublesome and insoluble stories about endemic and systemic criminality and deprivation, Tony Garnett's 'society where there's no hope or expectation … where all sense of community and stability has disappeared' (Garnett, cited in Lacey, 2007, p. 145).

My proposition is that together, these discursive contexts contribute to some very significant shifts in the settings, themes and concerns of the police series in the twenty-first century, and a broadcast environment which is deeply inimical to the type of realist contemporary drama with which I started, unless the programmes are actually about a crisis in policing (like *The Ghost Squad*, Channel 4, 2005 and *Line of Duty*, BBC, 2012–). The cancellation of the long running London-set police procedural *The Bill* in 2010 is significant here. *The Bill*, based in the fictional Sun Hill police station in a recognisable, contemporary London, had started in 1984 and had provided a steady, familiar image of British policing in a range of half hour and one hour formats. Stylistically, *The Bill* was characterised by what could be called banal television naturalism, presenting, without stylistic flourish, everyday contemporary life in an ordinary cop shop. *The Bill*, along with *Coronation Street* (ITV, 1960–), was one of the core fixed markers in the ITV landscape, and its cancellation was largely driven by the catastrophic decline in ITV's advertising revenues as the commercial television station, with its historically older audience, failed to rise to the challenges of the shift to digital and download cultures. Axing *The Bill* could be seen to both 'freshen the schedules' and save substantial production costs.[8] However, as the critic Tom Sutcliffe (2010) observed at the time, 'I couldn't help but wonder why this had been singled out for redundancy.' Peter Fincham, the ITV Director of Television, denied that the decision was made on cost-cutting grounds, asserting that 'times change, and so do the tastes of our audiences', emphasising a creative shift towards the commissioning of shorter prime-time shows such as *Collision* (ITV, 2009).[9] While the finer detail of the decision will always remain obscure, I suggest that the decision was partly conceivable because something about *The Bill* looked a bit last century, and this was because of the shift away from a 'law and order' context for policing to policing as part of the anti-terror state. *The Bill*, which was first broadcast in the early years of the Thatcher government, and in conception embodied a return to a particular British attachment to the 'Bobby on the beat', was a 'law and order' series. The dramatic rhetoric of the police series, so familiarly realised in *The Bill*, ('I know my rights, one phone call'), its characters (the desk sergeant, the suited superior officer, the duty solicitor), its narrative rhythms ('we've had to let him go, we've got no evidence'), depended on certain consensual understandings of what it is to be a citizen of the British state. Once the law actually dispenses with these and citizens can be held without trial in situations of duress, there is a hollowing out of the consensual legitimacy of policing in the contemporary British state and a kind of crisis in the integrity and trajectory of the genre.

This crisis is manifest in a variety of ways, the most significant of which is avoidance of this trauma at the heart of the justice system by setting dramas in populations, or contexts, or eras or with generic inflections which avoid the possible invocation of the anti-terror state. There are perhaps three main strategies, of which I will have the space to discuss only one, the new prominence of women in the genre, which is in turn often bound up with the new prominence of 'bad sex' narrative causality. Too often, in too many investigative dramas of the twenty-first century, does some kind of 'bad sex' history explain contemporary trouble. 'Bad sex' and serial killing become the crimes which can be solved. The other identifiable strategies are the use of isolated non-metropolitan communities (*Shetland*, BBC, 2013–; *Hinterland*, S4C/BBC, 2014–; *Broadchurch*, ITV, 2013–) and the retro-setting which is characteristic of many of the successes of the twenty-first century, be it the costume drama of *Ripper Street* (BBC, 2012–13; Amazon Prime, 2014–) or the time travel of *Life on Mars* (Kudos/BBC, 2006–07) and *Ashes to Ashes* (BBC, 2008–10); *Inspector George Gently* (BBC, 2007–), *Endeavour* (ITV, 2012–) and *Whitechapel* (ITV, 2009–13) too, allude to pre-twenty-first-century policing worlds, which, in addition to avoiding the anti-terror state, permit a range of anachronistic, and often rather smug, forms of retrospective political correctness.

However, at the same time, in other places on the schedule, often in shorter 'serious' dramas – one or two episodes – we find an obsessive meditation on the 'new' narrative questions of the anti-terror state, accentuated by the London bombings of 2007. Who is a terrorist? Can you tell by looking at them?[10] What are the legitimate means of finding out? Is resisting surveillance suspicious? Can you use torture? This is not the generic material of the police series, but of other, un-uniformed operatives, who appear increasingly on our screens, in conspiracy dramas such as *Spooks* (BBC, 2002–10) and *The Shadow Line* (BBC, 2011), and MI5 dramas *Britz* (Channel 4, 2007) and *Complicit* (Channel 4, 2013). So it is not that these questions are not known, or not present, but that they don't quite fit in the police genre world. This is partly because, on the whole, this is a world which assuages, rather than augments, anxiety. However, it is also because so much of the state involvement in the monitoring, investigation and prosecution of matters deemed to be matters of national and international security are, very literally, outside representation. Certainly, outside the representation of the police station, the unarmed junior officers, the squad room and the duty sergeant. This is shown most elegantly in *Line of Duty* when Gates (the senior officer being investigated for corruption), decides to invoke the trump card of (invented) suspected terrorism to defend his position.[11] His move is more successful than he could hope, and he is henceforth excluded from the relevant rooms and meetings as more senior officers are shown to be thrilled with the seriousness of their new mission.

Police Officers with Personal Lives

I want to conclude by considering how these arguments might be pertinent to the increase of female lead characters in the police series itself, from Rebecca Front playing Lewis's line manager in *Lewis*, to the series which are actually fronted by women: Brenda Blethyn as *Vera*, and Suranne Jones and Lesley Sharpe in *Scott and Bailey*. There are two points to note. First, the noticeably – and perhaps rather over-optimistic – increased diversity of senior officers, to include actors such as Idris Elba (*Luther*, 2010–13) and Steve Toussaint (*Scott and Bailey*) is partly the result of struggle and campaigning outside television as well as of particular histories of the genre in Britain.[12] However, if I am right about a kind of moral bankruptcy/crisis of legitimation in the traditional police series, then one of the effects of more women (and some non-white men) is as a cover job: a 'beard.' The stagnation in the genre is screened by the relative novelty of having different types of person in key roles. Old stories can be told again, and slightly differently. Sometimes I wonder if I will ever see another male pathologist on television again. The second is what happens to the traditional concerns of the police series if there is much more focus on the private lives of the officers (as opposed to the conventional broken-marriage loner heroes). This takes us back to John McGrath's concern in the early days of *Z Cars* when, as he put it, 'the pressure was on to make them the subjects, rather than the device' (McGrath cited in Laing, 1991, pp. 42–3). Here, *Scott and Bailey* (ITV, 2011–) is instructive and I will use it very briefly to illustrate my argument, although it would also be worth considering how much screen time is devoted to the John Luther/Alice Morgan narrative in *Luther*.[13]

Scott and Bailey is set in the Major Incident Team (MIT) of the Manchester Metropolitan Area with three central female characters, DS Janet Scott, DC Rachel Bailey and the team head, Jill (Amelia Bullmore). What I want to argue is that, in this show too, the police are a device. For John McGrath and Tony Garnett, the police were a device to explore social inequality, the world never shown on television. Here, the police are a different type of device, being used to explore a different type of reality. It is not the reality of the sink estate, of the people being policed, that is the desired focus here, but the lives of professional women doing a difficult, demanding and responsible job with irregular and unpredictable hours. The series has many of the characteristics of the female ensemble drama, with narrative questions about traditional female destinies: Will Janet leave her husband? Will Rachel have a baby? However, these personal life questions are imbricated into the fabric of the police series, not just in terms of character, but also through the ways in which the women's personal lives affect the performance of their professional duties. Most significant in the first series is the series-long narrative arc about Rachel Bailey and her lawyer lover, the story with which the whole series opens as Rachel discovers not only that she has been dumped, but that he was already married. This personal life event is carefully juxtaposed in the first episode with the investigation of the murder of a young wife of an adulterous husband, and the audience is shown the way in which Rachel's own situation gives both intensity and insight to her interrogation of the dumped girlfriend who eventually confesses to the murder.

This, necessarily, in my view, involves the greater use of the generic codes of melodrama rather than the police procedural, and shifts the balance of the programme.

This can be extremely witty in relation to the conventions of the genre, as well as slyly demonstrating how much more effective listening to – rather than hitting – suspects can be as a strategy. Arguably, it proposes policing as a much more complex and difficult project. It also entails a different type of crime and criminal. The programmes favour psychological rather than social causation, and they prefer crimes with a gendered element, particularly ones which in some ways relate to the personal lives of their core trio. These programmes are not interested in the crimes of social deprivation and inequality, although 'bad sex' is present. Instead, they are interested in the ways in which the protagonists juggle their own lives with their professional commitments, and particularly in questions of the intersection of personal and professional lives. Thus, both Scott and Bailey are shown at different points to be vulnerable to plausible male serial killers, and in several of the investigations a question is placed on the judgement of the women. There is a tendency towards melodramatic generic convention, rather than the police procedural, in the resolution of cases and the concluding of episodes, with vigilantism and perpetrator suicide providing emotional resolution without recourse to the justice system.

There is much more to say about *Scott and Bailey*, the pioneering work of Sally Wainwright and RED productions.[14] However, in the context of my wider discussion of twenty-first century television cop shows, *Scott and Bailey* is an example of the television police show refigured so that there is a much greater emphasis on personal life than citizenship and the public sphere. And this presents certain paradoxes for those, such as myself, who have long wanted to see the genre refigured. For this new presence of police with personal lives (*Broadchurch*, ITV, 2013–; *Happy Valley*, BBC, 2014–; and even *Line of Duty*), so noticeable in the last couple of years, and thus perhaps marking the end of my tentative periodisation (2002–12), while making for some great television, also screens the void in the heart of the genre in the current historical context, and some very uncomfortable questions about the changing role of the police in the contemporary state.

Notes

1. Brian True-May, the producer of *Midsomer Murders*, observed in 2011 that Midsomer was 'the last bastion of Englishness and I want to keep it that way', agreeing with the interviewer's query that: '"Englishness" includes other races', 'Well it should do, and maybe I'm not politically correct ... I'm trying to make something which appeals to a certain audience which seems to succeed' (Wilson, 2011, p. 20).
2. McGrath, 1975, pp. 42–3, cited in Laing, 1991.
3. Garnett, 1998, cited in Lacey, 2007, p. 145.
4. McGrath, 1975, pp. 42–3, cited in Laing, 1991.
5. A coinage of Richard Hamblyn's, cited by Marina Warner (2015).
6. See the series' writer/producer Jed Mercurio (2012) on this culture. World Productions, the company started by Tony Garnett was also responsible for the 1992–93 police corruption series, *Between the Lines*.
7. *DCI Banks* (ITV), Series 4, Episode 4, 'Buried 2/2'. Transmitted 25 March 2015.
8. In 2009, the programme had been moved from its earlier, soapier 8pm slot to the prime time 9pm one, but the hoped-for increased audiences didn't follow (see Turnbull, 2014, pp. 59–63).
9. *Collision*, which was broadcast stripped over five days, has higher production values, but, as a short production is a more flexible financial commitment than a continuing serial with salary costs. Fincham's comments, presumably from a press release, appeared in almost identical form across a range of media outlets on the announcement of the cancellation (Anon, 2010a; Anon, 2010b; Sweney, 2010).
10. Yvonne Tasker (2012) has discussed the significance of racial profiling to the narratives of what she nominates US 'terror tv.' While the contexts, the television and our arguments are different, there are evident overlaps and, in the British context, one of the most 'troubling' character figures in twenty-first-century crime and conspiracy drama is the identifiably observant Muslim.
11. Joy (2014) provides a useful analysis of the opening of *Line of Duty* in relation to terrorism.
12. See Brunsdon (2011) for a much more detailed discussion of the post-1978 crisis in the genre.
13. On *Luther*, see Piper (2015, pp. 122–9).
14. See, for example, Ruth McElroy's 'Women Cops on the Box: Female Detection in the British Police Procedural' in this volume and her 'The Feminization of Contemporary British Television Drama: Sally Wainwright and Red Productions' in Moseley, Rachel et al (eds.) (2016) *Television for Women*, Routledge.

References

Anon., 2010a. ITV axes *The Bill* after 27 years. *BBC News*, [online] 26 March. Available at: http://news.bbc.co.uk/1/hi/entertainment/8588941.stm [Accessed 24 March 2015].

Anon., 2010b. ITV axes *The Bill*. *The Independent*, [online] 26 March. Available at: http://www.independent.co.uk/arts-entertainment/tv/news/itv-axes-the-bill-1928353.html [Accessed 24 March 2015].

Brunsdon, Charlotte, 1998. Structure of anxiety: recent British television crime fiction. *Screen*, 39(3), pp. 223–43.

Brunsdon, Charlotte, 2010. Bingeing on box-sets: The national and the digital in television crime drama. In: Jostein Gripsrud, ed. 2010. *Relocating Television: Television in the Digital Context*. London, England: Routledge. pp. 63–75.

Brunsdon, Charlotte, 2010. *Law and Order*. London, England: British Film Institute/Palgrave Macmillan.

Joy, Stuart, 2014. Policing across borders: *Line of Duty* and the politics of national identity. *Journal of Popular Television*, 2(2), pp. 155–72.

Lacey, Stephen, 2007. *Tony Garnett*. Manchester, England: University of Manchester Press.

Laing, Stuart, 1991. Banging in some reality: the original 'Z Cars.' In: John Corner, ed. 1991. *Popular Television in Britain: Studies in Cultural History*. London, England: British Film Institute. pp. 125–44.

Lawson, Mark, 2010. *The Bill* killed off due to ratings slump. *The Guardian*, [online] 26 March. Available at: http://www.theguardian.com/media/2010/mar/26/itv-bill-dropped-ratings-slump [Accessed 24 March 2015].

McElroy, Ruth, 2016. Women cops on the box: female detection in the British police procedural. In Ruth McElroy, ed. 2016 *Contemporary British Television Crime Drama*, London, England: Routledge.

McElroy, Ruth. 2016 The feminization of contemporary British television drama: Sally Wainwright and Red Productions. In Rachel Moseley, Helen Wheatley and Helen Wood, eds. *Television for Women: New Directions*, London, England: Routledge.

Mercurio, Jed, 2012. Paperwork and a target culture have taken their toll on our police. *The Guardian*, 27 June. p. 28.

Piper, Helen, 2015. *TV Detective: Voices of Dissent in Contemporary Culture*. London, England: I.B.Tauris.

Stubbs, David, 2010. What killed *The Bill*? Chronic revamp syndrome. *The Guardian*, [online] 26 March. Available at: http://www.theguardian.com/tv-and-radio/tvandradioblog/2010/mar/26/the-bill-revamp-syndrome [Accessed 24 March 2015].

Sutcliffe, Tom, 2010. Last night's TV: *The Bill* ITV1, *The Deep* BBC1: Why shouldn't this drama plod on? *The Independent*, 25 August.

Sweney, Mark, 2010. *The Bill*: ITV drops police drama after 27 years. *The Guardian*, [online] 26 March. Available at: http://www.theguardian.com/media/2010/mar/26/the-bill-itv [Accessed 24 March 2015].

Tasker, Yvonne, 2012. Television crime drama and homeland security: from *Law & Order* to 'Terror TV.' *Cinema Journal*, 51(4), pp. 44–65.

Turnbull, Sue, 2014. *The TV Crime Drama*. Edinburgh, Scotland: Edinburgh University Press.

Turner, Graeme, 2009. Television and the nation: does this matter any more? In: Graeme Turner and Jinna Tay, eds., *Television Studies After TV: Understanding Television in the Post-Broadcast Era*. Londo, England: Routledge. pp. 54–64.

Warner, Marina, 2015. Learning my lesson. The disfiguring of higher education. 19 March 2015. *London Review of Books*, 37(6).

Williams, Raymond, 1977. A lecture on realism. *Screen*, 17(1), pp. 61–74.

Wilson, Benji, 2011. Solved: the mystery of the missing black faces in *Midsomer Murders*, interview with Brian True-May. *Radio Times*, 19–25 March. pp. 20–3.

2 Unlocking the Mechanism of Murder[1]

Forensic Humanism and Contemporary Crime Drama

Martin Willis

While a great deal of critical attention has been given to US forensic crime drama, and especially to *CSI: Crime Scene Investigation* (CBS, 2000–), there is relatively little on its British equivalents. *CSI* has proved influential in several fields of inquiry, from its industrial and network settings (Kirby, 2013), through the technical innovations it has pioneered (Weissmann, 2007; Pierson, 2010) to the legal contexts in which it has been controversial (Cole and Dioso-Villa, 2006–07; DiFonzo, 2007). However, British forensic crime dramas should be of greater interest because of their primacy in presenting forensic science on television and their greater attention to its complexity. What is most interesting, and the focus in this chapter, is the relationships between forensic science and medicine and the human stories in which they intervene. British forensic crime dramas stage what I shall call forensic humanism: the dramatisation of interconnections between science and society where conflict is to be found not in the traditional battle between criminals and their pursuers but in the clash of scientific and human stories.

Silent Witness (BBC, 1996–) premiered four years before *CSI*, and was a leader in distributing forensic drama as a global television format. *Waking the Dead* (BBC, 2000–) also premiered before *CSI* (if only by a month) and introduced the high-tech mise en scène that became a staple of the *CSI* franchise. In the scholarship on forensic crime drama, a consensus has been reached on how, and in what contexts, the genre should be read (Jermyn, 2003; Nunn and Biressi, 2003; Pierson, 2010; Ridgman, 2012). First, forensic drama should be seen as a form of realism in which scientific work provides the foundational realist framework for what is otherwise standard police procedural television. Second, forensic investigation should be regarded as a method for shifting the focus of crime drama onto the victims of crime rather than their perpetrators or investigators: the corpse as a silent witness given a voice by forensic procedures. While these interrogations of British forensic crime drama offer valuable readings, and are revealing of what is new and interesting about the televising of forensics, they emerge from specific theoretical and even subject-specific contexts; they focus on understanding and analysing both televisual realism and Michel Foucault's influential idea of the gaze as a paradigm for the power relationships that develop from looking at one another. Understandably, these readings of forensic science on television privilege television. What might emerge if a reading began, instead, with the science? What different conclusions would be reached from an analysis that situated forensic crime drama within histories, and present understandings, of scientific medicine?

In television production, the links between medicine and crime have been extensive. In the United States, for example, in the 1950s the creator of medical drama *Medic* (NBC, 1954–56) James Moser, was also the producer of the influential crime drama, *Dragnet* (NBC, 1951–59). This crossover continues into the present day in both Britain and the United States with, for instance, the writer Jed Mercurio, who wrote the innovative medical drama, *Cardiac Arrest* (BBC, 1994–96) and who went on to write the award-winning crime drama, *Line of Duty* (BBC, 2012–). While connections clearly exist in the writing and production of crime and medical television, there are also parallels in the structures and narratives of such dramas. As Frances Bonner (2005) has shown, medical drama is 'marked by the display of technology' (p. 110) in ways comparable to forensic crime drama, and additionally provides a fictionalised 'accelerated hyperreality' (p. 109) in which medical crises are resolved within a short timescale just as forensic examinations take place in a speeded up fictional world where, for example, DNA typing takes a matter of moments rather than months in order for the narrative of human relationships to continue without undue fragmentation. As these examples reveal, it is the relationships between scientific medicine and human subjects, whether in history or on television, that provides the most valuable context from which to consider contemporary forensic crime drama.

The Problem of the Speaking Body

One key problem that critical readings of forensic crime drama have struggled to negotiate is the somewhat contradictory notion of forensic examination, and especially forensic pathology, as a conduit for greater empathy with the victims of crime. Deborah Jermyn (2013) recognises that forensic crime drama attempts to show a 'victim more worthy of attention' (p. 108), but also notes the discomfort when such attentiveness comes close to voyeurism. It is, however, commonplace to argue, as Weissmann (2007) has done, that forensic science gives victims 'the agency to be able to look and talk back at the investigators.' Indeed, this is how dramas such as *Silent Witness* and *Waking the Dead* appear to place themselves: first and foremost in their titles, which contrast the normal and assumed passivity of the lifeless body with the active testimony that they will come to provide via forensic efforts. *Silent Witness*, in particular, reinforces this message in its evocative, liturgical title music. The central lyric, sung in Latin, is 'co-witness from the spirit', indicating the connection between the corpse and the forensic scientist.

From the perspective of the history of medicine, however, there is a fundamental opposition between scientific medicine like forensics or pathology and the agency of the victim. Scientific medicine does not enable the subject of medical investigation to speak, but rather reduces the power of that speech by shifting the burden of truth from personal testimony to scientific fact. Indeed, such has been the silencing power of scientific medicine that new forms of what are often called patient-centred medicine have, for several decades, been fighting to regain some of the rights and privileges that human subjects had lost to diagnostic machines and unsympathetic physicians. Forensic science also followed this pattern of an increasing scientific dominance silencing the voices of victims. As Sarah Dauncey (2010) points out, forensic science's history and success has been built on its ability to turn the body into 'a different kind of authority, of proof rather than testimony' (p. 167).

Television drama is not, of course, historical reality, and forensic drama writers and producers need not concern themselves with the contradiction of privileging scientific medicine and the voice of the victim simultaneously. Yet it is clear that, in offering both to their audiences, the makers of forensic television wish to negotiate a position for these crime dramas that displays some understanding of the complex relationships between the scientific and the human stories they tell. Nevertheless, this is not how US forensic dramas such as *CSI* perform. David Kirby (2013), in a series of interviews with key *CSI* personnel, concludes that 'what we see in contemporary television's forensic fictions is the triumph of science over humanistic modes of detection' (p. 94). Since forensic science is 'always certain' (Kirby, 2013, p. 101) in the *CSI* franchise, Kirby is right to make his claim of that drama. Yet British forensic crime drama cannot, as Kirby appears to suggest, be placed in the same category. Unlike *CSI*'s promotion of scientific mastery (the franchise tagline is 'the evidence never lies'), British dramas offer a more nuanced interrogation of the meanings of scientific investigation as they pertain to institutions of authority and to the individual people who represent them or come into conflict with them. It is in these British dramas that what I have called forensic humanism is most commonly introduced and tested.

Uncovering the Past

Both the most important British forensic crime dramas of the last decade, *Silent Witness* and *Waking the Dead*, present the conflict between forensic and human stories as negotiations between the past and the present. For both dramas, but particularly for *Waking the Dead*, whose unique selling point is the resurrection and solving of 'cold' or historical criminal cases, the past is a vital element in uncovering the human activity that led to, and forms a part of, the crimes under scientific investigation. The importance of knowing, and even understanding, the past is also an essential aspect of scientific medicine. The medical case history, which physicians take from patients presenting their symptoms for the first time, is one of the most vital interrogative and exploratory tools at the disposal of the medical profession. It was during the rise of scientific medicine in the nineteenth century that taking a case history became an essential feature of the newly objective doctor-patient relationship. In order to stage an appropriate conflict between human stories and forensic discovery, British crime dramas maintain a sense of forensic evidence as only ever partial and always liable to contestation. As the forensic pathologist Sam Ryan (Amanda Burton) states in the first episode from *Silent Witness*'s third series, titled 'An Academic Exercise' (19–20 March 1998), forensics 'is a science of debatable facts' that must never forget its own fallibility.

This is a long way from the epistemology of the *CSI* franchise, where forensic science is both technically infallible and also immune to human error or intervention. However, Ryan is reflecting accurately the historical reality of forensic science's own past; particularly in Britain. As Roger Smith (1988) explored in an important essay on the use of forensic evidence in criminal court proceedings, from the late 1960s and intermittently through to the late 1980s, forensic science often found itself in 'a period of unwanted attention' (p. 72) where its methods and claims were placed under severe scrutiny. In particular, Smith draws attention to the contested convictions by forensic evidence of several supposed Irish terrorists for the bombing of two British cities: Guildford and Birmingham. Although the outcomes of appeals were not known when Smith published his essay, an extensive undermining of the validity of forensic evidence had already taken place. Much of this was reported in the media and thus reached a large audience. Smith concludes that 'forensic scientists may thus increasingly find themselves in an uncomfortable world where scientific knowledge no longer has self-evident credibility' (p. 85). The convictions of the 11 individuals imprisoned for the bombings were quashed by 1991, and the story of one of those was turned into the BAFTA-nominated film, *In the Name of the Father* (directed by Jim Sheridan, 1993). What Deborah Jermyn calls the 'cultural turn towards forensic fascination' (2013, p. 103) in the 1990s must therefore also be seen in this context as forensic fragility. Indeed, as Alison Adam has revealed in her recent book-length study of the history of forensics in Britain, forensic science was prone to error and misprision long before its problems with terrorist investigation (Adam, 2015, p. 102).

It was into this forensic reality that *Silent Witness* first appeared on British screens in February 1996. In an interview given to the *Radio Times* by Amanda Burton to support the launch of the drama, the interviewer draws attention to the fact that Burton's character is 'living and working in Cambridge where her mother moved after her husband, who was in the RUC, was blown up in a booby-trapped car when Sam was 13' (Duncan, p. 16). For Burton, there is public interest in forensic science because 'they're the things we most worry about politically' (p. 18). On the day of the screening of the first episode (21 February 1996), several newspapers led with a story of the renewal of the Irish Republican Army's bombing campaign on the British mainland (e.g., 'IRA') and this was reported, too, on the BBC News at 9pm, which *Silent Witness* directly followed. The first episodes also drew attention to the problems of forensic evidence and this, too, was noted by reviewers. Peter Paterson, writing one of the first reviews of the drama on 22 February 1996, asked – under the title 'Amanda, yes – propaganda, no' – whether the writer of the drama, Kevin Hood, aimed to depict Ryan as corrupt: 'at any rate, he included a sequence in which Dr. Sam told a bare-faced lie to the coroner's court' (Paterson). Whether viewers were aware of a broader 'public crisis in confidence' (Naughton, 2010, p. 1) over forensic evidence, as the Criminal Cases Review Commission put it, there was ample opportunity to be reminded of the parallels between problems within the British justice system and *Silent Witness*'s portrayal of forensic science.

It was in *Silent Witness*, too, that two types of scene commonly used in forensic crime drama to display forensic science and its reading of the past evolved. They are the crime scene analysis, and the reconstruction (often a flashback sequence). These scenes enable dramas to draw the relationship between scientific and human interpretations. Both are staged examinations of historical events. That is, despite being presented in the on-screen present, such scenes are commonly conducted in the past tense. The crime scene, for example, must be forensically secured: a means of trapping a specific location in a period of past history rather than allowing it to accrue the detritus of the present. It is, in fact, important that the crime scene is a *scene*, for it has theatrical connotations entirely appropriate to its role in providing for the forensic scientist a repeated, discrete segment of narrative action bounded on either side by its previous and consequent temporality. Every on-screen actor involved in the dramatic tension of the crime scene is fascinated by the past, as is indicated by the desire always to know the time of death of any victim. Almost the first words spoken by *Silent Witness*'s new forensic specialist, Jack Hodgson, in his first screen appearance in 'Change' (10 January 2013) are 'He hit the corner of the table as he fell. He instinctively put his hand to his head. It's bleeding. He transfers the blood to his hand, so when he falls again he leaves it on the carpet.' Jack is immediately identified as a forensic scientist with a keen ability to read the past in the traces it leaves on a crime scene. The response of the pathologist, Nikki Alexander – 'I guess it's plausible' – immediately delimits Jack's perspective and reminds audiences that forensic evidence is only ever an interpretation of the past, not its totality.

Waking the Dead frames forensics rather differently. Unable to access historic crime scenes, it dramatises forensic knowledge of the past in reconstruction scenes. In the episode titled 'Magdalene 26' (7 September 2009), a middle-aged woman describes the events leading to a 1960s double murder at which she was present. This moment is the key revelation of the drama, since the double murder is the historic case on which the detective and forensic teams have been working. In an earlier scene the forensic pathologist, Eve Lockhart, had explained the likely events based on the remaining forensic evidence. As the woman begins her testimony, a cut takes the viewer back to the 1960s, to witness the double murder for themselves. *Waking the Dead*'s reconstruction begins with a human story rather than a

story emerging from forensic expertise, although, as we shall see, it is forensic expertise that the reconstruction scene will confirm. The reconstruction
scene aims not at a highly technological scientism, but instead to produce
a more granular image that connotes the past and employs popular music
from the 1960s to do so: in this instance, Dusty Springfield's *You Don't
Have to Say You Love Me* (1966), whose lyrics reflect the human story at
the heart of the episode.

Most important in the reconstruction scene, however, is the subtle slowing of the actors' movements as well as of the tracking and panning camera
(which otherwise moves quickly in depicting a violent fight) in order to
stress the forensic evidence of which the viewer is already cognisant. One
such slowing of the pace of the dramatic action shows the thuggish night-
club owner first slap and then kiss the young woman, transferring her blood
to his own mouth (a forensic trace of the past that is puzzling to Lockhart
40 years later). There is no narrative that explains the connection between
the on-screen action and the forensic evidence. Instead the episode assumes
a form of forensic insight on the part of the viewer, allowing the screen to
show us both human and forensic truths simultaneously. Indeed, in terms
of the on-screen chronology, forensic evidence leads not to an appreciation
of the wonders of forensic science but to the human narratives and actions
that created that evidence.

Reconstruction scenes are widely employed in *CSI*, and commonly discussed in its scholarship (Kirby, 2013; Pierson, 2010; Weissmann, 2007).
In fact, the vivid visual reconstructions of the effects of a weapon on the
body, for example, are even called the CSI-shot. This filmic technique promotes forensic science's ability to recover past events, certainly, but it does
so only in order to promote a sense of the mastery of forensics. More than
that, these scenes also use false and heightened colouring for the interior
of the body and ally this with a soundscape that overemphasises biological
damage (noisy squelching is common), while also linking forensic explanation to contemporary rock music. This has the effect of denuding the scene
of any humanity (these are rarely scenes in which a complete human body
appears, and never as a person), whilst aiming to suggest that the technical
skill of forensic investigation is both filled with wonder, and also powerfully
masculine and interestingly maverick. This last, of course, is supposed to
denote the work of science although it is a very nineteenth-century version of heroic, dangerous science. Reconstruction in *Waking the Dead* never
takes the audience inside the human body. Rather, it privileges human interaction whilst enabling the now forensically aware viewer to see the events
which left vestiges of forensic evidence for later discovery.

Locating Expertise

British forensic crime dramas draw attention to the partiality and frailty of
forensic knowledge through consistently foregrounding an essential component of forensic work: expertise. *Silent Witness*, in particular, but also

The Body Farm (BBC, 2011) – a spin-off series from *Waking the Dead* – often ask the audience to consider who has expertise, of what kind, and in what relation to other forms of knowledge. Expertise has always been essential to both forensic science and forensic fictions. From a medical juris-prudence perspective, for example, forensic science 'hinges on expertise in constructing factual statements' (Smith, 1988, p. 91). Likewise forensic fictions, beginning with the groundbreaking novels of Patricia Cornwell, attempt to walk a line between authenticity and imagination. In her early publicity materials, Cornwell was always at pains to stress her years of work with the Virginia County Medical Examiner's Office. Forensic tele-vision dramas are no different. *Silent Witness* parades its forensic pathol-ogy consultant on its official website; in fact, it provides a video-recorded interview with Dr. Stuart Hamilton, one of only two recordings that does not include a key member of the on-screen talent (BBC, 2013). Hamilton makes a key argument in his 2-minute interview to camera: 'I had a con-ception that really they [the producers of *Silent Witness*] weren't bothered about accuracy ... Now that I've dealt with *Silent Witness* ... it's just really eye-opening how much effort all these people put into balancing accu-rate forensic facts with a good story.' Similarly, the producer of *Waking the Dead*'s final series, Colin Wratten, claimed, in a more light-hearted vein, that from working on the show he 'could probably kill someone 20 different ways now and have an above average chance of getting away with it' (Wratten, 2011).

Wratten's comment concerning his own improved forensic knowledge also speaks to the most widely discussed phenomenon of forensic exper-tise, the so-called 'CSI-effect.' Investigated by media scholars and, more prominently, by legal experts, the *CSI*-effect is the perceived influence of the television series on juror behaviour in American courtrooms (Cole and Dioso-Villa, 2006–07; Deutsch and Cavender, 2008; DiFonzo, 2007). The *CSI*-effect is actually a series of different effects, including the potential belief amongst jurors that they have gained real forensic expertise from viewing *CSI* and are therefore in a position to pass expert judgement upon forensic evidence presented in court. For legal scholars, the *CSI*-effect either tells a story of science overtaking the law as a 'truth-making enter-prise' (Cole and Dioso-Villa, 2007, p. 469) or alternatively gives a 'mis-leading presentation of forensic evidence in the guise of scientific truth' (DiFonzo, 2007, p. 507). The same phenomenon has been observed in scientific medicine, where Catherine Belling, for example, identified the medical documentary, *The Operation* (Discovery, 1993–2001) as contrib-uting to the emergence of the expert patient who was sometimes unable to see that expertise gained from television was 'fragile indeed' (Belling, 1998, p. 14).

British forensic crime dramas, led by *Silent Witness*, accept and interro-gate forensic expertise as unstable and contested. Uniquely, they highlight how truth-making might be found outside of science in the human stories that non-scientific investigators tell of crimes and criminals. It is important to note that *Silent Witness* has not arrived at this questioning of forensic expertise in response to *CSI*. Rather, it has from its origins in the mid-1990s, always considered forensic expertise to be incomplete and only ever able to solve crime in collaboration with other forms of knowledge. The series' original forensic pathologist, Sam Ryan, was often placed in scenes where her evidence was challenged, as it was in 'An Academic Exercise' by both a science student and by police officers. Likewise, the three pathologists who led the cast through the 2000s – Leo Dalton, Harry Cunningham and Nikki Alexander – were continually placed in storylines that saw them in conflict with one another over the interpretation of evidence. A good example of this is the episode 'Voids' (7 January 2010) in which Nikki and Harry are employed by opposing legal teams to offer directly contrasting, yet still expert, opinions on the same victim's death.

More recently, *Silent Witness* has offered a vision of a more fine-grained expertise than was the case in the 1990s. Since 2013, the key protagonists have not been forensic pathologists alone, but pathologists and forensic scientists (who work with trace evidence from crime scenes rather than with human remains) represented by Nikki Alexander (Emilia Fox) and Jack Hodgson (David Caves). Their early encounters, and subsequent encounters with police officers, highlight how the series aims to show different forms of expert knowledge which clash with and complement one another. In Jack's first episode, 'Change' (10 January 2013), he, Nikki and police officers DS Gold and DC Cook discuss the nature of a man's death whilst standing in his hotel room over his corpse. The dialogue from the scene is worth setting out in full:

> GOLD: Oh, I love these [reaching for a bowl of sweets].
> JACK: No! It's a crime scene.
> GOLD: I'll decide if it's a crime scene.
> DC COOK: Druggies?
> JACK AND NIKKI: [talking over one another] No paraphernalia/No visible …
> NIKKI: I'll know more later.
>
> …
>
> JACK: He fell.
> NIKKI: I'll know more later [Jack and Nikki share a look of mutual annoyance]. The victim is …
> DS GOLD: John Briggs, yes. Already on the web. One of you on retainer or do you tip them off a la carte?
> NIKKI: You're not really insinuating that one of us …? [Jack and Nikki share a look of mutual incredulity]
> DS GOLD: No, no, of course not, it'll be the chambermaid or one of the girls on reception.
> JACK: Not a policeman?

Heather Nunn and Anita Biressi (2003) argue that forensic crime dramas show us a consensual science underwriting 'the authority of the law' (p. 196), but as is clear from this scene, expertise is just as likely to be envisioned as diffuse and antagonistic. Indeed, here the antagonisms are tripartite: Nikki's pathological expertise conflicts with Jack's forensic science expertise and in turn Jack's knowledge clashes with DS Gold's assertion of police expertise. At various points the scene shifts the dynamic so that viewers are invited to sympathise with the police (as Jack unnecessarily attempts to dominate Gold), pathology (as Jack over-asserts the truth of his own expert knowledge), and finally forensics in toto (as Gold wrongly accuses Jack and Nikki of speaking with the media). What is most revealing here, however, are the ways in which forensic expertise and human narratives blend and clash. While we might expect Jack to privilege forensic knowledge, it is actually his desire to tell stories of the evidence that Nikki undermines. By contrast, Jack's annoyance with Nikki's hesitation in drawing conclusions arises because of her unwillingness to put her expertise to imaginative use in constructing a storyline for the evidence around them. Gold, meanwhile, asserts a different kind of expertise: a knowledge of the relative strengths of different stories that will ultimately allow her to decide whether the hotel is, or is not, a crime scene.

Silent Witness continually pits humanistic storytelling against forensic evidence. In a later episode, 'Undertone' (23–24 January 2014), this is spelt out to Jack by another policeman, DI Brooke, who tells him: 'Not your job to have theories, Jack. Facts. Physical evidence. That's what we look to you for.' Ultimately, *Silent Witness* undermines the usual assumption about the relationship between the police and forensic sciences as mutually legitimating (Cavender and Deutsch, 2007, p. 73). It does so, however, in order to place forensic expertise in conflict with humanistic detection so as to show that *both* are necessary in the solving of crime. This asks viewers to think of forensic expertise as liable to error in the same way that humanistic knowledge – detective's hunches, possible stories, what ifs – is already seen to have epistemological fragility. Unlike *CSI*, *Silent Witness* and other British forensic crime dramas reduce the presentation of scientific mastery to more mundane, but more humanist, concerns with forensic expertise.

Surveillance and Sousveillance

The forensic gaze is, for most scholars of this genre of television, the most vital aspect of the power of forensic science on screen (Pierson, 2010; Weissmann, 2007). It is not: it is, rather, the archive. As Allan Sekula (1986) argues in his reading of historical photographic archives, 'the central artefact of this system is not the camera but the filing cabinet' (p. 16). The same applies to forensic crime drama: the central feature of forensic investigation is not what forensic pathologists and examiners uncover through their expert and powerful looking, but which archival database provides them with relevant information. This is one aspect of such dramas that seems universal, applying equally to *CSI* and to *Silent Witness* and other British series. In a single episode of *Waking the Dead*, for example, titled 'Pietà' (19–20 May 2008), seven different archives and databases (British DNA records, CCTV footage, files from the former Yugoslavia, hospital personnel records, mobile phone data, Serbian military files and Soviet espionage records) contribute to the solution of the crimes at hand. Success in forensic television crime comes not from the discovery of DNA, say, but from finding a 'hit' or a 'match' in a database. More than this, each crime scene is transformed by forensic science into a new archive – converted into segments, photographed, documented, numbered, labelled and stored – against which other archives can be compared.

Such forensic archiving began in clinical medicine (Osborne, 1999), and has come to have power equivalent to legal systems (Manoff, 2004). It is a form of surveillance that operates, as Vian Bakir (2010) argues, through 'data banks' (p. 19) and other assemblages of surveillant technologies and systems. This poses a problem for forensic crime drama which, in replicating this contemporary assemblage, reduces the corpse of the victim to nothing but a repository for the material traces of someone or something else (a fibre that will connect to a place or a fingerprint that belongs to another person). To enter into the archive as a victim is to become reified: to be turned into a machine and made part of a larger, mechanistic knowledge-base in which uniqueness (one's own DNA, for example) is transformed into similarity (how far is one's DNA like someone else's). Indeed, the victim often plays a useful role only if the DNA sample in the archive is not their own and can be identified as *the same as* one in another archive somewhere else. For example, it is common for forensic dramas to create dramatic tension by discovering that a DNA sample associated with a victim belongs to another individual and has been matched to a sample from that individual within another archive, such as the archive of members of the Armed Forces. Yet forensic crime dramas also resist the totality of such archives. They do so by undermining archival surveillance with various forms of subversive sousveillance. Sousveillance is defined by its creators and later commentators as the reuse of technologies of surveillance for personal purposes so as to offer a 'watchful vigilance from underneath' (Steve Mann, cited in Bakir, 2010, p. 16). It aims to 'take a stance against the surveillant state' (Bakir, 2010, p. 16). Importantly, and in a fascinating doubling of their identity, British forensic crime drama places its central forensic experts as employers of sousveillance techniques when, officially at least, their role is to support the surveillant state.

It is to counter the dehumanising procedures of archival surveillance that forensic crime drama introduces its sousveillant antagonists. The episode of *Waking the Dead* ('Pietà') that employed the vast range of archives and databases to come close to discovering the identity of two Serbian war criminals concludes with a privileging of sousveillance, announced angrily by Superintendent Boyd who, in interviewing the suspected criminals shouts: 'Why is my account so accurate?' It is because, he continues, he has three witnesses who have provided their own account, and which means he does not need to rely on DNA and other archival evidence to secure a trial. As Boyd's angry monologue comes to an end, the camera shifts attention to the three witnesses who are gathered outside the interview room – using the surveillance technology of the one-way mirror to spy on the proceedings within. The scene ends with Boyd drawing back a screen to reveal the witnesses in the act of their sousveillance and to invite them to enact the power of that position by coming forward to identify the men personally. Not only does this dramatise, very theatrically, the actions of sousveillance, it also makes the process of identification a human story rather than an archival discovery.

Silent Witness also uses sousveillance as a humanist tool, and indeed has done so across its 17 series. Its first forensic pathologist Sam Ryan, for example, makes connections using a private photograph that she was unable to do using laboratory images ('An Academic Exercise') and, across her seven series from 1996 to 2003, was continually in conflict with state-sanctioned law enforcement over the potential truths of forensic evidence. Recently, *Silent Witness* has extended its sousveillance, perhaps to respond to the increasingly archived society of contemporary Britain where 'surveillance and … sousveillance coexist [in a] fragile equilibrium' (Ganascia, 2010, p. 491). One 2014 episode ('Undertone') sees Jack Hodgson undertake a series of sousveillance activities – accessing mobile phone records and retrieving data from a car's SatNav system – in order to reveal the corruption of a police officer who is blocking Jack's and Nikki's efforts to seek justice for a victim. Jack's sousveillance not only enables that justice, but also uncovers a further human story in the officer's desire for fatherhood despite infertility. Sousveillance offers 'access to … intimacy' (Ganascia, 2010, p. 492) that the unnatural authority of surveillance cannot, and provides a humanist corrective to the cold, archival culture of forensic examination.

Of course, forensic crime dramas cannot subjugate all forensic data to alternative means of finding solutions to crimes. Were they to do so they would fall foul of their generic conventions, as Kirby (2013, p. 100) has argued. What is depicted on screen, however, is not a fight between surveillance archives and sousveillance resistance in the ways that expertise is often characterised as conflict. Rather, sousveillance is seen to support the activities of forensic surveillance. While this tends to undermine the politically radical nature of contemporary sousveillance outside the television industry, it does humanise the clinical scientific medicine of forensic science on screen. In the example above, Jack's sousveillant investigation of the police officer comes after his own forensic examination has been questioned and the archival evidence he has collected has been tampered with. His sousveillance is therefore a means to protect the security of the forensic archive rather than to question it. Ultimately, it is the forensic database (this time of car interior fabrics) that reveals the guilt of the police officer and reaffirms Jack's expertise as well as the forensic archive's centrality to criminal detection.

Not coincidentally, *CSI*'s scientific mastery is only called into question when material scientific evidence gives way to sousveillance. In the series' sixth season, in an episode titled 'Rashomama' (27 April 2006), the Las Vegas team loses all the forensic evidence related to a murder at a wedding. Confined to the office whilst waiting for internal affairs to interview them, the team solves the murder through a combination of personal recollection and a private wedding video. Although it is additional forensic evidence that ultimately confirms their conclusions, both the video and their own stories determine the direction of their further examinations.

Conclusion

British forensic crime dramas, unlike their US counterparts, mediate forensic science with humanist detection. They offer up a challenge to the hegemony of law and the power of the state and although ultimately they always fall on the side of law and confirm state-sanctioned authority, they illuminate the fragility of that support. They also offer a mature vision of forensic science as a mode of knowledge production that is only ever partial and is continually contested. In doing so, they replicate how scientific knowledge operates in the real world. It is in this depiction that British dramas depart most dramatically from *CSI*, whose vision of infallible scientific mastery and heroic investigators looks, from the historical and contemporary perspectives of scientific medicine, somewhat one-dimensional.

British forensic crime dramas reveal that it is the introduction of a humanist perspective that opens up the possibility for complexity in both dramatic and scientific territories. Without humanist narratives with authority equal to the forensic science stories on display, the drive would always be towards reduction: towards the promotion of a science that always has the answers since the generic formula for television crime fiction demands that answers are provided. In partnering forensics with humanism, British crime dramas can provide solutions and complex narratives that do not place demands on forensic science always to control access to the truth. To conclude in this way is also to illuminate the important role that human narratives – and humanities scholarship – play in balancing scientific interpretations of the world and scientistic philosophies that enable them. There is particular significance not only in paying attention to the ways in which popular television might portray human-science interactions on screen but in understanding how to interrogate such representational narratives so as to recover the humanist endeavour at the heart of civic society.

Note

1. This phrase was inspired by the first episode of forensic crime drama *The Body Farm* (BBC, 13 September 2011), which begins with the narration of forensic pathologist, Eve Lockhart. Her desire is to bring justice to victims by unlocking the mechanism of the murders she investigates.

References

Adam, A. 2015. *A History of Forensic Science: British Beginnings in the Twentieth Century*. London, England: Routledge.

Bakir, V., 2013. *Torture, Intelligence and Sousveillance in the War on Terror: Agenda-Building Strategies*. Farnham, England: Ashgate.

BBC, 2013. *Silent Witness*. BBC.co.uk. [online] Available at: http://www.bbc.co.uk/programmes/P012yd2c> [Accessed 10 November 2014].

Belling, C., 1998. Reading *The Operation*: television, realism, and the possession of medical knowledge. *Literature and Medicine*, 17(1), pp. 1–23.

Bonner, F., 2005. Looking inside: showing medical operations on ordinary television. In: G. King, ed. 2005. *The Spectacle of the Real: From Hollywood to 'Reality' TV and Beyond*. Bristol, England: Intellect. pp. 105–15.

Cavender, G., and Deutsch, S.K., 2007. CSI and moral authority: the police and science. *Crime Media Culture*, 3(1), pp. 67–81.

Cole, S.A. and Dioso-Villa, R., 2006–07. CSI and its effects: media, juries, and the burden of proof. *New England Law Review*, 41(435), pp. 435–69.

Dauncey, S., 2010. Crime, forensics, and modern science. In: C. Rzepka and L. Horsley, eds., 2010. *A Companion to Crime Fiction*. Chichester, England: Wiley-Blackwell. pp. 164–74.

Deutsch, S.K. and Cavender, G., 2008. CSI and forensic realism. *Journal of Criminal Justice and Popular Culture*, 15(1), pp. 34–53.

DiFonzo, J.H., 2007. Devil in a white coat: the temptation of forensic evidence in the age of CSI. *New England Law Review*, 41(503), pp. 503–32.

Duncan, Andrew, 1996. Amanda Burton gets tough in BBC1's Silent Witness. *Radio Times*, 17–23 Feburary. pp. 16–18.

Ganascia, J-G., 2010. The generalized sousveillance society. *Social Science Information*, 49(3), pp. 489–507.

'IRA Renew Bombing Campaign', 1996. *Daily Mail*, 21 February. p. 1.

Jermyn, D., 2003. Women with a mission: Lynda La Plante, DCI Jane Tennison and the reconfiguration of TV crime drama. *International Journal of Cultural Studies*, 6(1), pp. 46–63.

Jermyn, D., 2013. Labs and slabs: television crime drama and the quest for forensic realism. *Studies in History and Philosophy of Biological and Biomedical Sciences*, 44, pp. 103–09.

Kirby, D.A., 2013. Forensic fictions: science, television production, and modern storytelling. *Studies in History and Philosophy of Biological and Biomedical Sciences*, 44, pp. 92–102.

Manoff, M., 2004. Theories of the archive from across the disciplines. *Portal: Libraries and the Academy*, 4(1), pp. 9–25.

Naughton, Michael. ed., 2010. *The Criminal Cases Review Commission: Hope for the Innocent?* Basingstoke, England: Palgrave Macmillan.

Nunn, H. and Biressi, A., 2003. *Silent Witness*: detection, femininity, and the post-mortem body. *Feminist Media Studies*, 3(2), pp. 193–206.

Osborne, T., 1999. The ordinariness of the archive. *History of the Human Sciences*, 12(2), pp. 51–64.

Paterson, Peter, 1996. Amanda, yes – propaganda, no. *Daily Mail*, 22 February. p. 55.

Pierson, D.P., 2010. Evidential bodies: the forensic and abject gazes in C.S.I.: crime scene investigation. *Journal of Communication Inquiry*, 34(2), pp. 184–203.

Ridgman, Jeremy, 2012. Duty of care: crime drama and the medical encounter. *Critical Studies in Television*, 7(1), pp. 1–12.

Sekula, A., 1986. The body and the archive. *October*, 39, pp. 3–64.

Smith, R., 1988. The trials of forensic science. *Science as Culture*, 4, pp. 71–94.

Weissmann, E., 2007. The victim's suffering translated: CSI: crime scene investigation and the crime genre. *Intensities: The Journal of Cult Media*. [online] Available at: http://intensitiescultmedia.files.wordpress.com/2012/12/weissmann-victims-suffering-translated.pdf [Accessed 15 January 2016].

Wratten, C., 2011. Waking the dead: maggots, jam and mouldy corpses. BBC.co.uk, [blog] 11 March. Available at: http://www.bbc.co.uk/blogs/tv/posts/waking-the-dead [Accessed 15 January 2016].

3 Walking Whitechapel

Ripper Street, *Whitechapel*, and Place in the Gothic Crime Drama

Rebecca Williams

In her comprehensive analysis of the crime drama, Sue Turnbull (2014) identifies television series including *Dexter* (Showtime, 2006–13), *Hannibal* (NBC, 2013–), *The X-Files* (FOX, 1993–2002) and *Profiler* (NBC, 1996–2000), which possess a distinctive '"Gothic tone" and horror movie aesthetic' (2014, p. 139). However, when she notes that the crime genre resembles a 'primordial soup' 'that includes true crime, melodramatic plays, the detective story, the hard-boiled thriller, film noir, the semi-documentary feature film, the radio crime show, and the routine representations of crime in the news' (2014, p. 42), the Gothic genre is notably absent. Indeed, there has been a tendency to overlook crime drama's debt to the Gothic in favour of an inclination to 'frame … crime television in terms of realism, emphasizing the ways in which the genre … deals with societal perceptions of crime, deviance and danger in a risk society' (Tasker, 2011). Seeking to redress this apparent neglect, this chapter explores the generic hybrid of the Gothic crime drama through two recent British examples, ITV's *Whitechapel* (2009–13) and BBC's *Ripper Street* (2013–). Firstly, it outlines the key tropes of the Gothic crime drama, considering examples such as British shows *Wire In The Blood* (ITV, 2002–08), *Cracker* (ITV, 1993–96) and *Waking the Dead* (BBC, 2000–11) and the US-produced *Criminal Minds* (CBS, 2004–), *Millennium* (FOX, 1996–99), *The X-Files* (FOX, 1993–2002) and *Hannibal* (NBC, 2013–). These series engage differently with the Gothic; for example, *The X-Files* drew on Gothic tropes such as the tension between the supernatural and the ordinary, including the use of premonitions and possessions, and an unclear division between 'good' and 'evil' (Delasara, 2000, pp. 138–9), whilst the Gothic cop drama *Millennium* emphasised the contested Gothic space of the home alongside these other tropes (Wheatley, 2006, p. 189). American police procedurals such as *Criminal Minds* and British crime dramas including *Waking the Dead* and *Wire In The Blood* share a Gothic aesthetic and have deployed the 'widespread use of macabre, Gothic imagery – particularly the low key lighting and expressionist aesthetic associated with gothic film' (Tasker, 2011).

Secondly, the chapter explores the representations of the Gothic and space in *Ripper Street* and *Whitechapel*, since the Gothic has often been concerned with 'returning history and constrictive geography' (Spooner, 2006, p. 155). Whilst *Ripper Street* is explicitly set in the Whitechapel of late Victorian

London, *Whitechapel*'s contemporary landscapes draw on the history of this area, both via associations with the Whitechapel murders and a broader historical background of crime. Drawing on Jack the Ripper in both series means presenting an established cultural understanding of the type of place Whitechapel is and the type of landscape – haunted, dangerous, uncanny – that it represents. This chapter thus builds on analysis of *Ripper Street* as a Victorian crime drama (Pyke, 2013; Hindes, 2013) and *Whitechapel*'s use of place and history (Williams, 2014) to consider both as examples of Gothic crime drama and their places within this subgenre. They offer opportunities for analysis of how location operates within the genre, bringing together the haunted landscapes and geographies of the Gothic with the familiar spaces of the crime drama and its streets, homes and police stations.

Monstrous Origins: Identifying the Gothic Crime Drama

The crime drama has its roots in the nineteenth century, which saw an increased public interest in sensational murders that were reported to the growing numbers of literate city dwellers of the late nineteenth century in newspapers and 'broadsides' (single sheets of paper that were sold more cheaply than newspapers) (Turnbull, 2014, p. 21). The seriality of such reporting allowed narratives of often gruesome crimes to be consumed by readers who were entertained by such tales of sensational murder. Furthermore, fictionalised representations of crime also became hugely popular in that century (Flanders, 2011, p. 99), best exemplified by the interest in the works of Edgar Allan Poe and Arthur Conan Doyle's *Sherlock Holmes* series, as well as in theatre (Turnbull, 2014, p. 22). The contemporary case studies discussed here – *Ripper Street* and *Whitechapel* – hark back to this formative period of Gothic crime drama since both are linked to Jack the Ripper, often considered to be 'a figure of "fiction", a Gothic image, constructed almost immediately after the murders themselves, who belongs with a larger cast of such nineteenth-century characters, including Sherlock Holmes, Jekyll and Hyde, Dracula and Dorian Gray, populating an imaginary fog-engulfed city' (Cunningham, 2007, p. 167). This is linked to the fact that:

> The Ripper murders ... compel us because they were never solved. Reported in the newspapers as sensation narratives, the story withholds exactly what nineteenth century detective *fiction* promised: the conclusion, the confession, the sense of order: the *intellect* of the detective (and modern nation) more powerful than brute force.
>
> (Pyke, 2013)

Such dramatisations of crime and the Gothic can now be commonly seen on our television screens. However, discussion of these has often focused on the distinctions between the Gothic and the horror genre. Although there has 'never been a convincing definition of "the Gothic" that definitively separates it out from horror' (Hills, 2005, p. 199), in general terms the Gothic is more likely to imply terror via mood and atmosphere rather than to explicitly show it as is more common in horror texts. Matt Hills argues that '"Gothic TV" function[s] as a discursive other to TV horror – the latter being associated with gore and low culture, and the former carrying connotations of historical tradition, and "restrained" suggestion or implication rather than graphic monstrosity and splatter' (2005, p. 120). Gothic television is inherently unstable, since the Gothic has been 'alternately described as an aesthetic, mode or style, as a set of particular themes and narrative conventions, as a sub-genre of fantasy, and, initially, as an isolated historical movement' (Wheatley, 2006, p. 2). However, Gothic television does possess certain characteristics including 'a mood of dread and/or terror inclined to evoke fear or disgust in the viewer; the presence of highly stereotyped characters and plots' and 'representations of the supernatural' (Wheatley, 2006, p. 3).

In addition to the presence of these aesthetic and narrative features, there are three clearly identifiable trends in Gothic crime drama; a shift towards the depiction of the ruined body as a site of evidence (see Willis in this collection); an increasing focus on investigators as profilers; and the use of supernatural or fantastic elements alongside more traditional modes of crime-solving. In these cases the supernatural becomes part of the generic structure of the narrative of detection and is integrated into certain examples of the genre.

There are clear links between television horror and investigative and hospital drama, since each of these genres shares a preoccupation with the body as 'evidence.' As Deborah Jermyn points out, for example, *Prime Suspect* (ITV, 1991–2006) offered 'forensic sequences featuring graphic imagery and graphic detail' (2010, p. 5) whilst subsequent US series such as *Bones* (FOX, 2005–), *CSI* and *Criminal Minds* and UK crime drama such as *Silent Witness* have all featured an emphasis upon the evidential body, the study of which is central to the solving of a crime. However, such crime dramas are not themselves 'constructed as horror' (Jowett and Abbott, 2013, p. 21) and instead 'draw upon a language of horror to highlight the often diabolical qualities of serial killers, ... to highlight the monstrousness of the crime through graphic depiction of what was done to the victim' (Jowett and Abbott, 2013, p. 21). Thus, whilst bodily invasions and mutilations are often seen in medical and crime series, such as *CSI*, these usually function to resolve a narrative and lead to resolution of a crime or a case.

Alongside this increase in displays of the ruined body, the crime drama has shifted toward an emphasis upon the figure of the investigator who 'bring[s] to the case in question a particular gift or knowledge that equips him or her with the necessary powers to solve the crime' (Turnbull, 2014, p. 125). These are often criminal profilers such as the UK's *Cracker* or the Behavioural Analysis Unit of the US's *Criminal Minds*. Alongside this, we can trace a preoccupation with the figure of the serial killer, perhaps since the expert profiler requires a suitably worthy adversary. Serial killers, such as the murderous judge Paul Millander (in seasons one and two), 'The Miniature

Killer' Natalie Davis (in the seventh season) and Nate Haskell (also known as 'The Dick and Jane Killer' in seasons nine through eleven) occupy the narrative of *CSI* whilst *Dexter*'s eponymous serial killer and blood spatter analyst, Dexter Morgan, provided audiences with a morally grey anti-hero who dispatched his own victims whilst facing other killers including the Ice Truck Killer, the Trinity Killer and the Doomsday Killer. NBC's recent *Hannibal* represents graphic examples of the violated and destroyed body alongside the investigations of Will Graham, an FBI profiler who possesses an uncannily accurate insight into the minds of serial killers, including the Minnesota Shrike and the eponymous Hannibal Lecter. Graham, as with many other fictional profilers, combines expert knowledge with the visions of the killer or his motives – what he refers to as the killer's 'design' - that often categorise the profiler, and suggest a more supernatural slant to his or her skillset. Indeed, a distinctive characteristic of the Gothic crime drama is the role of the investigator or detective as both a rational solver of crimes and as a figure in touch with the unexplained through his or her link with those pursued.

Finally, and related to the figure of the intuitive investigator, several crime dramas have invoked the Gothic via their use of supernatural tropes and imagery, often blessing (or cursing) their lead investigative characters with supernatural insights or contact with the 'otherworldly.' In examples such as the British series *Sapphire and Steel* (ITV, 1979–82) and *The Saint* (ITV, 1962–69) and the American *Medium* (NBC, 2005–09; CBS, 2009–11) and *Ghost Whisperer* (CBS, 2005–10), contact with the spirit world is essential to solving the crime since 'visions and/or communication with the dead initiate and are central to the development of the investigative plot' (Tasker, 2011). However, Jowett and Abbott argue that, fundamentally, 'the supernatural is rendered safe' (2013, p. 22) in such series, since the 'supernatural [must] yield to mortal laws when the crimes are resolved and criminals brought to justice' (2013, p. 22). Here, the Gothic and supernatural are forces for good, reporting unjust deaths or crimes to the sympathetic investigator who is able to put these right. As discussed below, *Whitechapel*'s Chandler displays this trait. Drawing on the past to solve the crimes of the present allows him an insight into crimes that his colleagues cannot share, and he possesses 'a heightened intuitive sense which allows a sort of resurrection of the dead, amidst a stirring up and re-staging of past events' (Tasker, 2011).

Jack the Ripper and the Horrors of Place

The 'image of the London East End, particularly the nineteenth-century East End, has an international currency, and has historically attracted a gaze which is both fascinated and horrified' (Brunsdon, 2007, p. 150). This fascination can be seen in *Whitechapel* and *Ripper Street*. *Whitechapel* aired in the United Kingdom on ITV1 between 2009 and 2014. Following Detective Inspector Joseph Chandler (Rupert Penry-Jones), his Detective Sergeant Ray Miles (Phil Davis) and the policemen and women of Whitechapel, the show's first series dealt with Jack the Ripper copycat murders, before subsequent series featured copycats of the Kray Twins, and the third and fourth series began to feature different cases which were solved by reference to historical crimes. Despite attracting high audience figures – the first series' debut attracted 8.3 million viewers whilst the third series averaged 7 million (Fletcher, 2013) – it was announced in 2013 that the show had been cancelled. *Ripper Street* debuted on BBC One on New Year's Day 2013 and aired its second series in October 2013. In December 2013, the BBC announced that it was axing the show due to low viewing figures although it was later revived via a co-production deal with online retailer Amazon, airing its third series on Amazon Prime in 2014 and BBC One in 2015. Whilst *Whitechapel* takes place in modern-day London and deals with copycats of historical crimes, *Ripper Street* is set in the late nineteenth century and focuses on the efforts of DI Edmund Reid (Matthew Macfadyen), DS Bennet Drake (Jerome Flynn) and the American surgeon and pathologist, Captain Homer Jackson (Adam Rothenberg). Set in the immediate aftermath of Jack the Ripper's killings, it presents a forward-thinking approach to solving crime with the character of Jackson demonstrating early skills in pathology and analysis of evidence (Levente Palatinus, 2014). The crimes dealt with in *Ripper Street* involve pornography, drugs and arson alongside murder and, whilst the series is not as aesthetically or thematically dark as *Whitechapel*, it still owes a clear debt to the Gothic since it utilises 'a Gothic narrative form, featuring key figures and/or events associated with the genre (e.g., the victim-heroine and villainous anti-hero, or the presence of a disturbing secret from the past)' (Wheatley, 2005, p. 12). In *Ripper Street*, these secrets include Captain Jackson's true identity as a fugitive who may have committed murder and the ongoing narrative involving the disappearance of Reid's young daughter.

In contrast, *Whitechapel*'s publicity materials explicitly describe it as a 'Gothic cop show.' Commenting on the final series, producer Patrick Schweitzer stated: 'We entered into this series with the remit of making a very visual, very exciting gothic drama on the backdrop of a TV detective show' (Whitechapel Press Pack, 2013). A sustained mood of dread is created via its aesthetics which include gloomy interiors; the dark streets and alleys of London; ambiguous suggestions of the supernatural; evocative montage sequences to demonstrate the furthering of plots or the deciphering of clues; and the use of shadows, dark visuals and other elements associated with the Gothic. *Whitechapel*'s debt to both Gothic and horror conventions was often highlighted in promotional materials, such as the interview for the third series in which stars Rupert Penry-Jones and Phil Davis commented:

> PHIL: I think we're in a place almost where horror movie meets the cop show …
>
> RUPERT: … I missed the horror that we had in the second [series]. I'm glad it's back now. It's this very gothic feeling that we get which is, I think, what makes *Whitechapel* special and different. (Wightman, 2012)

This emphasis on the Gothic in the show's promotional discourse counters the claim that 'Gothic television is not a category which is utilised by television industry professionals to define their programmes' (Wheatley, 2005, p. 2). As the quotation above attests, the foregrounding of Gothic elements allows the series to position itself as original amongst the crowded television schedules of other crime drama. Generic hybridity, as Robin Nelson (2007) has argued, has 'historically has been a useful way of informing and attracting viewers' (p. 22).

The first series of *Whitechapel* draws on the figure of Jack the Ripper to establish the district of Whitechapel as a deadly and sinister place. Jack the Ripper was apparently responsible for killing five prostitutes in East London between 31 August 1888 and 9 November 1888, although it is debatable whether these 'canonical five' (Gray, 2010, p. 31) victims were killed by the same killer, or whether there were actually more than five victims. The first series draws on both widely known elements of the case and more implicit references; for example, Chandler is named after the first Inspector to respond to the Annie Chapman crime scene in 1888 (Rumbelow, 2004, p. 36), whilst pathologist Dr. Llewellyn shares a name with the original doctor at the first Whitechapel murder (Rumbelow, 2004, p. 25–7). This linkage between place and the horror of Jack the Ripper is highlighted most clearly in *Whitechapel* through the only copycat killing to take place on the actual spot where a murder occurred in 1888. Since this location at Mitre Square remains to this day, place here is imbued with particular significance. Chandler, and expert 'Ripperologist' Edward Buchan, are certain that the allure of being able to commit a crime on the physical site of Jack the Ripper's crime will prove too strong for the killer to ignore. Buchan is sure that 'Mitre Square's too important to miss', continuing 'It's the only murder site that still exists. You can go and stand on the exact same spot today. I think he'll definitely be tempted by that. It's so authentic.' *Whitechapel* is thus well aware of its own representations of a past that is self-reflexively constructed for the viewer. The series' use of Mitre Square enables the fictional text to exploit the value of a tangible location with a gruesome history, and functions as a marker of authenticity and of 'the real.' Many of Jack the Ripper's murder sites are 'possessed of a celebrated history which [they] cannot display' (McEvoy, 2012, p. 142) due to demolition and gentrification (Cunningham, 2007). However, Mitre Square offers the promise of a material connection to the past, relatively untarnished by modernisation or the march of progress. Across all four of its series, the Whitechapel district is positioned as deadly and dangerous; Chandler's decision to take over the police team there is questioned by his superiors in the police force, and it is considered 'a bit of a rough squad.' The special 'quality' of Whitechapel, and its specific history of violence and dread, becomes the main focus. In the final scene of the first series, Miles cautions Chandler about the more mundane violence typical of the district:

> [I]t's not all serial killers and car chases and saving the girl at the end, you know ... There's gangland murder, drug-related murder, domestics, aggravated burglary, knock-on-the-head-for-no-reason-on-a-Friday-night murder. That's Whitechapel. You up for that?

It is not only the extraordinary – the famous serial killers and evil – that renders Whitechapel a deadly locale. Here, the mundane and everyday are also held up as an example of the district's long-standing status as 'a dreaded name, the East End Murderland, infamous throughout the world' (Walkowitz, 1992, p. 195).

Whilst *Whitechapel* uses the past to shed light on crimes in present-day London, *Ripper Street* is a historical crime drama that borrows from the Gothic. Set in the late 1890s *after* Jack the Ripper's reign of terror, *Ripper Street* nonetheless constructs the Whitechapel district as dangerous, frightening and unstable. The official press description summarises thus:

> April 1889 – six months since the last Jack the Ripper killing, East London is emerging into a fragile peace, hopeful that this killer's reign of terror might at last have run its course. Nowhere is this truer than in the corridors of H Division, the police precinct charged with keeping order in the chaos of Whitechapel. Its men hunted this maniac; and failed to find him ... *Ripper Street* is not another backward-looking 'Hunt the Ripper' story, but a fictionalised trek into the heart of a London borough living in the blood soaked aftermath of that forever anonymous killer.
>
> (BBC, 2013)

By distancing *Ripper Street* from previous stories which have focused on hunting Jack the Ripper, the press release promises a new take on the genre of crime drama which will be both historical and forward-thinking, again carving out a space for the programmes' uniqueness in a crowded television marketplace.

Ripper Street's first episode represents the Jack the Ripper case, with the police keen to avoid a public frenzy when a suspected new victim is discovered. The episode opens with a tour guide leading a group of well-dressed tourists through Whitechapel. He intones, 'Ladies and gentlemen, welcome to Whitechapel ... follow me for the haunts of Jack the Ripper. Our men in blue are still cloaked in ignorance of Jack.' He then leads the visitors to Millers' Court, the scene of Jack the Ripper's final murder. Upon discovering the corpse of a young woman, the tour is interrupted and the caption 'East London 1889' appears on-screen. In its opening moments, *Ripper Street* establishes its location and time-frame, drawing on the real-life crimes of Jack the Ripper to set up its own narrative. The 'ghost' of the Ripper is present throughout this first episode. Reid fears that 'Hell will rise again' whilst a local newspaper reporter reminds him that Jack remains uncaught and that 'the man and his works abide.' The murder in this case is eventually revealed to be a cover-up for a pornography ring, but the spectre of Jack the Ripper looms large over the first series of the show even though it begins after his final murder, and the viewer is not witness to the first-hand investigation of his crimes by Reid's team. In this sense, Jack the Ripper functions as a structuring absence in *Ripper Street*; the very title of the series invokes his name and the cultural associations of grisly murder that accompany this alongside an image of a specific nineteenth-century version of London. Jack the Ripper can never be caught or made 'real', but in many ways this is merely a reflection of the 'artifice and cultural construction' (Gray, 2010, p. 18) of the Ripper myth. The murders were not solved 'in real life', nor can they be in *Ripper Street*, casting a shadow of uncertainty and fear over the London that it depicts. Whilst *Whitechapel*'s first series re-presents the Jack the Ripper myth, *Ripper Street* avoids visual depiction of it, allowing it instead to be a shadowy reminder of the wider unease and danger inherent in the Whitechapel district at the time, a location that was 'stigmatise[d] … [by the press] as a place apart' (Walkowitz, 1992, p. 195). Both series invoke an idea of a fictional London, specifically a constructed version of the Whitechapel district, much as the press reports of the time were media constructions of the district for Victorian readers. Charlotte Brunsdon discusses how such fictional Londons represent ideas about the city. The myth of late Victorian London, with its figures of Jack the Ripper, Jekyll and Hyde and Sweeney Todd remains one of the most enduring: 'This London requires only a gas street lamp, a cobbled street, a horse-drawn carriage and a wisp of mist to be identified, and begins to demonstrate the ways in which landmarks signify genre as well as time and place' (Brunsdon, 2007, p. 24). *Ripper Street*'s use of figures' names such as Inspector Abberline, and DI Reid, as well as the location of the police station in Leman Street, are historically correct and the series offers the viewer a sense of the imagined East End at this time. Part of *Ripper Street*'s sense of the past is constructed via its invocation of the Jack the Ripper murders, as well as its iconography of place within a recognisable, albeit fictionalised, Whitechapel district. Gothic crime drama thus offers a place where history and place can be represented alongside the generic trappings of the crime drama, speaking to its generic hybridity and its engagement with Gothic themes of the past and place.

Whitechapel, the Police Station and the Gates of Hell

It is not only through their engagement with the figure of Jack the Ripper that these series position Whitechapel as a haunted Gothic place. Elsewhere, I have discussed how *Whitechapel* negotiates representations of both place and the past in its first three series and how 'the area's violent, bloody past' means that it represents history as 'doomed to repeat itself in vicious cycles of murder and violence' (Williams, 2014, p. 83). Here, I focus on the fourth and final series of the show, which demonstrated a move towards the supernatural and away from the fact-based deductions of the first three series. Whilst the previous series represented Whitechapel's famous criminals – Jack the Ripper, the Kray twins and a range of murders which depicted the invasion of Gothic domestic spaces – the final series positions the police station as *the* defining place of the series. Alongside the streets and homes of Whitechapel, the police station itself becomes the locus of terror and is the centre of the horrors that have been inflicted upon the district. As actor Steve Pemberton explained in the series four promotional material: 'In this series everyone is affected by the station, a bit like *The Shining* where the hotel takes over the characters. There is a sense that there is something supernatural that we can't control' (Whitechapel Press Pack, 2013).

The police station functions as a space of often masculinised professional identity which is frequently contrasted with the feminised domestic spaces of the home in crime drama. Despite this, the workplace in the crime drama is often deeply personal and in some series also a space where the domestic enters. For example, the uncanny police station is also seen in *Life on Mars* and *Ashes to Ashes*, two police series that blurred generic boundaries via their 'combination of realism and fantasy, of science fiction time travel and traditional cop show' (Lacey and McElroy, 2012, p. 2). The station in both of those series presents the space as frequently threatening and the site of mystery and secrets. They thus present the uncanny, but share generic overlaps with the genre of fantasy and the fantastic, since they offer a hesitation about whether the events we see (and which the protagonists experience) are 'real' or 'fantastic.' In contrast, the police station in *Whitechapel* is positioned in the realm of the Gothic (although it is also fantastic in its final series' questions over whether Whitechapel is actually afflicted by evil), due to its thematic and aesthetic depictions and the fact that it is 'visually dark, with a mise-en-scène dominated by drab and dismal colours, shadows and closed-in spaces' (Wheatley, 2006, p. 3).

In the opening episode of *Whitechapel*'s fourth series, Ripperologist and police advisor Edward Buchan launches his new book *A History of Murder in Whitechapel*. He intones:

> Why Whitechapel? Why was this the birthplace of the serial killer? Why the bloody history of murders and unnatural deaths? How can so much horror be visited on such a small area? There are those who believe that the Gates to Hell can be found in the shadows of Christchurch Church. That this is the reason Whitechapel is plagued with terrors.

Buchan later refutes these statements, explaining that his book publicist forced him to play up this supernatural angle of the crimes that have occurred in Whitechapel. However, the fourth series places Buchan's questions at the centre of its narrative, moving towards an exploration of *why* Whitechapel is the scene of so many horrific crimes. The first story of the series (episodes 4.1 and 4.2) involves a poisoned killer who, in a delirious state, is hunting down and murdering the 'witches' he blames for his recent bad luck. This storyline also involves an MI6 whistle-blower named Wingfield who claims to have tracked an Agent Provocateur to the Whitechapel police station. This Provocateur is apparently the instigator of much of the chaos and crime in the district and has infiltrated the station itself in order to derail investigations. Wingfield claims that 'The Krays, The Ripper. An immortal enemy was behind them all. Planting the seeds, watching the horror grow.' Although initially dismissive of the informant, each of the Whitechapel squad is tormented within the police station across the rest of the series. Chandler is haunted by constantly dripping taps in the bathroom and thick black sludge spewing from them; Buchan's office and historical files are threatened by the spread of the 'black death' of mildew and mould in his walls; Mansell receives a string of phone calls from distorted, creepy voices whilst Kent repeatedly sees grotesque distortions of his reflection in mirrors and other reflective surfaces. Although the viewer has seen occasional glimpses of the policemen's homes in previous series, *Whitechapel* has routinely represented the police station, and the incident room in particular, as a surrogate 'home' where the police characters are most commonly seen and where they eat, celebrate and socialise. When the police station itself becomes threatening in the fourth series, then, the surrogate home of the team is violated. In particular Miles, the character who has previously been the most reluctant to embrace the need to use unorthodox methods of policing, is the most 'haunted', hearing high-heeled footsteps following him around the station corridors. The police station here becomes threatening, the familiar is rendered dangerous and deadly, a mood that is conveyed through the use of low and high-angled dark shots of the station staircases, corridors and offices, flickering lights, distorted use of mirrors and reflections, and buzzing noises on the audio soundtrack. Each of these techniques works to heighten a sense of unease and dread, rendering the previously safe space of the police station uncanny. It is in these shots that *Whitechapel*'s aesthetic debt to the Gothic can be most clearly seen. In one sequence, Miles walks down a corridor followed by the sounds of high-heeled footsteps. He calls out 'Who's there?' and the footsteps retreat, as the camera pulls backwards away from the character down the corridor. The corridor is suddenly darkened as the lights flicker and Miles begins to run. A point-of-view shot follows behind him until he turns. The corridor is empty. Miles consults with Buchan, suggesting that Wingfield may have been correct and that there may 'be a demon in this station.' Through the use of CCTV in the station, Miles eventually determines that the Agent Provocateur is an elderly woman named Louise Ivor, who has been hammering nails into the water pipes at the station and likely causing the issues that have plagued the team across the series. He tries to convince Buchan that she can be seen in old drawings from the Jack the Ripper case and in photographs with The Kray Twins, asking him 'What if she placed ideas in their heads? What if it were her? For years and years and years?' Buchan dismisses him, claiming that 'Evil is human. It always has been.' However, the series leaves this possibility open to interpretation and in its final scenes strongly favours Miles' interpretation of events.

DI Chandler is also seen to be exposed to events that appear more supernatural in origin; he suffers flashbacks and dreams and, in the final episode he encounters a psychic whose powers are revealed to be more genuine than he believes. Having rejected what he supposes will be generic declarations of love from his dead father from the psychic, Chandler eventually reads the message after his successful arrest of eight members of a cannibalistic religious cult, the first time he has captured a criminal in the series. Having placed them all in the same police van for transfer to the station, the van crashes and explodes after the suspected Agent Provocateur, Louise Ivor, steps in front of the traffic, essentially causing the crash. As Miles enters the room to inform Chandler that, yet again, he has failed to catch a criminal alive, Chandler reads the message from the psychic which informs him: 'DON'T PUT THEM ALL IN THE SAME VAN.' Through his own failure to believe in the other-worldly, Chandler again fails to bring criminals to traditional forms of justice. Here, the series allows a more supernatural interpretation of events to be not only presented, but sanctified. As the safe space of the police station – the surrogate home of the policemen – is threatened, series four of *Whitechapel* draws again on Gothic tropes involving threats to the familial, the homely and domestic. In the final series, *Whitechapel*, moves further towards the Gothic and the realm of the supernatural than the crime drama. Whereas prior series balanced this more delicately, the events of the final episode indicate a willingness to embrace these aspects of the Gothic. However, given ITV's decision not to renew the show for a further series, *Whitechapel*'s engagement with the Gothic and the supernatural ends there. Definitive answers for the final series' move towards the Gothic and the supernatural are unclear. However, the pre-publicity for the series indicates a desire for the show to return to suspense and terror alongside its more graphic horror. Actor Rupert Penry-Jones explained: 'There's lots of scary stuff going on! I think what they realised from the last series is that people really enjoyed the scary, suspenseful elements of Whitechapel not just the horror – though there is still going to be some gore of course' (Whitechapel Press Pack, 2013). He also noted how: 'we also have this kind of dark, psychological thing that each character has to deal with across the entire series. Everyone is being spooked in one way or another and we don't know whether it can be explained logically or whether there's something else going on' and that the series would propose 'the idea of something other worldly going on within Whitechapel' (Whitechapel Press Pack, 2013). The discourse from promotional materials thus suggests a move away from graphic gore towards psychological horror and suggestion, and modes of terror rather than horror, echoing pre-existing discussions of Gothic fictions.

Conclusion

Despite the difficulty in identifying what constitutes a Gothic text, the success of a range of Gothic crime dramas indicates an ongoing fascination with this hybrid genre. In many ways, the two genres sit well alongside one another, both speaking to potential anxieties about contemporary society and able to reflect social change and unease through their narratives, characters and aesthetics. Indeed, 'the television crime drama has often played a critical role in bringing current social issues and anxieties into the public domain' (Turnbull, 2014, p. 2) whilst the Gothic genre also has the potential to disrupt a range of established assumptions about gender, sexuality, place and the past through its capacity to be 'reordered in infinite combinations' (Spooner, 2006, p. 155). The examples discussed here – *Ripper Street* and *Whitechapel* – allow consideration of how place functions within the British Gothic crime drama combining the haunted locations of the Gothic with the established spaces of the crime drama: its streets, homes and police stations. Indeed, both series offer a combination of tropes from the Gothic genre with the crime drama to 'generate a specific sense of threat and horror emerging from specific location' (Williams, 2014, p. 70). As Brunsdon argues, we need to pay attention to how 'generic convention and expectation governs the way in which location is produced in the audio-visual media' (2009, p. 169). The examples of *Ripper Street* and *Whitechapel* suggest that the genre of the Gothic crime drama is one place where representations of place and space in contemporary television can be detected and analysed.

References

BBC, 2013. *Ripper Street*. BBC Media Centre, [online] 1 January. Available at: http://www.bbc.co.uk/mediacentre/proginfo/2013/01/ripper-street-ep1 [Accessed 14 November 2014].

Brunsdon, C., 2007. *London in Cinema: The Cinematic City Since 1945*. London, England: BFI.

Brunsdon, C., 2009. Introduction: screen Londons. *Journal of British Cinema and Television*, 6(2), pp. 165–77.

Cunningham, D., 2007. Living in the slashing grounds: Jack the Ripper, monopoly rent and the new heritage. In: A. Warwick and M. Willis, eds., 2007. *Jack the Ripper: Media, Culture, History*. Manchester, England: Manchester University Press. pp. 159–75.

Delasara, J., 2000. *Poplit, PopCult and The X-Files: A critical explanation*. Jefferson, NC: McFarland.

Flanders, J., 2011. *The Invention of Murder: How the Victorians Revelled in Death and Detection and Created Modern Crime*. London, England: Harper Press.

Fletcher, A., 2013. *Whitechapel* returns for series four: First look trailer. Digital Spy. [online] Available at: http://www.digitalspy.co.uk/tv/news/a506703/whitechapel-returns-for-series-four-first-look-trailer.html#~pfYoDDyP9WChnw [Accessed 18 June 2015].

Gray, D. D., 2010. *London's Shadows: The Dark Side of the Victorian City*. London, England: Continuum.

Hills, M., 2005. *The Pleasures of Horror*. London, England: Continuum.

Hindes, J., 2013. CSI: Whitechapel: *Ripper Street* and the evidential body. *Journal of Victorian Culture Online*. [online] Available at: http://myblogs.informa.com/jvc/2013/01/28/ripper-street-csi/ [Accessed 14 August 2014].

Jermyn, D., 2010. *Prime Suspect*. London, England: BFI.

Jowett, L. and Abbott, S., 2013. *TV Horror: Investigating the Dark Side of the Small Screen*. London, England: I.B. Tauris.

Lacey, S. and McElroy, R., 2012. Introduction. In: Stephen Lacey and Ruth McElroy, eds., *Life on Mars: From Manchester to New York*. Cardiff, Wales: University of Wales Press. pp. 1–15.

Levente Palatinus, D., 2014. The spectres of crime: Haunting iconographies on/off the screen. CST Online. [online] Available at: http://cstonline.tv/the-spectres-of-crime-haunting-iconographies [Accessed 12 October 2014].

McEvoy, E., 2012. West End ghosts and Southwark horrors: London's Gothic tourism. In: L. Phillips and A. Witchard, eds., *London Gothic: Place, Space and the Gothic Imagination*. London, England: Continuum. pp. 140–52.

Nelson, R., 2007. *State of Play: Contemporary High-End TV Drama*. Manchester, England: Manchester University Press.

Pyke, J., 2013. Imagining the Ripper. *Journal of Victorian Culture Online*. [online] Available at: http://myblogs.informa.com/jvc/2013/01/04/imagining-the-ripper/ [Accessed 12 August 2014].

Rumbelow, D., 1975. *The Complete Jack the Ripper*. 2004. London, England: Penguin.

Spooner, C., 2006. *Contemporary Gothic*. London, England: Reaktion Books.

Tasker, Y., 2011. Haunting crime: The Gothic, the grotesque and the paranormal. *Flow*. [online] Available at: http://flowtv.org/2011/01/haunting-crime/ [Accessed 22 June 2014].

Turnbull, S., 2014. *The TV Crime Drama*. Edinburgh, Scotland: Edinburgh University Press.

Walkowitz, J., 1992. *City of Dreadful Delight: Narratives of Sexual Danger in Late-Victorian London*. Chicago, IL: University of Chicago Press.

Wheatley, H., 2006. *Gothic Television*. Manchester, England: Manchester University Press.

Whitechapel press pack, 2013. ITV Press Centre. [online] Available at: http://www.itv.com/presscentre/press-packs/whitechapel# [Accessed 3 March 2015].

Wightman, C., 2012. 'Whitechapel' Rupert Penry-Jones, Phil Davis, Steve Pemberton Q&A. *Digital Spy*. [online] Available at: http://www.digitalspy.co.uk/tv/news/a361644/whitechapel-rupert-penry-jones-phil-davis-steve-pemberton-qa.html [Accessed 17 July 2014].

Williams, R., 2014. 'The past isn't dead … it's deadly': horror, history and locale in ITV1's *Whitechapel*. *Journal of British Cinema and Television*, 11(1), pp. 68–85.

4 Crime and Punishment – Jimmy McGovern's *Accused* and *Common*

Steve Blandford

In the time it takes to climb the steps of the court we tell the story of how the accused came to be there. We see the crime and we see the punishment. Nothing else. No police procedure, thanks very much, no coppers striding along corridors with coats flapping. Just crime and punishment – the two things that matter most in any crime drama.

—(McGovern, 2010)

In the last three years, one of postwar Britain's most prolific and versatile writers for television has devoted the valuable prime-time space that he has been given to two programmes that are both, in significant ways, out of step with much contemporary television crime drama.[1] Although they are different in format, both *Accused* and *Common* (BBC One, 2014) are linked by a strong focus on individuals accused of crimes and their relationship both with the law and wider ideas of justice. As Mc Govern suggests in his description above, in the context of this volume what is particularly significant is that neither programme devotes much screen time either to the police themselves or to police procedure, or in McGovern's own words 'No police procedure, thanks very much, no coppers striding along corridors with coats flapping.' This chapter will examine the significance of this removal of the police as the focus of popular crime dramas in an era where, it is argued, personality-driven series centred on police women and men are the norm on British television.

It is necessary, therefore, to start by saying a little about the context into which Jimmy McGovern has made his most recent (at the time of writing) interventions into the crime genre. In the early 1990s McGovern made a significant contribution to the shift in the crime genre towards agents of detection outside the police themselves through the introduction of the forensic psychologist, Edward Fitzgerald (Robbie Coltrane) in *Cracker* (ITV, 1993–2007). McGovern's return to explicit questions of law and order in *Accused* and *Common* comes in the context of a range of work shown on British television that has the detective's role inscribed at the core of our interest, either through their name being the title – *Wallander, Scott and Bailey, Lewis* and *Vera* – or where the critical attention is so firmly on the individual that *The Killing* may as well be called *Lund* or *The Bridge, Saga and Martin*. The range of this list of central characters that have tended to dominate British television screens in recent years is, admittedly, much more extensive than once would have been the case. It is therefore now much less tenable to claim, as the BFI's *Screenonline* site still does, that 'the television image of the police is still dominated by the traditional male sleuth in a suit, sometimes avuncular, sometimes grumpy' (Delaney, 2014).

However, what does seem to have become much more solidly the case during the last decade is the increasing tendency for writers to create fallible, but ultimately heroic, crime fighters. This chapter will argue that McGovern's most recent work has reacted against such a tendency. Much academic analysis has tended to view the role of dominant police characters as inscribing reactionary ideas about the contemporary functioning of law and order at the heart of the police and crime television genre though, as Nichols-Pethick argues, there has also been a counter-balancing tendency to exempt some kinds of work that fall into the very fluid category of 'quality television':

> Scholarly criticism of the television police drama has had a tendency to approach the police series as an inherently conservative form that repeatedly rehearses a dominant 'common-sense' ideology of law and order. This vein of criticism often focuses on 'traditional' series which are structured as morality tales ... On the other hand, there has also been a tendency to celebrate a few series as part of a broader spectrum of 'quality television.' (2012, p. 6)

Nichols-Pethick's work in fact goes on to question this polarising tendency in scholarship, but his book's conclusion is undoubtedly convinced of the centrality of the police series to the wider formation of society's ideas about crime. It will therefore be argued here that McGovern's very conscious decision to shift the focus away from the police and back towards 'criminal' motivation remains a key political act, even in the context of a number of series that present complex, nuanced portrayals of policemen and women that would undoubtedly fall into most definitions of 'quality' television.

This chapter is far from being a criticism of the quality of many of the shows listed above. The pleasures and sophistication of most so-called 'Nordic-noir' discussed by McCabe in this collection are plain to see, as are the many acute observations of contemporary Scandinavian society contained within them. However, what I am arguing here is an attempt to define the current context of television crime drama in the pursuit of an idea about the genesis of McGovern's *Accused* and *Common*. This is a context, I would argue, that has become dominated by a galaxy of well-written and fascinating policemen and women but with far less consideration of the moral, philosophical and motivational complexity of crime and criminal activity itself. The result, it is argued, has been to limit the police series' potential for serious political and moral debate around key issues of law and order. This is not to say that no such debate takes place in work with police characters at the centre, rather it is an important question of emphasis, one that McGovern consciously seeks to address.

The trend that I have described is not of course universal, and some recent European and American crime drama is, on the whole, more likely to be interested in complex criminals than British shows. From the now classic *Sopranos* (HBO, 1999–2007) through to the more recent *Breaking Bad* (AMC, 2008–13) via *The Wire* (HBO, 2002–08) and *The Killing* (DR1, 2007) there has been a string of high concept dramas whose central cast is dominated by fascinating and morally complicated criminal characters. Such offerings are, though, very different from the aesthetic and moral universe inhabited by McGovern's work. Whereas the shows described above tend to be high concept, with characters that are baroque in their complexity, McGovern is interested in individuals who are close to the popular audience in the way that they live their lives until, that is, they become caught up in circumstances that propel them towards their fate. In ways that McGovern himself has compared to certain forms of Victorian fiction (Blandford, 2013, pp. 75–6), his work shows us how apparently insignificant encounters with events outside the character's control can lead to profound and life-changing consequences. Frequently such encounters involve crimes of various kinds committed under morally ambiguous circumstances.

McGovern's characters though, are never presented as worthy victims. On the contrary, his strong writer's instincts lead him to provide us with a string of central figures who are, frequently, anything but easy to like. The very first episode of *Accused*, 'Willy's Story' (dir. David Blair), featured one of the least likeable of them all. 'Willy's Story' centres on a man who both possesses ultra-traditional McGovern tendencies – he gambles, smokes, drinks and is an uneasy Catholic – and has a range of other qualities that make him difficult to like on most levels. Christopher Eccleston, who played the eponymous Willy Houlihan, tells an anecdote about the cast of the episode taking a vote on whether or not Houlihan deserves a jail sentence for his crime at the end of the episode. The vote was split 50/50 with Eccleston himself claiming to be undecided (BBC, 2010a).

Willy Houlihan, perhaps most importantly, is more ambiguous in his class position than most of McGovern's central male characters. He is a plumber, but one who has clearly prospered over time and who lives in the kind of semi-detached house, complete with conservatory, that recalls McGovern's *Brookside* (Channel 4, 1982–2003) days (though Houlihan's house is loomed over by two gas holders that act as kind of a reminder of the precarious nature of the family's relative prosperity). Houlihan's life looks representative of the prosperous lower-middle classes that supposedly brought Margaret Thatcher to power, and who continued to pre-occupy Tony Blair's governments. He is a self-employed plumber whose successful business is derailed, not by his own profligacy, but by the bankruptcy of a major client.

For Rachel Cooke, Houlihan's many flaws were enough to make the drama too deeply flawed to be judged against McGovern's best work, describing Houlihan as 'a bully, a loudmouth and a misogynist', and going on to state that she 'felt no pity when he was sent down' (Cooke, 2010). In my view, the flaw in Cooke's statement is not her dislike of Houlihan, but her somewhat dismissive description of McGovern's supposed tendency to create 'decent Everyman figures.' One of the ways that *Accused* complicates the traditional tropes of television crime drama is to test the relationship between moral judgements and the criminal justice system much further than most crime drama. By focusing the narrative of *Accused* away from the police, McGovern creates the space in which to do this by removing the concentration on generic conventions such as detailed procedural matters. In the case of Willy Houlihan, it is as if McGovern was determined to open the series with the kind of character that would deliberately fly in the face of any sense that *Accused* would be about working class heroes who had fallen foul of a system of state justice consistently biased against them.

Whilst all this may make Houlihan look more sinned against than sinning, McGovern also provides him with an impressive series of opportunities to demonstrate not just his frailties, but also his boorish contempt for the feelings of others. Near the start of the episode, Houlihan is seen making a pact with his much younger lover, Michelle (Emma Stansfield), that they will both tell their respective spouses that they are leaving them at the exact same moment. The precision, and chilling banality of that arrangement, is captured in telling McGovern fashion as Michelle chooses the moment: '… half-six. When the woman says "Now it's time to join the BBC news teams where you are".' Houlihan seems to enter the pact with something approaching callousness but, in a moment of spectacular melodramatic surprise, at around six twenty-nine, Houlihan's daughter, Laura (Joanna Higson) enters with her boyfriend to announce that they are to marry.

This wrecking of Houlihan's plans, by what seems to be a malevolent fate, is just the first of a series of similar moments in 'Willy's Story' that remind us of the interweaving of social realism and a storytelling that, as suggested above, has its roots in aspects of the Victorian novel. Throwing himself into his daughter's wedding plans, whilst postponing his flight with his lover (until the evening of the wedding!), Willy's testosterone-fuelled pride leads him to book an expensive venue and insist on paying for an expensive dinner for his future in-laws, only to discover that his client's bankruptcy has left him with almost nothing.

The fable-like structure of the narrative becomes more and more overt as the episode proceeds. At one point Houlihan visits his bank manager to plead for some grace. He starts his plea with: 'There's this Western, I think it's a Western, I'm not sure. Anyway, there's this bloke who walks into a bank and asks for a loan …' after recounting the story he ends with: 'I know it's not Hollywood but …' tailing off as he sees the bank manager's blank expression. In this moment, McGovern's narrative technique is allowed to surface as we see the grim reality of Houlihan's situation played against the extraordinary events that are buffeting him. The obstacles that are put in front of him remind him of some of the great popular myths of the twentieth century, and he casts himself as the John Wayne-like anti-hero able to battle his way out with the use of his fists and his heart. Sadly though, there are no happy endings as Willy discovers that any fragile status he has inside a bank in front of a man in a pin-stripe suit is entirely dependent on his continuing prosperity.

Willy is undoubtedly unlucky but in writing surely one of his least sentimental leading roles McGovern works very hard to make him repel us. This is most telling not so much in the deceptions and hubris of his long-term plans, but in the coldness and bullying that characterise his daily human transactions. He doesn't so much speak to his sons as bark at them; when he meets his in-laws he brow-beats them with his tastes and opinions in a relentless onslaught that has his wife, Carmel (Pooky Quesnel), dying from embarrassment and even his sympathy for his lover's blackened eye (the result of telling her husband she is leaving) is expressed not through tenderness but by 'sorting him' with his fists. Willy's natural discourse is the relentless harangue, even when he is in a good mood, and even without trying hard, he comes over as a bully.

Despite all this, McGovern succeeds in at least making us doubt whether Willy deserves to be in the dock. This is mainly by showing us the effect on him of the collapse of all the belief systems by which he has lived – hard work bringing its just rewards, the last remnants of Catholicism, and a belief in the romance of the male hero, have all let him down when malign fate decides it is his turn. The laws of evidence and the criminal justice system do the rest.

The place where the central tropes of *Accused*, and those of many crime show/police series, do coincide, however, is in the ways that they play out contemporary constructions of masculinity. Despite the many exceptions, some of which I have already mentioned, the contemporary police and crime genre generally still produces what Rebecca Feasey has called both 'some of the most tired and passé representatives of hegemonic masculinity on the small screen'; however, there are also examples of 'some of the most tormented and troubled images of the male on contemporary television' (2008, p. 80). In the case of *Accused*, there are clear attempts to produce less polarised representations of masculinity, and to therefore look at such a key area of debate in ways that are both more sophisticated and consistent with popular television.

Perhaps the most explicit engagement with such questions comes in the final episode of series one of *Accused*, 'Alison's Story.' The episode ostensibly focuses on Alison Wade (Naomie Harris), a teacher of children with learning disabilities whose husband David (Warren Browne) becomes the main carer for their two children because he is out of work. At first, McGovern avoids the clichés of such commonplace stories, as David seems both content with, and good at, being a full-time parent. However, subsequent events suggest that beneath the relatively cosy domestic surface of their lives some extremely primitive feelings exist. They are revealed in relatively conventional fashion when Alison has a brief fling with a work colleague producing a reaction in David that is shocking in its barbaric ferocity. David's rape of his wife is brutal enough, but his subsequent chilling observation that 'after battle there's always rape' completely shatters any remaining illusion that there is any substance to the attractive and well-lit surface of their relationship.

'Alison's Story' represents something of a return to an old McGovern battleground as David's old-school policeman father, Detective Sergeant George Wade (Tony Pitts), enters the fray. The territory of the conflict is all too clear as Wade stands on the doorstep of his small house towering over Alison, every inch the macho bully, and with the self-righteousness of white working class anger behind him. First of all he uses that most reductive of contemporary terms of abuse of women, 'slag', and then follows it with an unsolicited diatribe about his views on contemporary gender politics: 'I grew up with women like you, always spouting about their rights, equality, feminism. Shall I tell you what I know about women like them? Give them the same rights as men and they start acting like men. Using, abusing, shagging.' To which McGovern has Alison retort with 'Must stop you reading that *Guardian* George!' ably demonstrating that one of his much-overlooked writer's weapons is black humour at moments of high tension.

It is surely of some significance that the one fully realised policeman to appear in Series One of *Accused* is not there as an upholder of the law, but as an abuser of power as he conspires with his wronged son to try to get rid of Alison from their life for good by that most tried and tested means of planting evidence, in this case some class A drugs. In one of the least open-ended and morally ambiguous stories of the series, McGovern has the bent copper and his son exposed and Alison triumphant. While this is satisfying given what has taken place, there is a gnawing sense that McGovern's policeman is not one of his most subtle creations and perhaps an indication of why the series is successful through its lack of police characters.

In Series Two of *Accused*, McGovern focused even more explicitly on questions of masculinity in 'Tracie's Story.' This opening episode casts Sean Bean as Simon, by day an English teacher who, by night, comes closer to his true identity by dressing in feminine clothing and becoming Tracie. The casting of Bean was not only inspired, but of some significance to this discussion, because of Bean's long-standing ultra-masculine persona, perhaps best exemplified through his appearances in the title role of *Sharpe* (ITV, 1993–97).

McGovern uses Simon/Tracie's transvestite identity in a story that openly explores questions about male sexuality in ways that are, at best, rare in police-centred crime drama. McGovern (and co-writer Sean Duggan) creates a romance between Tracie and a married man, Tony (Stephen Graham). Tony's anxiety and reluctance to confront his complex identity eventually leads to violent and tragic consequences, but along the way the writers mix a touching tenderness between the unlikely couple with a number of scenes that press home the story's wider analysis of the reality of a great deal of contemporary macho (and frequently homophobic) behaviour. The realist generic imperatives of the majority of police-centred drama generally still require that the 'hero' conforms to conventional ideas about masculinity. The hero of 'Tracie's Story' is not only Simon, the self-confessed 'most boring man in the world' who each day squeezes himself into his sensible grey suit, but also Tracie, the lover of nails made from 'real French cultured ivory' and 'hand-stitched' red Italian stilettos. Like much of *Accused*, 'Tracie's Story' uses its focus on those who end up in the dock, rather than those who solve crime, to offer us lives that are messy, multi-layered and complex. Above all, the series offers a recurring plea to resist a view of human motivation and justice that is too simple and focused on the detection and solving of crimes.

'Frankie's Story', the second episode in the first series of *Accused*, is worth a brief mention here because of the way that it reinforces how McGovern took the crime-centred series into anti-establishment territory that would be extremely difficult if police officers had been central to its construction. At an historical moment of some sensitivity for the British Army, 'Frankie's Story' offered a narrative centred on an account of an episode of horrific bullying amongst young recruits in Afghanistan. The failure of the army's macho culture to deal with such behaviour eventually leads to the murder of the main culprit by his victim.

It is perhaps something of a leap to directly equate this kind of behaviour in the army to that traditionally exhibited by the police in crime drama. However, the central critique of an outdated masculinity within one of the key branches of the establishment is consistent with the series' overall implicit critique of the police as agents of justice.

Not surprisingly, 'Frankie's Story' provoked a series of outbursts from senior serving army officers who felt that its treatment of the subject of young recruits involved in bullying incidents at a British army base in Afghanistan was not only a distortion, but potentially had the effect of undermining morale among serving troops. The power of McGovern's anti-establishment critique was perhaps best evidenced by the fact that a recent former head of the army felt it appropriate not only to comment, but to call for the programme to be banned:

> General Sir Richard Dannatt ... accused the BBC of 'a gross error of editorial judgment' and 'gross arrogance' for screening what he described as 'a nasty show' in defiance of objections from the army. Dannatt told the Today programme the episode 'portrayed bullying that's got no place in fact or fiction in the 21st century.' He said: 'BBC1 stands indicted for gross insensitivity while the army's conducting difficult and dangerous operations in Afghanistan.'
>
> (Robinson, 2010)

One suspects, of course, that McGovern was back where he has always enjoyed being. As he said at the time,

> Why have a BBC complaints unit in the first place? They tell me, 'Jimmy, it is in case you offend anybody', and I say, 'I am a writer. That is my job.' Just imagine if it said on my headstone that I had never offended anybody – I would turn in my grave.
>
> (Thorpe, 2010)

In 'Frankie's Story' the offence he gave was in suggesting that the army was likely to condone what would be criminal activity in any other context, whilst the police only became interested once the natural order of things had become disturbed by the murder of the bullying NCO. This is the kind of offence that is much easier to give once freed from the centrality of police characters to a crime series.

In the context of this collection, 'Frankie's Story' is a clear reinforcement of McGovern using his late career status to return to more solidly anti-establishment territory, and to a place where the consideration of law and order is of a very different order from most contemporary crime dramas. In an era in which there are many varieties of treatment of police officers, but also in which there appears to be something of a resurgence of the tendency to valorise police work, McGovern's emphasis on the moral and political ambiguity of many crimes represents a distancing of his writing from most of his contemporaries. That he has used the umbrella of the anthology series to reintroduce the single play to prime time commissioning by stealth tends to further reinforce the sense of a writer getting as close to the freedom once enjoyed by writers of one-off drama as it is possible to get. In this instance at least, such freedom is used in the pursuit of an effective counterweight to much contemporary police and crime fiction on British television.

I would argue, therefore, that McGovern's decision to remove the police (and also the other agencies of criminal investigation) almost completely from *Accused* is itself implicit commentary on the genre, and an approach that is rare in today's climate. It is also an approach that speaks so directly to a contemporary politics in which the increased exigencies of poverty, homelessness and other forms of social injustice put people into positions similar to those in the dock in *Accused*. Whilst accepting, to a large extent, the conclusions of recent scholars (Turnbull, 2014; Nichols-Pethick, 2012) that the police and crime genres are much more varied and difficult to define than had been previously suggested, it remains the case that series which place police characters at their heart also suggest an emphasis on the police perspective to the understanding of crime and criminal activity. To take just one particularly admirable recent example, *Happy Valley* (BBC One, 2014–), there is undeniably an extensive, sympathetic representation of the social world in which the series is set (the eponymous, ironically named valley in West Yorkshire, so-called because of the areas' widespread drug problem).

Ultimately though, the series cannot quite escape the compelling narrative logic of good and evil that drives the audience in the direction of willing the capture of the brutal criminal at the heart of the story.

McGovern's approach in *Accused* is avowedly different. The police are almost absent, and we are forced to concentrate on the true complexity of motivations at play in the crimes that the 'accused' have committed. This is an approach to wrongdoing that McGovern has rarely deserted entirely (see, for a number of examples, *The Street*, BBC One, 2006–10) but his status as a writer whose work brings both popular and critical success has bought him the freedom to return to it in *Accused* with increased vigour. Where this situates the series within the crime and/or police genre is open to some debate, and there is perhaps a case for more attention being given to a kind of sub-genre within which the police themselves are reduced in significance.

Arguably even more direct in its approach to questions of the law and justice is McGovern's single, 90 minute drama, *Common* (BBC One, 2014). Before going on to look at the film in detail, it is worth pausing to note the achievement of a single drama being commissioned and screened on BBC One, particularly one that was likely to arouse a degree of controversy. I have noted above how McGovern has been one of the very few writers in recent times who has managed to carve out space for single dramas [albeit under the guise of the anthology format, first in *The Street* (BBC One, 2006–10) and then *Accused*]. *Common* takes this a stage further by becoming one of only a tiny handful of original feature length dramas shown on British television in 2014. What is particularly remarkable is that McGovern has used such privileged commissioned space to produce a piece of work which, in his own estimation, harks back to the 'campaigning' drama of the 1960s and 1970s (Midgley, 2014).

McGovern's impulse to write *Common* developed very directly from his encounter with victims of miscarriages of justice:

> The inspiration for *Common* came, in part, from a meeting McGovern had with Janet Cunliffe, whose son, Jordan, is serving a life sentence for the murder of Garry Newlove in Warrington in 2007. It was, says McGovern, 'a notorious case. But then Jan told me her version of the story. Jordan was with the group [who attacked Newlove], but took no part in the attack. He went up the road to make sure the ambulance got to the injured man, and bumped into a policeman. And that's why he was apprehended.'
>
> (Midgley, 2014)

Common is not, though, a documentary drama but a work of fiction that focuses on a 17-year-old man, Johnjo (Nico Mirallegro) who is accused of murder after driving a group of friends to fetch pizza, only for one of them to stab a young boy to death inside the shop. In a pattern close to that used in *Accused*, *Common* spends far less time on questions of detection and far more on the difficult territory on which the law meets fairness and a sense of natural justice.

The case of Jordan Cunliffe mentioned above is only one of a large number in recent years that campaigners cite as evidence that the comparatively little-known British law of joint enterprise is being used more and more extensively and, in many cases, inappropriately. Since both *Common* and a BBC documentary, *Guilt by Association* (first broadcast 7 July 2014), were screened the momentum to change or amend the law has increased considerably and has been the subject of a highly critical report by the House of Commons Justice Select Committee.[2]

The inclusion of *Common* in a chapter discussing the treatment of the police on television is principally motivated less by the comparatively minor police roles in the drama, and more by this further example of McGovern's focus away from police personalities and a radical view of the way that justice is operating, particularly in an era during which many detect a worsening of the UK's record on civil liberties. Whilst much of the attention of groups such as Liberty is inevitably on UK counter-terrorism activities, McGovern's drama reminds us that this is only one dimension of the continuous vigilance about the operation of the law that is vital in a healthy democracy.

At a key moment in *Common*, Shelagh Wallace (Michelle Fairley), the mother of Tony (Philip Hill-Pearson), one of the boys accused of murder, screams in anger that the law of joint enterprise is 'about getting working-class scum off our streets', something borne out at least in part by the conclusions of the Select Committee referred to above. McGovern's drama is, then, firmly underpinned by a sense that whilst such a law is in itself a bad thing, its disproportionate impact on already marginalised sections of society makes its reform even more urgent. To further emphasise this point, the Justice Select Committee drew specific attention to another dimension to the impact of the law, namely the disproportionate number of black and mixed-race young men convicted under joint enterprise.

Campaigning drama inevitably leaves itself open to charges of being too polemical, and *Common* attracted its share of criticism. One particular line dealt with what one reviewer called the 'pantomime villainy' of the police, particularly the character of DI Hastings (Robert Pugh). Early in the film Johnjo, somewhat naively as it turns out, goes to the police to tell them that he drove the car that had been picked up on CCTV beside the scene of the murder. His assumption is that his explanation will be believed, but his fate is sealed when he refuses to name the real culprit and Hastings exclaims with relish that it's all fine with him because he can charge Johnjo with murder anyway because of the law – 'It's called Joint Enterprise, y'know, and I love it.' Some reviewers found this level of relish hard to take (Jones, 2014) and it must be said that Hastings, practically the only policeman portrayed in this crime drama lasting 90 minutes, is not one of McGovern's subtlest creations, but to an extent that is part of the point. Our focus is directed away from the kind of individualised 'character' policeman and on to those whose lives are devastated by crime, whether as accused or victim.

This latter point is also important to any analysis of *Common*. Whilst at one level the film is strongly polemical about the iniquity of Joint Enterprise law, McGovern's script is also at pains fully to represent the enormous trauma suffered by the family of the victim. In order to do this he focuses strongly on the estranged parents of the murdered young boy, Thomas Ward (Harry McMullen). The vivid portrayals by, for example, Susan Lynch as Margaret Ward, situate the complex motivations and consequences of crime in the central narrative position that is most often occupied by the police work involved in its detection.

McGovern's overriding point in both *Common* and *Accused* is to write powerful stories around serious crimes that, against the prevailing trend, are genuinely interested in the marginalised people who make up by far the largest percentage of both perpetrators and victims of serious, violent crime. In doing this, he highlights the danger of a political vacuum developing at the heart of so much critically acclaimed work that has dominated the UK schedules in recent times. As I have already stated, this is frequently work which, in so many respects, is of the highest ambitions, particularly with regard to production values and the creation of fascinating characters (usually policemen and women). However, what has so often been lost is what I think McGovern would regard as one of the historic missions of drama that deals with crime and the criminal justice system, namely a constant questioning of what constitutes a proper criminal justice system in which all citizens can have confidence.

As long ago as 1998, Charlotte Brunsdon identified a move away from such a mission, a mission exemplified by the likes of *Law and Order* (BBC Two, 1978) and *Between The Lines* (BBC One, 1992–94). Brunsdon's emphasis was, admittedly, much more on the way crime drama in the late 1990s was moving away from questions of policing to what she called the 'medicalization' of crime. However, I would suggest that her concerns remain important in the second decade of the new millennium for slightly different reasons. As we can see here, Brunsdon's concern was about the absence of policemen and women in crime drama that could be part of a wider questioning agenda: 'I would suggest that the dynamism of the questions about policing – who can police? who is responsible? has become diminished, and instead there is a detectable tendency towards a spectacularization of the body and the site of crime' (1998, p. 242).

I have argued here that whilst crime drama on British television, both imported and made in the United Kingdom, now has no shortage of policemen and women, what it has tended to lack is a sustained critical edge about the kinds of questions (and more) that Brunsdon raises and revisits in this volume. Arguably, a kind of exception to this is contained in work such as *Line of Duty* (BBC Two, 2012–) which is discussed elsewhere in this collection and which has continued the rich vein of drama to be found in the likes of *Between The Lines* (BBC One, 1992–94). Centring on various incarnations of police complaints units, such dramas do focus on the fallibility of the police as the guardians of law and order, only to imply that there are important safeguards in place to protect us (albeit ones that contain their own problems).

In both *Accused* and *Common*, McGovern has sought his own path to rebalance the representation of law and order. This has been partly through the relegation of even 'complex' policemen and women to the background. Instead, he uses the voices of those at the bottom of the criminal justice heap to again bring difficult questions about the criminal justice system onto the popular television agenda. As we have seen above, he has succeeded in attracting the opprobrium of key sections of the establishment, something which he regards as central to his job description. It is perhaps not entirely facetious to end by suggesting that he must be doing something right.

Notes

1. For the sake of clarity, it should be stated at the outset that although both programmes were created by McGovern and referred to as his work in this chapter, *Accused* (BBC1, 2010–12) also featured co-writers on a number of the episodes, a practice adopted by McGovern on a number of occasions, especially on his later work. For a full list of co-author credits on both series of *Accused* see: http://www.imdb.com/title/tt1769411/fullcredits?ref_=tt_ql_1.
2. For a fuller account both of the complexity of the law itself and of the pressure for it to change, see: http://www.theguardian.com/law/2014/dec/17/joint-enterprise-law-mps-call-review.

References

BBC, 2010a. Accused – Christopher Eccleston plays Willy Houlihan. BBC [online] Available at: http://www.bbc.co.uk/pressoffice/pressreleases/stories/2010/10_october/26/accused2.shtml [Accessed 3 December 2014].

BBC, 2010b. Jimmy McGovern army drama "fails soldiers" says veteran. 16 November 2010. BBC [online] Available at: www.bbc.co.uk/news/entertainment-arts-11764240 [Accessed 6 January 2015].

Blandford, Steve, 2013. *Jimmy McGovern*. Manchester, England: Manchester University Press.

Brunsdon, Charlotte, 1998. Structure of anxiety: recent British television crime fiction. *Screen*, 39(3), pp. 223–43.

Cooke, Rachel, 2010. *Accused*: Rachel Cooke gets the feeling Jimmy McGovern is his own biggest fan. 18 October 2010. *New Statesman*. [online] Available at: http://www.newstatesman.com/film/2010/11/mcgovern-willy-mistress-money [Accessed December 4 2014].

Delaney, Sean, 2014. TV police drama. British Film Institute *Screenonline*. [online] Available at: http://www.screenonline.org.uk/tv/id/445716/ [Accessed 3 December 2014].

Feasy, Rebecca, 2008. *Masculinity on Popular Television*. Edinburgh, Scotland: Edinburgh University Press.

Jones, Ellen, 2014. *Common*, BBC1, TV review: Jimmy McGovern's harrowing crime drama is another cracker. 7 July 2014. *The Independent*. [online] Available at: http://www.independent.co.uk/arts-entertainment/tv/bbcs-common-jimmy-mcgoverns-harrowing-crime-drama-is-another-cracker-9587781.html [Accessed 7 January 2015].

McGovern, Jimmy, 2003. *The Lakes*. Complete Second Series [DVD commentary]. BBC Worldwide Ltd.

McGovern, Jimmy, 2010. On *Accused*. RSJ Films [online] Available at: http://www.rsjfilms.com/ [Accessed 9 January 2015].

Midgley, Neil, 2014. Jimmy McGovern: 'You have to write stories that matter.' 4 July 2014. *Daily Telegraph*. [online] Available at: http://www.telegraph.co.uk/culture/tvandradio/10927886/Jimmy-McGovern-You-have-to-write-stories-that-matter.html [Accessed 6 January 2015].

Nichols-Pethick, Jonathan, 2012. *TV Cops: The Contemporary American Television Police Drama*. London, England: Routledge.

Robinson, James, 2010. BBC: Accused is 'a piece of fiction.' *The Guardian*. [online] Available at: http://www.theguardian.com/media/2010/nov/23/bbc-defends-mcgovern-drama [Accessed 6 January 2015].

Thorpe, Vanessa, 2010. TV drama must stop relying on irony and costumes, says Jimmy McGovern. *The Guardian*. [online] Available at: http://www.guardian.co.uk/tv-and-radio/2010/nov/07/jimmy-mcgovern-tv-drama-irony [Accessed 6 January 2015].

Turnbull, Sue, 2014. *The TV Crime Drama*. Edinburgh, Scotland: Edinburgh University Press.

Part II
The Police

5 Women Cops on the Box
Female Detection in the British Police Procedural

Ruth McElroy

'I know these telly shows all have to be entertaining, but our USP was that we were going to get it right', explained Sally Wainwright in a press interview with Danuta Kean (2011) just ahead of transmission of her police procedural, *Scott & Bailey* (ITV, 2011–). 'We were going to show people how it really is and I think that has paid off because people have responded well to it.' This chapter approaches the question of realism in the police procedural from a critical feminist perspective in order to explore the links between claims to verisimilitude at the level of policing with much broader televisual and social concerns about how professional women are represented on screen. It seeks to advance existing debates about realism and crime drama by arguing that the police procedural provides a distinct generic space in which the gendered nature of the social order, and in particular of changing gender relations in the workplace, is investigated and worked over, sometimes explicitly but often more obliquely as part of the main focus on police detection. The chapter acknowledges the enduring importance of verisimilitude but also detaches – or at least loosens – the rather constrictive association between verisimilitude and realism that has characterized so many analyses of crime drama. In particular, I want to explore how a narrative- and character-based emphasis on emotion and empathy allows for a more nuanced combination of realism and melodrama in the female-lead police procedural.

One of the longest-standing debates in crime fiction, both literary and televisual, has been the degree to which writers accurately capture the actual procedures of police investigations. This emphasis on authentic detail and expert insight is normally realised through research, occasionally through first-hand knowledge, and more commonly through employing expert police advisors to the production. There is valuable cultural capital to be gained by a production in making such investments, not least as they ground the genre's claims to realism and the privileged insights it seems to offer viewers of a world largely unknown to law-abiding citizens. The origin narratives of police series as diverse as *Cagney and Lacey* (CBS, 1982–88), *Prime Suspect* (Granada for ITV, 1991–2006), *The Wire* (HBO, 2002–08) and *Z-Cars* (ITV, 1962–78) all include the role real-life police stories and officers have played in inspiring realist fiction, and it is the highly mediated relationship with the truth of crime and policing which the subgenre and its viewers negotiate. So pervasive are these accounts that we need to understand them as an integral hallmark of the police procedural's own production values, providing supporting evidence for the subgenre's claim to privileged insight to the working of those who have the power to arrest citizens and detain them behind bars. Furthermore, this 'know-how' marks out this form of the crime drama from other, more fanciful, examples including the numerous adaptations of Agatha Christie's crime fiction involving amateur sleuths whose quirky personalities and clever instincts, rather than professionalism, lead them to reveal the truth of whodunnit.

In this regard, the police procedural shares a claim to verisimilitude with other popular television genres, such as the medical drama and legal drama, where audience pleasure emerges not just from the credibility of the professional world portrayed on screen, but also from the incremental knowledge the regular viewer gains of procedures that are played out on-screen *as if* true to life. The pleasure of the police procedural's detection lies not only in guessing whodunnit but also in working alongside the investigative pair or team and knowing how each element of their evidence-gathering, from forensic evidence being processed at the lab, to getting extensions from judges to allow further questioning of detained suspects, works collectively to capture the criminal and hold them responsible for the crime(s) committed. The allure of proximity to investigative police officers is what gives the genre both a good and a bad name; good in that it is pleasurable to see the complexity of an ensemble investigation work together and realise its objective, bad in that it does so by positioning the audience ideologically on the side of the police in a hegemonic viewing position whereby crime and criminals are always reduced to the interpretative power of the law. As Jonathan Nichols-Pethick (2012) has argued of the American cop show, 'much of what has been written seems to repeat the same basic contention: that television police dramas are limited by the genre's formulaic nature' which 'provides moral reassurance and champions an inherently conservative social agenda by focusing on the essential wisdom and virtue of those who enforce the law … and offer protection from all who threaten the social order' (p. 2).

Wainwright's claim to getting it right, even when making fictional entertainment, tells us something not just about the generic position of the police procedural and its unique purchase on representing contemporary crime and policing, but also of the appeal of this particular form of crime drama to the viewer. In one key regard, however, it is doubtful whether contemporary British police procedurals are reflecting the police reality, and that is in the preponderance of female police detectives now populating our television screens. In 2011, the same year in which series one of *Scott & Bailey* was transmitted, the Home Office published data showing that just 14.8 per cent of senior rank (that is Chief Inspector and above) officers in the police forces of England and Wales were women (Dhani and Kazia, 2011, p. 14) Even at the lowest constable rank, women only constitute 29 per cent of the police service (ibid.), albeit this results in an overall average of a quarter of police officers in England and Wales being women, one of the highest such levels internationally. Yet if you have been watching police procedurals on British television in the past decade or so, you will have been struck by the plethora of female police officers who have been the protagonists of both domestic series such as *Broadchurch* (ITV, 2013–), *Blue Murder* (ITV, 2003–09), *Case Sensitive* (ITV, 2011–), *Happy Valley* (BBC, 2014–), *The Commander* (ITV, 2003–08), *The Fall* (BBC, 2013–), *The Ghost Squad* (Channel 4, 2005), *Line of Duty* (specifically series two, BBC, 2014), *Murder in Suburbia* (ITV, 2004–05), *New Tricks* (BBC, 2003–15), *Scott & Bailey* (ITV, 2011–) and *Vera* (ITV, 2011–), and of international series acquired by BBC Two and BBC Four (see McCabe in this collection) and fronted by female detective leads such as *Top of the Lake* (BBC, 2013), *The Bridge* (originally *Bron/Broen*, 2011–), *The Killing* (originally *Forbrydelsen*, 2011–) and *Spiral* (originally *Engrenages*, 2006). Even series with titular male detective heroes such as ITV's *DCI Banks* (2010–) or escapist series such as the BBC's feel-good melodrama, *Death in Paradise* (2011–) see them flanked by ambitious, accomplished women officers. The rise of female policing even extends retrospectively to historical crime as witnessed in the current series (2015) of the BBC's *Inspector George Gently* (2007–), which charts the rise of a woman police constable to the rank of police sergeant. As Charlotte Brunsdon (2012) has argued, these series' 'simultaneity suggests a greater confidence on the part of commissioners and schedulers of their ability to entice audiences with that combination of generic familiarity and women cops' (p. 17). Simultaneity is as much a symptom of the television industry's notorious risk aversion as it is a reflection of the genre's response to changing positions of women in the police force; less a question of social mimesis and more a case of commissioners mimicking earlier proven successes. Yet it is also striking to observe how many of the British-made series listed above are ITV dramas. As Ross P. Garner argues in this collection, ITV's audience is skewed female and the development of popular prime time fictions with women leads may well help to secure that audience whilst not alienating the crime genre's traditional male viewership. Moreover, between 2007 and 2013 when many of these series were getting commissioned and transmitted, ITV drama was being fronted by two key women in the TV industry, Laura Mackie (Director of Drama) and Sally Haynes (Controller of Drama Commissioning), though both have since left the broadcaster to establish their own independent production company, Mainstream Pictures. Reflecting on her earlier crime thriller *Unforgiven* (ITV, 2009), Sally Wainwright (2009) described how the decision to submit the script to ITV was an expedient, rather than creative, move based on her conviction that 'Laura [Mackie] would say yes or no quite quickly.' While it is dangerous and rather essentialist to assume that having women in senior commissioning and production roles will in itself transform the representation of women on screen (Hallam, 2013), it is nonetheless striking how important women's relationships have been in the making of women-lead police procedurals. Looking back at the history of women police officers on television, Sue Turnbull (2014), for example, has noted the importance a few key figures have made including the late Verity Lambert's (then Head of Drama for Thames Television) support for Lynda La Plante's first drama *Widows* (ITV, 1983). In her groundbreaking analysis of the landmark US police procedural *Cagney and Lacey* (CBS, 1982–88), Julie D'Acci (1994) notes how the series creators, Barbara Avedon and Barbara Corday, were inspired by Molly Haskell's *From Rape to Reverence: The Treatment of Women in the Movies* (1974) and by their direct observation of New York policewomen with whom they spent time researching female officers' daily experience of policing. Moreover, 75 of the series' 125 scripts were by women (p. 207). It is unsurprising given the enormous impact of *Cagney and Lacey*, both in its depiction of professional female detectives who are friends and partners on screen, and within the TV industry where the series had a turbulent ride from network chiefs, that it continues to hold a special place in the memory of many women who were watching TV in the 1980s. Indeed, Suranne Jones (who plays Rachel Bailey) and Sally Lindsay (who plays her sister, Alison), who created the original idea for *Scott & Bailey,* have recounted how they framed their idea for a female lead police procedural as 'a Manchester-based *Cagney and Lacey*' (Jones cited in Rochlin, 2013), which would address the restrictive acting roles facing women in their 30s and 40s, what Jones termed 'the wife-of, sidekick-to, mother-of, mistress-to' roles. Interviewed in the pre-publicity phase for the fourth series of *Scott & Bailey*, Lesley Sharp (who plays Janet Scott) noted:

> When Scott & Bailey [sic] started it was sort of a lone wolf. But there's an appetite out there for really interesting, complicated, female heroines. And now we have women like Keeley Hawes and Vicky McClure being brilliant in Line of Duty [*sic*] and Gillian Anderson being amazing in the Fall [*sic*]. It's wonderful that there's now writing out there that gives them the chance to get their teeth into something, rather than being an appendage to the man as a wife or a mother.
>
> (Sharp in Brown, 2014)

Scott & Bailey has earned its writers and actors numerous nominations, including for the BAFTA Best Drama Series in 2012 and again in 2013, where it lost out to another ensemble drama by Sally Wainwright, *Last Tango in Halifax* (BBC, 2011–). Indeed it is notable that three of the four nominations had female leads (the other being the BBC's legal drama, *Silk*); the fourth male-lead series was the BBC's crime drama, *Ripper Street*. Sharp's celebratory tone belies relief at finding a broader range of roles for women on screen, together with a claim for a growth in television writing (in which Wainwright has played no small part) placing women centrally as protagonists who hold genuine appeal for audiences. Series one of *Scott & Bailey* was the fourth most popular new TV drama series in 2011, as measured by UK audience ratings (Conlan, 2011). Announcing the commission of series five of *Scott & Bailey*, Steve November, ITV Director of Drama Commissioning (2015) said that 'Scott & Bailey [*sic*] is a firm favourite with ITV viewers who relate to the characters' busy professional and working lives.' Read from this vantage point, the rise of female detection on British TV screens cannot be understood solely in terms of the realist representation of crime and policing. If the police procedural may be disproportionate in its representation of abundant female detective officers at middle and senior ranks, it is nonetheless the case that there are substantive social and televisual realities which help explain the rise of female detection and its widespread appeal.

The Police Ensemble

In her analysis of early British police series, Susan Sydney-Smith (2002) points to the structural emphasis placed by *Z-Cars* on the collective police unit as opposed to a single police officer or heroic detective. The diverse units that exist within UK police forces (drugs, vice, missing persons, traffic, CID and so on) provide writers with an opportunity to distinguish their series from the many others likely to be onscreen at any one time by making their specialism integral to the series' identity and the crimes it investigates. Ensemble series such as *Waking the Dead* (BBC, 2000–) or *New Tricks*, for example, are defined by their specialism in investigating cold cases and distinguished further from each other by their expertise in forensics in the first instance, and by the experience of mainly retired officers in the other. Because the police forces in England and Wales remain regionally constituted (there is no single English or Welsh police force), it is also possible to exploit place as part of the police unit's identity as is the case in *Scott & Bailey*'s Greater Manchester Police Major Incident Unit. The police procedural thus adopts a genuine structural characteristic of the English and Welsh police forces for its own televisual purposes of making each iteration of the genre distinct from any other, whilst retaining the appearance of realist representation. A further characteristic of the police procedural is its tendency, to varying degrees, to exploit the dramatic and narrative potential of a group of characters working together as an ensemble. This allows for the depiction of diversity in characters and ranks, for interpersonal relations to develop, and for the portrayal of an actual workplace where – as in the experience of many viewers – many different types of people may be encountered. Whilst crime obviously lies at the heart of the police procedural's narrative action, its social examination of everyday life and major issues at work in contemporary society are as likely to emerge from the interplay of the ensemble. As Charlotte Brunsdon notes in this collection, this potential was recognised from the subgenre's inception most notably perhaps by John McGrath's desire to 'use a *Highway Patrol* format, but to use the cops as a key or a way of getting into a whole society ... a kind of documentary about people's lives in these areas, and the cops were incidental – they were the means of finding out about people's lives' (McGrath cited in Brunsdon this volume 2016). Latterly, however, the focus of the police procedural has been as much the ensemble of police *workers* themselves (the term is used here deliberately, as will become evident), as the array of criminals and social types they encounter. The police station is neither homogenous nor hermetically sealed, and the diversity gained by decades of equality policies, whilst nothing like as extensive as might be hoped for, have nonetheless allowed writers to exploit further the ensemble format. For some critics, such as Brunsdon, this implies a hollowing out of the genre and its sociological investigation of crime, law and order. For my part, however, I am more concerned here with how the police procedural's ensemble foregrounds the world of work and family life as a distinct kind of moral and emotional order that is interwoven with – but not reducible to – the moral order of policing itself. In this I am inspired by the work of Vicky Ball (2012) and her analysis of the supposed feminisation of British television.

The claim that from roughly the mid-1990s onwards British television has been feminised has emerged from several quarters including scholars, TV professionals and journalists reviewing British television output. A diverse array of evidence has been marshalled to support this analysis ranging from genre and the emergence of popular factual entertainment especially lifestyle and reality formats in prime time (Brunsdon, 2003; Moseley, 2000), to cultural change and the emergence of new scripts articulating emotional and reflexive approaches to life management (Tania Lewis, 2008; Glen Creeber, 2004), to personnel changes which saw women such as Jana Bennett, Dawn Airey, Jane Root and others (including Mackie and Haynes discussed above) occupy senior roles in British broadcasting. More importantly here though, Ball (2012) points to how female ensemble dramas became increasingly prominent in British television schedules from the 1990s, providing 'a distinctive form of feminine-gendered fiction in the way it focuses upon particular communities of female characters and pluralized senses of female identity at the level of region and class' (p. 256). To my mind, a police procedural such as *Scott & Bailey* very much fits this description. Rather than sacrificing its generic distinctiveness, a reading that approaches the series as a female police ensemble drama enables us better to appreciate how the criminal investigative narrative provides writers and actors with the dramatic and cultural space to explore questions of power, agency and gendered labour. Placing women as detective leads enables writers to examine how women perform their professional identities both in the field and in the station. Here the capacity to undertake the painstaking, regulated procedural labour of modern policing is combined with the performance of diverse forms of affective labour, from managing teams (as in the case of DCI Gill Murray, played by Amelia Bullmore in *Scott & Bailey*) to interviewing both the victims and perpetrators of often horrific crimes. Hence, the rise of police procedurals starring women detectives needs to be understood as a direct response to how women's lives and labour have been remade in contemporary society and, in particular, to how the figure of the professional woman has become such a pervasive focus of conflictual and often highly emotional discourses of power and femininity.

This is not to say that an exclusively female police ensemble is necessary for such tensions to emerge. Indeed, one of the most shocking depictions of the police ensemble in recent years is to be found in the second series of *Line of Duty*. Jed Mercurio's writing problematises the idea of the police ensemble and reveals its closed ranks to be the very source of police corruption and its bullying, immoral social order. Keely Hawes' performance as DI Lindsay Denton is an outstanding example of how resistance to women's professional success is dramatically and violently enacted in the main police workplace, the police station. Awkward, aloof and ambitious, Denton makes few friends amongst her police colleagues. Hawes plays her in such a way as to seem always outside the action, as a sometimes calculating, sometimes overawed observer. The heavy cut of her fringe provides a kind of cover from under which Denton seems to look at the world. In the contemporary police procedural, the female detective's face is core to the drama of the narrative action affording exceptional actors the opportunity to convey so much of the feeling I've been discussing here through facial expression. Whilst Denton's battles may echo some of those endured by *Prime Suspect*'s Jane Tennison, she has none of her flair and much more of her vulnerability. On more than one occasion in the first episode, we see Denton holding back tears. There is an awful inevitability (understood more in retrospect than at that point in the narrative) to Denton finding herself in episode one with her head forced down a toilet at her own police station by her colleagues, who take the law into their own hands to punish her for what they believe to be her failure adequately to support fellow officers whom she despatched unarmed to their deaths at the ambush that lies at the heart of the series' corruption plot. 'No firearms, no back up! Should be you we're burying you stupid bitch' torments her sergeant as he holds her forcibly by her brace-collared neck (Denton has previously been injured in the ambush) ready to dunk her a second time while several police officers, including her own superior and a single young female officer, look on enraptured, smugly enjoying the vindictive authority of their own retributive moral order. Yet, whilst Denton's flawed character helps account for why she is singled-out this way, it is deeply and profoundly shocking to watch such visceral, gendered bullying onscreen. And it *is* dramatically shocking precisely because the scene has been carefully plotted and played to produce a thoroughly false sense of secure camaraderie as, just minutes earlier, both her sergeant and superior officer had publicly expressed concern and greeting for Denton on her return to work. The scene's narrative power emanates from the way the acting forces the viewer to *feel* the power of policing. It is melodramatic not in narrowly generic terms but in precisely this capacity to examine questions of gender, power and belonging through the aesthetics of emotional effect. What seems is not the case; Denton does not belong, is not wanted, and despite police officers' ability publicly to perform the collegial role, the truth that emerges in her attack belies the enduring realities of violent sexism and a deeply corrupt police service which the series goes on to investigate and reveal. Whilst Denton herself is ultimately imprisoned for her limited part in the events leading to the death of two officers, the viewer of this scene is left in little doubt that her sex makes Denton vulnerable in a way that her male colleagues are not. The police ensemble is portrayed as a vicious pack, intolerant of any difference Denton may be trying to make.

Procedural Intimacy

In the remainder of this chapter I want to explore how *Scott & Bailey*, as a female police ensemble drama, uses the generic conventions of the procedural investigation to explore the culture of contemporary police work, and women's place within it and in relation to one another. My argument rests on the assumption that the representation of police work in the series is indicative of wider changes in the world of modern work, and in which many supposedly feminine skills (including empathy, communication and collaboration) have become increasingly important. These transformations in post-industrial workplaces have led to increased emphasis on affective forms of labour, with which both women and femininity have traditionally been associated. Indeed, some argue that the capitalist workplace has itself been feminised not only by the increased participation of women as both full-time and part-time workers, but also 'because of the feminine skills of flexibility and constant adaptability demanded within current precarious employment systems' (Jarrett, 2014, p. 15). The binary established between the public world of work and the private world of home is itself disrupted in such a formation, as many of the supposedly private emotional competencies thought of as familial and domestic come to be required of modern workers. Eva Illouz (2007) has theorised these changes as 'the making of emotional capitalism' in which the therapeutic culture that emerged in the early twentieth century combined with new economic models of American corporations to develop a new model of good management:

> Elton Mayo revolutionized management theories because at the same time that he recast the moral language of selfhood into the dispassionate terminology of psychological science, he substituted a new lexicon of 'human relations' for the engineers' rhetoric of rationality that had hitherto prevailed ... being a good manager increasingly meant displaying the attributes of a good psychologist: it required being able to grasp, listen to, and deal dispassionately with the complex emotional nature of social transactions in the workplace. (pp. 14–15)

Empathy, and the capacity to listen attentively to others, thus became integral to the procedures of modern management. In *Scott & Bailey* this is especially evident in the figure of DCI Gill Murray (Amelia Bullmore) who leads and manages the unit with considerable authority. Whilst we see her experience the stresses and frustrations of leading an investigation, the tone of Bullmore's delivery is predominantly one of assured calm and confidence. A set-piece of the series' production design positions Murray at the head of a boardroom table around which the whole team are seated and invited to speak and report on their specific work to date for the investigative whole. Murray alone has the authority to chair, but she is seen listening to others and consulting with her juniors, Scott and Bailey, and on occasion her female superior, Detective Superintendent Julie Dodson (Pippa Haywood), who sits alongside her. Women *as* professionals largely control these spaces and are *in* control in these spaces. Their capacity to collaborate and communicate is foregrounded in their methodical approach to police procedure. This reflects Wainwright's desire as a writer to avoid a common instance of melodramatic performance found in the police procedural, the furious commander, 'they always show DCIs shouting in interrogation rooms. DCIs never interview anyone it's all [done by] detective constables or sergeants. And nobody shouts' (Wainwright in Kean, 2011). Notable here is Wainwright's claim to realism which is based both on her relationship with police advisor and former detective, Diane Taylor, and her experience of observing working police stations. One of the striking things about Murray is the mixture of fear, respect, admiration and often agreement that she elicits from her team through her by-the-book approach. This contrasts with the more common opposition – established from the days of *The Sweeney* and which is reprised/reversed so effectively in *Life on Mars* – between the police duo and their boss. Instead, *Scott & Bailey* establishes Murray's pervasive professionalism as the normative approach to police investigation management. This greater ambivalence and tacit acceptance of modern managerialism is vital to the series' take on the police procedural and to the space it provides for exploring affective skills in the professional workplace. Design is again important here not least in the space of Murray's office. The separating off of the senior investigating officer into a half-glass office is a common staple of the police procedural, allowing them to be both part of and aloof from the factory floor of everyday policing. Murray is frequently placed behind her desk, wearing a formal, fitted skirt suit that could be worn by any professional woman, at furniture that looks like it has been ordered from Staples (or any other standard office supplier). Only the map on her noticeboard, and the branded identity badge she wears on her lapel, distinguish this from any other office in the country's workplaces. The design is mundane, ordinary, deliberately common. Murray's stance is often angular, composed with body language half-open as she peers over her glasses, a tick that enhances her authority and emphasises her active gaze; both we the viewer and her junior officers subject to its power (Figure 5.1).

Figure 5.1 DCI Gill Murray (Amelia Bullmore) at her desk.

Of course, her workplace extends beyond the station and here Murray is again seen articulating the procedural steps to secure and work through a crime scene and direct operations. In doing so, she is also seen repeatedly communicating with other investigators, reporting back to her Superintendent and, as is now vital to any modern cop show, working with a forensic pathologist, the brilliantly named 'scary Mary' for whom Murray has absolute respect despite the dark humour in her nickname. The world of work is everywhere populated by women in this police procedural which, whilst it may lack mimetic accuracy given the data on female officers, does capture a different truth of the everyday professionalism of women's working lives and many of the skills which those workplaces demand. Whilst the police procedural's appeal thus lies partly in how it takes us into a world we hardly know, it also seems especially malleable to representing the known world of work and the routine tensions, communications and conflicts we, as viewers who work in such places, will recognise and readily identify. Wainwright's objective with *Scott & Bailey* was to write a script where it was 'perfectly acceptable to be a woman and high-powered in an interesting job and it goes uncommented upon because you're surrounded by women who are doing a similar caliber of job' (Wainwright cited in Rochlin, 2013). This tacit, taken-for-granted nature of a feminised workplace contrasts with earlier series such as *Cagney and Lacey*, *Prime Suspect* and *The Gentle Touch*, where the argument for women's right to be in senior roles, undertaking serious criminal investigation is far more overt. As Lorraine Gamman argued, *The Gentle Touch*'s Maggie Forbes is an isolated specimen, devoid of female peers with the series offering 'no suggestion that, given the opportunity, women are as capable as men' (Gamman cited in Lamb, 2014, p. 208).

One area where *Scott & Bailey* dramatically exemplifies women's particular professional policing capabilities is in the titular detective's interviewing skills. The police interview room is a carefully designed set-piece to which the series returns in each episode, imbuing it narratively with the significance of plot development (it is where suspects are often hoisted by their own petard). Performatively though, it also provides a space of accomplishment where Scott and Bailey's emotional and professional competence can be observed. Whilst interviews across a simple table are a hallmark trope of police procedurals, here the detectives routinely come out from behind the interrogation desks and sit to one side, allowing a greater degree of intimacy and proximity. Repeated use is then made of the two-shot (at both mid-shot and close-up levels) to show how the posture of the interrogator mirrors empathically the person being questioned. Such performance of professional control and semblance of fellow feeling is achieved by the careful performances of both actors who remain calm and overtly oriented to the suspect in their body language (Figure 5.2).

Figure 5.2 DC Rachel Bailey (Suranne Jones) interviews a witness.

Posture, as much as gesture, works symbolically to tell the story of police officers' authority. This dramatic embodiment requires actors, as well as directors and camera operators, expressively to inhabit the space of police stations, interview and incident rooms as well as scenes of crime, in such a way as to convey these complex interpersonal relationships that are both professional and personal. In their interviewing skills, Scott and Bailey evidence a methodical approach, working through lines of questioning that are periodically reviewed both by the interrogator (who is seen reflecting on whether that line of approach is working) and by Murray in scenes where she directs changes in the interview from her observation of them and receipt of new information from the rest of the team. This contrasts sharply with the more commonly hierarchical use of desks in most police procedurals' interview rooms that function to separate police officers defin-itively from civilians being questioned opposite, on the other side of the desk which acts as a firm physical and ideological barrier between the two parties. The design of *Scott & Bailey*'s procedural intimacy is self-conscious as Wainwright indicates in a press interview: 'They showed me one they had done with a 28-year-old man who had stabbed a five-year-old boy 64 times ... The way they interviewed him was really kind and calm, not shouting at him. They would get nothing if they shouted at him. It was really empathic' (Wainwright in Kean, 2011).

Empathy is integral to both women's procedural control of the criminal investigation, and is integral to their professional competence which Murray, as their senior officer, both directs and admires. As Illouz (2007) argues:

> Empathy – the ability to identify with another's point of view and with his or her feelings – is at once an emotional and cognitive sym-bolic skill, for the prerequisite of empathy is that one must decipher the complex cues of others' behavior. To be a good communicator means to be able to interpret others' behavior and their emotions. To be a good communicator requires a fairly elaborate coordination of emotional as well as cognitive skills: one can only empathize fully if one has mastered the complex web of cues and signals through which others simultaneously hide and reveal their selves. (p. 20)

Illouz's attention to the diverse skills necessary to empathise reveals how much routine detective work is involved in accomplishing such an emotion. Televisually, empathy is also amenable to being performed and captured by the camera, making this aspect of the police performance a visually, and not just emotionally, appealing element of the investigation:

> Great television is about conversation – and confrontation. It takes two people and closes in on their faces as they talk, so that we can see the emotion animating every flicker and expression.
>
> That's TV at its purest. As soon as the camera pulls back, to show us action or scenery or explosions, some of the intensity is lost. *Scott & Bailey* understands the power of question-and-answer, face-to-face.
>
> (Stevens, 2013)

Rather than being the product of police gut instinct, empathy stands as a distinctly modern competence possessed by Scott and Bailey by dint of their professional training and capacity to stand imaginatively in others' shoes. Often reinforced through dialogue, the capacity for empathy stems also from their own personal lives. Both women have troubled family lives; Scott separates from her husband early in series one and has her mother living with her to help with childcare, whilst Bailey goes through numerous calamitous heterosexual relationships while maintaining a close relationship with her sister with whom she bonds over their mothers' years of neglect and continued shambolic existence. In this regard they are very much like Christine Cagney and Mary Beth Lacey, though the distinct northern working-class speech and intimacy owes much to Wainwright's years as an accomplished writer of the soap opera, *Coronation Street* (ITV, 1960–).

Conclusion

The list of police series above starring female police protagonists provides strong evidence of the diversity of women detectives now known to viewers of the police procedural. Many of these roles have elicited extraordinary performances from actors who have played women detectives as simultaneously strong, vulnerable and as the bearers of complex secrets from often painful pasts. Prominent here is Keeley Hawes' DI Denton in *Line of Duty* (nominated for 2015 BAFTA for Best Drama Series), Sarah Lancashire's astonishingly vivid performance as uniformed police sergeant Catherine Cawood in Wainwright's ironically named *Happy Valley* (winner of 2015 BAFTA Best Drama Series), Olivia Colman's BAFTA-award winning detective Ellie Miller in *Broadchurch* (winner of 2014 BAFTA Best Drama Series) and Elisabeth Moss' powerful and elegiac role as detective Robin Griffin in the Jane Campion-directed, *Top of the Lake* (nominated for 2014 BAFTA Best Drama Series). This is a far cry from the frustratingly limited role which Lynda La Plante found herself working with in ITV's *The Gentle Touch*, and in response to which her *Prime Suspect* ultimately emerged. A balance is struck differently in each of these series between the commitment to the routine characteristics of the genre's criminal investigations, and the extent to which more explicitly gendered politics are played out, whether directly through *Top of the Lake*'s explicitly feminist alternative living group, or *Scott & Bailey*'s more mundane working through of the challenges faced by working women in managing their careers and families simultaneously. In the introduction to this chapter, I pointed out how claims of verisimilitude work to distinguish the police procedural and to enhance its claim to represent the social world of law and order. The rise of female detection both testifies to the malleability of the police procedural and reminds us of the value of women viewers to broadcasters, producers and writers. More importantly, however, this chapter demonstrates how the police procedural lends contemporary women writers and actors the opportunity to develop a narrative and performative approach that speaks to distinctly gendered concerns and experiences most especially through the procedural's mediation of social transgression and moral order. While this may superficially appear as a continuation of the genre's realist roots, the emotional expressivity that lies at the heart of these female detectives' performances of professional, gendered identity actually operates, and arguably innovates, on the dynamic continuum between realism and melodrama.

References

Ball, V., 2012. The 'feminization' of British television and the re-traditionalization of gender. *Feminist Media Studies*, 12(2), pp. 248–64.

Brown, D., 2014. *Scott & Bailey*: Lesley Sharp, Suranne Jones and Amelia Bullmore reveal all about the new series. *Radio Times*, 10 September.

Brunsdon, C., 1998. Structure of anxiety: recent British television crime fiction. *Screen*, 39(3), pp. 223–43.

Brunsdon, C., 2003. Lifestyling Britain: The 8–9 slot on British television. *International Journal of Cultural Studies*, 6 (1), pp. 5–23.

Brunsdon, C., 2012. Television crime series, women police, and fuddy-duddy feminism. *Feminist Media Studies*, 13(3), pp. 375–94.

Conlan, T., 2011. X factor final Pips royal wedding to become most-watched show of 2011. *The Guardian*, [online] 20 December. [Accessed 3 August 2015].

Creeber, G., 2004. *Serial Television: Big Drama on the Small Screen*. London, England: BFI.

D'Acci, J., 1994. *Defining Women: Television and the Case of Cagney and Lacey*. London, England: University of North Carolina Press.

Garner, R., This volume. Crime drama and channel branding: ITV and *Broadchurch*. In: R. McElroy, ed. 2017. *Contemporary British Television Crime Drama*. London, England: Routledge.

Hallam, J., 2013. Drama queens: making television drama for women 1990–2009. *Screen*, 54 (2), pp. 256–61.

Haskell, M., 1974. *From Rape to Reverence: The Treatment of Women in the Movies*. Chicago, IL: University of Chicago Press.

Home Office, Dhani, A. and Kaiza, P., 2011. Police service strength, England and Wales, 31 March 2011. *Home Office Statistical Bulletin*. (HOSB: 13/11). [Report] London, England: Home Office Statistics.

Illouz, E., 2007. *Cold Intimacies: The Making of Emotional Capitalism*. London, England: Polity Press.

Jarrett, K., 2014. The relevance of 'women's work': social reproduction and immaterial labour in digital media. *Television and New Media*, 15(1), pp. 14–29.

Kean, D., 2011. Sally Wainwright talks to Danuta Kean. [online] Available at: http://www.danutakean.com/blog/interview-sally-wainwright-keeps-it-real/ [Accessed 10 December 2011].

Lamb, B., 2014. 'Ah! Our very own *Juliet Bravo*, or is it Jill Gascoine?': *Ashes to Ashes* and representations of gender. In: J. Bignell and S. Lacey, eds., 2014. *British Television Drama: Past, Present and Future*. Basingstoke, England: Palgrave Macmillan. pp. 203–13.

Lewis, T., 2008. *Smart Living: Lifestyle Media and Popular Expertise*. New York, NY: Peter Lang Publishing.

Moseley, R., 2000. Makeover takeover on British television. *Screen*, 41(3), pp. 299–314.

Nichols-Pethick, J., 2012. *TV Cops: The Contemporary American Television Police Drama*. London, England: Routledge.

November, S., 2015. ITV Commissions new episodes of Scott & Bailey. *ITV Press Centre*, [online] 31 July. [Accessed 3 August 2015].

Rochlin, M., 2013. A 'Cagney and Lacey' with constables. *New York Times*, 10 May.

Stevens, C., 2013. Hooray for Scott & Bailey … it's just a pity about the man hating. *Daily Mail*, 2 May.

Sydney-Smith, S., 2002. *Beyond Dixon of Dock Green: Early British Police Series.* London, England: I.B. Tauris.

Turnbull, S., 2014. *The TV Crime Drama.* Edinburgh, Scotland: Edinburgh University Press.

Wainwright, Sally, 2009. Writer Sally Wainwright on ITV's hit drama *Unforgiven. Screen Yorkshire.* [online] Available at: http://www.youtube.com/watch?v=1O5 qyXJfy9c.

6 Unfettered Bureaucracy, Narrative Collapse

Postmodern Enemies in *Line of Duty*

Manel Jimenez-Morales

Since the beginning of the Cold War, numerous television dramas have set out to explore the nature of bureaucracy and reveal it as a tainted, albeit pervasive, concept. This concern with the failings of modern bureaucracies has something to do with the fall of state socialism and the way in which the lifting of the Iron Curtain, after the collapse of the Berlin wall, lead to the exposure of centrally controlled economies' tendency to justify the inefficiency of their own systems. However, for many television dramas it is the role of bureaucracy in late capitalist democracies that is the main focus of critical investigation. In the last few years, two facts have confronted the representatives of social leadership and order within society: firstly, the policy of suspicion, settled by the destruction of the Twin Towers and its consequences, and secondly, the recent economic crisis. It is through their dramatic exploration of the shadows of bureaucracy that such dramas bring to light the normally concealed and corrupt forces that continue to operate in modern societies.

Line of Duty (BBC2, 2012–) explores the specific absurdities of the police bureaucratic system and the challenges faced by investigators tasked with exposing police corruption. There have been two series transmitted to date, the first consisting of 5 episodes transmitted in the United Kingdom in June/July 2012 and the second, comprising 6 episodes transmitted in February/March 2014, with both series enjoying popular and critical acclaim. A further two series have been commissioned by the BBC and the series has been exported internationally and is available as a DVD box set. The series is written by Jed Mercurio, a former doctor who has made a name for himself in British television drama as the author of intelligent scripts that examine critically the managerialism and target culture pervasive in public services such as the National Health Service in dramas such as *Cardiac Arrest* (BBC, 1994–1996) *Bodies* (BBC, 2004–2006) and *Critical* (Sky, 2014). Echoing *The Wire* (HBO, 2002–2008), *Line of Duty* captures the zeitgeist of the new police series, where the satisfaction for the spectator is no longer deferred to the final dénouement of the mystery, but lies instead in losing oneself at every stage in the plot's intrigue. The series follows in the wake of other contemporary British police series such as *M.I.T.: Murder Investigation Team*, (ITV, 2003–2005) and *Murder City* (ITV, 2004), especially regarding the pace and proximity of the subjects, and the way in which the narrative delves into the mechanism of investigation, questioning its procedures and values. *Line of Duty* is a relentlessly self-questioning series, exploring police methods and the practices of authority through the investigations of the fictional anti-corruption police unit, AC-12, lead by Superintendent Ted Hastings (Adrian Dunbar), with DS Steve Arnott (Martin Compston) and DC Kate Fleming (Vicky McClure) as the main investigators on the ground. The series is deeply self-conscious and for this reason it can best be conceived as meta-discursive in its observation of the police as themselves criminal. Not only are the series narratives intricate and self-conscious but also they bear a privileged proximity to actual events in British society which viewers might well watch on the news before or after viewing the fictional series. Reviewing the first episode of series 1, for example, Ceri Radford wrote, 'With police collusion in the phone-hacking scandal still lingering in the public memory, now is a good time for a new drama series about uniformed skulduggery' (Radford 2012). *Line of Duty*'s narrative, both within and across episodes, takes the viewer and the main anti-corruption investigators on a round trip of suspicions. The mechanics of good and evil – a characteristic feature of police series – lose their natural condition. The behaviour of the police officers under investigation reveals the demagogy of police stations: the mistrust of the methods, the block of different departments or officers within them, to develop an investigation or the prioritisation of some cases for economical or personal reasons are some of the issues that question the work of the police as we understand it. *Line of Duty* has a narrative effect that is repeated persistently in our times: the idea of discussing itself, questioning its own construction, referencing itself, and subverting the classic mechanism of the story and its characters by dealing with aberrant and disarming types of social behaviour.

The main focus of my analysis in this chapter is the relationship between the absurd mechanics of the bureaucratic system on the one hand and, the detective narrative itself on the other. *Line of Duty*, I argue, is emblematic of the kind of postmodern televison mystery series that disrupt our narrative expectations and creates a pervasive atmosphere of suspicion without the reassuring promise of a defintive resolution. This chapter studies firstly the condition of the characters of this kind of series, as well as the ambiguity of their morality and the reaction of audiences towards them. It seeks to categorise the series' main narrative devices and traces how the bureaucratic system itself produces distinct problems for the police officers. Secondly, the chapter then explores how the narrative turns into a complex spiral of facts to the point that the solution of the mystery is often regarded as a long and convoluted process. Finally, it explains how the show exploits one of the most typical devices of police dramas, the interrogation of the suspects.

Line of Duty begins its first series with the story of Steve Arnott, a street cop, fired from his department for a flagrant error and forced to move to another department. There he is asked to demonstrate the alleged illegality of the operations of a successful senior officer. The second season has Arnott confront senior officer Lindsay Denton who survived an incident which resulted in the death of other officers. The second series starts with this attack to a convoy escorting a civilian under a witness protection. Denton's short information after the attack makes her suspicious of the collaboration in the crime and is transferred to a missing persons unit assisted by Kate, while Arnott and Hastings investigate the case. The plot is apparently very simple, but it brings a crucial element to the narrative: the difficulty of proving a police suspect's guilt when they are protected by the administrative bureaucracy of the police force itself. Two main factors describe the running of this kind of fiction and reflect the complexity of their nature: corruption and the bureaucratic system.

Everybody has a Price

Corruption is at the core of *Line of Duty*'s narration and is integral to the emotionally complex relationship between its corrupt characters and the viewer. In his book, *Engaging Characters* (1995), Murray Smith emphasises the moral importance of allegiance understood as the extension of our sympathy and comprehension to the characters of any narration. As Jason Mitell argues, a 'common trait shared by many complex television series is the prominence of unsympathetic, morally questionable, or villanous figures, nearly always male... and their narrative centre' (Mitell, 2014, p. 275). Contemporary television drama's fascination with dramatising the flawed hero is also the subject of Noël Carroll's article on *The Sopranos* (2004, pp. 121–136). He links the success of the HBO series to the protagonist's questionable morality.

Line of Duty dives deep into this practice, giving over the centrality of the plot to several suspicious characters including DCI Tony Gates, the main focus of AC-12's investigations in series 1. Our immersion in Tony Gates' family and the close and dependent relationship between DI Lindsay Denton (Keely Hawes) and her mother in season 2 elicits empathy towards these characters. Viewers become involved with all these negative characters' activities throughout the story, discover their human dimension and forgive their less constructive qualities. Engagement with this type of character neutralises our suspicion and confuses the audience. At the same time, the fact that some of the characters experience an equal reaction – Steve Arnott, for example, feels a special complicity with Lindsay Denton in series 2 – contributes to our mistrust of any preceeding line of investigation and keeps open all the possibilities of the plot.

It is also meaningful, however, that these characters are not neutral: they are police officers integrated into the whole dynamics of investigation, so that sometimes their blocking decisions are understood not only as a mechanism to hide their own crimes, but to preserve some policy of intervention in the squad. The ingenious skill here is conniving the strategies between alignment and allegiance, where *alignment* is the shared knowledge with the protagonists. In *Line of Duty* the audience's level of alignment is always in shortfall. There is a lack of information about the whole process these characters are following to achieve their plans. Obviously the link between allegiance and alignment is extremely systematic. The more the audience knows the characters, the more they can sympathise with their imagery. For Carroll, audiovisuals are 'criterially prefocused' (2003, pp. 69–70), meaning spectators have always a sort of 'pro-attitude' regarding the plot depending on the genre, the characters, the outlying elements of the narration, etc. Stories like the one presented in *Line of Duty* constantly disrupt this pro-attitude, hiding the basic information from the audience and creating an uncanny and undecipherable atmosphere.

In contrast to film, television series provide a longer period of reflection for audiences allowing for a more complex circuit of judging the characters. This protracted evolution of the story allows for the character nuances and a fickle and fluctuating policy of suspicion to emerge. At the end of series 1, for instance, Gates rescues Arnott from the gangsters threatening him which makes Arnott think that Gates could be innocent after all and leads the spectator to consider and reappraise the crime suspect's attitude. Only the over-dimension and the expansion of the time guarantees this kind of change in the characters' consideration and in the audience's response.

Moreover, the dark corners of the protagonists' character produces confusion in the audience. None of the main characters are exempt from dubious behaviour. They are neither holders of certainty, nor trustees of morality. This is very much the case with DC Kate Fleming who, in series 2, is revealed as having had an affair in the second season with Rich, the husband of Jayne Akers, one of the police officers shot in the ambushed convoy that motivates AC-12's investigation. This revelation could easily lead audiences to distrust her and suspect her implication in Akers' murder. Instead, in a narrative where the borders of morality are not clearly visible and where the characters live always in this vagueness of motivations, any conclusion about Fleming's guilt is endlessly deferred. Indeed, the second series plays extensively on the opposition between the two main female officers, Fleming and Denton, to balance the suspicion in several fields. The secret of Fleming's affair is known only by Arnott and Denton, with Arnott proving an uncomfortable confidant and Denton using the knowledge as a threat against Fleming when she herself comes under supicion. At almost every turn, new suspicions and conjectures emerge for every character.

An important narrative element in the series' climate of suspicions lies in the figure of the spy in the police station. The *lieu comun* of the mole is frequent in dramas made after 9/11. Many of these mystery narratives and police dramas place the figure of a spy or a traitor at the centre of their plots. In some instances, an infiltrator appears in the organization to destabilize the whole structure. The infiltrator acts as a bridge element between the allegedly correct order and a sacrificial figure fighting for a renewal of justice. Usually, the correct order is revealed as being as rotten as the forces facing it. FOX's *24* is the clearest example of this corruption inside the organization. In practically every season the main character, Jack Bauer, deals with the idea of an infiltration. Narrative complexity emerges from this playful exercise between the mole and the agents secretly investigating other agents. *Line of Duty*'s Gates is not exactly a mole, he is just a corrupted officer taking advantadge of his position. But Lindsay Denton could be taken for an infiltrator: she is definitely somebody in contact with *the other side* of justice and, to a certain point, a leak in the established system to pass some information. Fleming, on the other hand, is the AC-12 undercover officer who gets close to the main suspects to get information about them. But there is always a lasting doubt in viewers' minds about these characters as potential double agents who rarely escape the shadows of suspicion.

Finally, one of the elements that increases the unforgiving climate is the level of cruelty and violence against the alleged villains of the story. This antagonism is usually played by characters who cross the limits of any morality. Therefore, villains are perceived as more positive characters in contrast with the other characters who always act against the integrity of any role. Denton's experience in jail during epsiode three of series 2 exemplifies this situation vividly and proves that the *tour-de-force* between characters relocates them into one or the other side. During the whole time Denton is in custody both the staff and the prisoners terrorise her. As she becomes a victim, the audience's engagement with her shifts, rekindling our pity and compassion.

Lost in the Bureaucratic Order

The second factor that exerts a strong influence on the plot is the bureaucratic system itself and the way in which it is deployed across all police procedures. The peculiar logic of bureaucracy is examined through the narrative. Indeed, the absurd bureaucratic structure arches ostensibly over the plot to the point that it becomes *the* main enemy for the hero and offers itself up as the perfect mechanism by which to develop the story. Typically *Line of Duty*'s plot develops when the anti-corruption investigation encounters a substantial obstacle that emerges from the bureaucracy and prevents the accomplishment of the investigative mission. We can catgorise some of the main problems related to the bureaucracy as follows:

- Informational. The lack of information about the procedures. On several occassions the officers do not know exactly the right way to solve a situation and embark on a long journey to find the solution. In the fourth episode of the first series, for instance, Gates suggests that a specific investigation into money laundering should be passed to another department. This decision does not benefit Arnott's interests, but he cannot show opposition to it because he doesn't know if he can take full responsibility on issues like money laundering.

- Executive. The taking of decisions belongs to another department. Once clear about the procedure, the main characters feel completely blocked because the responsibility and control of issues are not in their hands.
- Legal. The legal procedures take too much time. The course of action is sometimes too long because it requires the participation of other agents or because the approval of some decisions has its own time durations.
- Economic. Lack of budget. The economic situation is obviously one of the most obstructive elements, especially because it dictates whether to go ahead with the investigation.
- Factual. The confrontational opposition between characters and their different interests. The police do not act as a whole organism, as in more standard police procedurals so their own enmities and hostilities also provoke a deceleration of the pace of the investigation.

There is a high degree of suspense in the narrative with the viewer often knowing in advance much of the plot or having evidence of the suspect's guilt. This is part of the audiences' 'pro-attitude' mentioned previously. There is advanced knowledge to tracing the distance between what the viewer knows and the impossibility of moving things forward in AC-12's investigation in order to achieve the appropriate action. Mercurio's plotting plays with fulfilling the audiences' expectations, putting them off or completely fooling the viewers. The combination of frustration and anticipation in the viewer's engagement with the narrative is also the result of Mercurio's exploitation of the form of television series and their particular temporality. As John Fiske argues (1987, p. 145):

> Television's sense of time is unique in its feel of the present and its assumption of the future [...]. In series, the future may not be part of the diegetic world of the narrative, but it is inscribed into the institution of television itself: the characters may not act as though they will be back with us next week, but we, the viewers, know that they will. The sense of the future, of the existence of as yet unwritten events, is a specifically televisual characteristic, and one that works to resist narrative closure.

At the same time as this linear temporality drives the viewer forward with a will to know, the bureaucracy itself acts as a frustrating loop. Thus, the main difficulty for the hero is not just in discovering the mystery but also in overcoming the administrative barriers that inhibit or shape actual behaviour. Therein lies the difficulty of the story: to break the boundaries of that which is protected by the administration. The main obstacle in the narrative is the lack of interlocutors: sometimes the structure of the organisation is so complex and hierarchical that any worker takes the last responsibility of facts and passes it to another person. The administration acts as a whole institution which embodies an organism without visible leaders. Work is a chain and every worker has a responsibility but none has definitive account-ability. As Hannah Arendt argues (1969, p. 18), the bureaucratic system denies freedom and individual acts:

> In a fully developed bureaucracy there is nobody left with whom one could argue, to whom one could present grievances, on whom the pressures of power could be exerted. Bureaucracy is the form of gov-ernment in which everybody is deprived of political freedom, of the power to act; for the rule by Nobody is not no-rule, and where all are equally powerless we have a tyranny without a tyrant.

Bureaucracy is capricious and always plays into the hands of whoever is in charge. The hero of *Line of Duty* tries to find the major weakness of the bureaucracy and remove the partiality shown by the person who controls it. For instance, in series 1 Gates not only manipulates his job outcome to appear successful in terms of his arrest rates, but also takes advantage of his reach to protect his lover and acquire an alibi. In series 2, Deputy Chief Constable Michael Dryden uses the investigation for self-interest, as when he decides to draw attention away from his driving offence by revealing to the media that DI Lindsay Denton is under investigation. Following the sociologist Michel Crozier in *The Bureaucratic Phenomenon* (1964, p. 169):

> in situations where almost every outcome has been decided in advance according to a set of impersonal and predefined rules and regulations, the only way in which people are able to gain some control over their lives is to exploit 'zones of uncertainty' where the outcomes are not already known.

The protagonist, DS Steve Arnott, tries to follow these elements of uncer-tainty, and reveal the fragility of the police system. The investigative narra-tive becomes not only an exercise in self-reflection but also an attempt to prove that the police system has as many cracks as any other organization. The shadow of doubt settles on the police force itself creating a constant sus-picious regime. The increasing complexity of the narration is held together by what we might term *suture stitches*. They are the splits in the plot where some information is left. These *suture stitches* constantly avoid the main character's revelations. No sooner does Arnott discover a line of investiga-tion than he immediately encounters a barrier to progression, sometimes in the form of an accusation that endangers the investigation. In episode 2 of series 2, Denton is interviewed again but this time she has evidence of misbe-haviours by all the main characters; Arnott seems to have had a relationship with a witness; Superintendent Ted Hastings' financial problems could make him guilty; while Fleming has had an affair with Acker's husband. All the characters find themselves in a sort of dead-end situation that jeopardizes the evolution of the case.

Paradoxically, the final mystery is often solved when the investigation follows a seemingly random path that leads the protagonists to the right conclusion. This is exactly what happens in series 2 when Arnott and Fleming finally arrest DCC Dryden after evidence emerges that he has had an affair with Carly Kirk, a 15-year-old girl. Dryden immediately claims to have been set up by Denton and this apparently random or secondary detail brings the evidence to the main conclusion.

This apparently adventurous effect is not accidental. As a structure, the police organization itself blocks access to information required by Arnott and contributes to this tight-lipped climate where nothing can be revealed. Thus, the intrinsic values of the police force are subverted to the point that it becomes an absolutely rotten system, an umbrella under which to hide crimes committed by the police organization itself.

Moreover, the police force as depicted in *Line of Duty* is more interested in numbers than in people, and in this way, meets Michel Crozier's four characteristics of what he terms the bureaucratic phenomenon (1964, p. 184–195):

- The development of impersonal rules. In the first season, Arnott is in charge of investigating Gates' suspiciously high arrest rates. It is a mission imposed by the police force on Arnott, but he does not get help from the force to investigate it. On the contrary, the young detective has to overcome the difficulties of this assignment following the universal rules that complicate his investigation.
- The centralisation of decisions. The decisions are always taken by superiors with little respect for the real agents of the investigation. Here Ted Hastings has a strong responsibility and uses it to favour Arnott's decision, but he has his superiors and their decisions sometimes clash with the objectives of the mission.
- The isolation of strata and group pressure within strata. The whole structure is dominated by groups of pressure. This is a typical characteristic of complex seriality, where the continuity between seasons is sometimes lead by the fact that different characters are involved in the crime, acquiring influence in the plot and expanding the narrative. Detective Inspector Matthew 'Dot' Cottan is a clear example of this complicity and of creating pressure from inside.
- The development of parallel power relationships. Politics and press usually appear as an ally of biased interests and bring added complexity to the resolution of the investigation.

Opposed to this bureaucratic universe are individuals – ordinary police officers – whose experience on the streets differs from this bid for targets and figures. Fleming's situation throughout the second series responds to this contrast: In the middle of this complex case Fleming is separated from her husband and sleeping in her car rather than at home. At the same time, Arnott deals with the death of Georgia Trotman, his colleague and lover who is murdered in service at the end of the first episode of the second series. These personal events condemn the characters to a split reality, one characterised by the coldness of the working environment and the other wounded by their personal traumas and anguish. The title *Line of Duty* is paradoxical: not all that happens in the series takes place in the line of duty and what is left unsaid, sometimes only insinuated, has a direct impact on the characters' decisions. The fact that Arnott finally knows about Fleming's indiscretion and invites her to stay at his home becomes a very positive decision, where they summarise their knowledge and conclusions in order to put an end to the investigation.

Line of Duty explores two kinds of bureaucracy: one that represents the typical structure of a police system, and the other that portrays the global economic crisis and austerity policies. The cuts caused by the crisis and the prioritization of cases, especially with the aim of getting good results in order to justify a certain service to society, obey this second type, mostly manifested in the first season, but having consequences also in the second. This second, external factor – as opposed to the internal organisational one – is an innovative element of crime fiction. It makes the police appear more vulnerable and prevents the police force from appearing as an all-powerful organism. The economic obstruction is an obstacle that does not depend on any character. It is usually imposed on them as fate, only possible to avoid with extraordinary strategies and by disobeying the basic rules and protocols of the situation. This acceptance of the impossibility of unmasking the genuinely guilty ones in a modern situation is what Jacques Derrida (2003), in conversation with Jürgen Habermas, calls *auto-immunity*, a sort of ineffectiveness and frustration, because the figures to fight against are decentered, fragmented, constructions of our own society. The postmodern justice system depicted in *Line of Duty* is installed over a hierarchy of officers but this complex structure blocks all of them and deprives each of decision making. Although the series' main investigators, DS Steve Arnott and DC Kate Fleming, know that bureaucracy is not almighty, they act as if it is: bureaucracy has created a '*mise-en-scene* of fantasy that performs in social reality' (Linstead, 2005, p. 116). While Arnott is ostensibly opposed to the system, Fleming plays it strategically with better results. In the second series, Arnott becomes completely confused by Hawes whereas Fleming is far more suspicious of her. This also makes audiences mistrust the intentions of the characters, especially because affection is also mixed up in the plot. The latent amorousness that Fleming seems to feel for Arnott leads audiences to think some of her reactions in the investigation have to do with jealousy. This is always an effective approach which makes any professional decision more difficult. Historically most crime series split love and professional activities. Love was more commonly an accessory to the main investigation and usually acted as a joint element to solve the mystery of the series, adding an extra insignificant complication to the story. Now, love can be a real obstacle to finding out what is behind the main mystery of the series. In fact, feelings are always difficult to decode in this kind of drama because characters endlessly aim to fool others and take advantage of them.

Perambulating the Spiral

Line of Duty's narrative complexity and circularity is characteristic of postmodern mystery fiction. As with series such as *Southland* (NBC and TNT, 2009–2013) and *The Shield* (FX Networks, 2002–2008), *Line of Duty*'s narrative is a social critique and its mystery a cul-de-sac or labyrinth. All tracks begin and end in the same place, there is no release, no redemption. Even at the end of the series, when the mystery is allegedly solved, a twist revives the intrigue, as in an eternal return, and the viewer realizes that bureaucracy is a sort of indestructible ivy. The first season closes Tony Gates' case but leaves unsolved Tommy's links with the police. DS Matthew (Dot) Cottan, who infiltrated the squad and leaked to Tommy or Gates, remains in the anti-corruption squad and, by the end of the second series, is promoted to a permanent position. The second series also leaves some mysteries behind and above all, the presence of some characters who could return and bring with them some of the old plots and narrative conflicts.

The combination of bureaucratic and investigative narratives draws a hermeneutic path of causes and consequences where advance information helps to create suspense but always returns us to the same point, as in a circular trip. The death of characters who could provide important evidence is part of this starting point return: Tony Gates' suicide and the witness's death at the beginning of the second season exemplify this mechanism of restarting the narration from a different perspective, knowing that the path is now a different one.

The conjunction between bureaucracy and intrigue turns into something even more opaque. All bureaucratic systems consist of small segments that work in an integrated body for the benefit of the community. These segments operate without seemingly knowing what happens in the whole of that system. This applies, for example, to Gates' secretary, who has vital file information and, consequently, a key to the case. Nevertheless, she is unable to discover anything because her concentration on other aspects won't let her realise something crucial: she has a document in the database she usually manages with clear evidences on Gate's guilt. Les Hargreaves does something similar when he decides to question Richard Akers in episode 4 of series 2. Akers is involved as a suspect in the investigation after £20,000 is discovered at his house. Hargreaves believes it to be a bribe to betray the escort of the car attack and questions Akers. This questioning is a completely inopportune decision, as Arnott and Fleming just discovered some evidence about Akers's innocence. This movement proves how cops overlap and contradict their functions according to different considerations and interests.

Mystery narratives follow the chained structure of cause-consequence that fit very accurately with a bureaucratic way of work. To remove a part of the bureaucratic system is often to disassemble a track of the mystery chain. However, the component parts of the bureaucratic structure are so entrenched that in order to remove one of them, it is necessary to undermine the system from inside. In other police series, the investigation may well focus on just one character's action. However, here the investigation involves so many decisions and people that the mystery extends as a hydra, becoming increasingly perplexing and difficult to untangle. Sometimes it remains hidden in the heavy structure of bureaucracy. But to destroy the great structure of the bureaucratic system it is necessary to remove at least one of the pieces. With a piece gone, the bureaucratic body crumbles. The problem is that sometimes removing just one of the pieces means removing the whole thing. Cottan could be this permanent piece rotting the entirety of the organism. His dirty work is practically revealed to the audience from the beginning of the series because it is evident that the other characters are completely unaware of his murky actions and let him work on with impunity. If they do ever realise his objectives, removing him will be a difficult task for the main characters precisely because there is no evidence of his crimes.

The Obsolescence of Interrogation Methods

Whereas face-to-face interrogations in most police series contribute to the revelation of truth (see McElroy in this collection), in *Line of Duty* they perversely provide corrupt officers with cover, concealing the suspects' actions. In series 1, for instance, Gates undergoes Arnott's fruitless interrogation and emerges completely unscathed because the mechanisms and interrogation techniques, even with their standards and rules, enfold and justify him. The same is true for Lindsay Denton and Michael Morton, who use the format to further their own interests. This kind of questioning changes its role completely: the face-to-face interrogation mise en scène is a kind of battle where the officer who interrogates has more to hide than the suspect.

On some occasions the only real thing that heroes can do in this kind of narrative is to become as illegal as the system allows. In series 1, episode 4, for example, Arnott disobeys protocols for accessing information after an anonymous telephone call. The main characters' journey is a sort of *bildungsroman* to achieving a maturing knowledge: in this case, to discover that the only way to catch the criminal is to walk just on the line that separates legality from illegality. In one of the last scenes of the first series of *Line of Duty*, Gates finds Tommy and drags him to a car to get a confession. Gates is wearing a wire given by Arnott, who takes advantage of Gates's predicament and exploits it to solve the case. Such twists and turns illustrate how the hero must play with lies to find the truth. And for a moment at least, the viewer may feel that good and evil have changed places.

Some *Impossible* Conclusions

The real value of *Line of Duty* is its radical proposal to change the classic condition of the detective genre. By introducing several elements of the bureaucratic narrative to provoke some complexity, the series breaks the rules of the plot function and offers an absolutely postmodern vision of a serial problematic. While old police dramas face a classical narrative of good against evil, the construction of the *Line of Duty* narrative shows how bureaucracy challenges the existing investigative method as it introduces new devices such as the moles or the block of actions because of the diversity of criteria on the procedures. *Line of Duty* provides a reflection on our times and stands as a fully self-reflexive and metalinguistic series which asks questions about issues relating to both television genre and society. Through its two series to date, *Line of Duty* exposes both how the economic cuts affect police investigations and also how the police institution itself operates in a climate of mistrust. The criminals are inside and the investigators do not have the best tools to get the solution. Its construction escapes certain considerations and conclusions in the strictest sense because *Line of Duty* is a unique, innovative and elaborate reference for treatments of contemporary police television drama series.

References

Arendt, H.,1969. 'Reflections on violence', *The New York Review of Books*, 27 February, p. 18.

Carroll, N., 2003. *Engaging the Moving Image*. Yale University Press, New Haven, CT.

Carroll, N., 2004. 'Sympathy for the devil', in Greene, R., and Vernezze, P. eds., *The Sopranos and Philosophy*, Open Court, LaSalle, IL, pp. 121–136.

Crozier, M.,1964. *The Bureaucratic Phenomenon*, Tavistock Publications, London, England.

Derrida, J., 2003. 'Auto-immunity: real and symbolic suicides: a dialogue with Jacques Derrida', in Borradori, G. ed., *Philosophy in a Time of Terror: Dialogues with Jürgen Habermas and Jacques Derrida*, University of Chicago Press, Chicago, IL.

Fiske, J.,1987. *Television Culture*. Routledge, New York, NY.

Linstead, A. ed., 2005. *Organisation and Identity*. Routledge, New York, NY.

Mittell, J. 'Complex TV. The poetics of contemporary television storytelling', in Nannincelli, T. and Taberham, P. eds., 2014. *Cognitive Media Theory*, Routledge, New York, NY.

Smith, M., 1995. *Engaging Characters. Fiction, Emotion, and the Cinema*, Oxford University Press, Oxford, England.

7   The Blitz Detective

Foyle's War, History, Genre and Contemporary Politics

Stephen Lacey

There were a lot of wicked people around between 1939 and 1945. Not all of them were Germans.
—(*Foyle's War* creator and main writer Anthony Horowitz, 2009)

The scene is an idyllic one. A middle-aged couple is enjoying a picnic in the warmth of the early summer, the grass is long and lush, cliffs rear in the background and the sea shines blue. After a few seconds a caption appears, 'England May 1940', indicating that the England of this idyll is at war, although the couple seems oblivious of this as he takes a photograph of her. The action is witnessed by an ARP warden[1] passing on his bike. This summer scene is abruptly interrupted: it is now night-time, and torches cut through the darkness, their bearers unidentifiable. The couple are awakened from their sleep by loud knocks at the door. The man is identified as Thomas Kramer (David Horovitch), and he and his wife, Elsie (Elizabeth Bell), are being interned under the terms of a law restricting the movement of potential enemy aliens. The couple are taken to what looks like a police station and questioned separately. Their every action seems suspicious: washing on the line can be signalling to the enemy; cameras are prohibited for aliens with a 'B' classification; chess moves sent in a letter to a friend might be secret code. They are taken to an internment camp, a warehouse, along with several dozen others. They are forcibly separated on arrival and Elsie is in evident distress. The camera precedes her as she stumbles into the building and then collapses. She later dies.

This is the precredit sequence of 'The German Woman', the first episode of *Foyle's War* (ITV, 2002–15), (its working title was *The Blitz Detective*). It is worth describing at length because it indicates – as first episodes often do – much of what the series will be concerned with and how it will address its audience. Like all of the first six series (of eight), this episode of *Foyle's War* is set during the Second World War and is concerned not with the battlefields but with the home front and the experience of civilian society under pressure. As the precredit sequence indicates, however, it does not always take the well-trodden route into that experience. As if to mark its distinctiveness further, *Foyle's War* is set not in London, the location of much of the drama and most of the mythology of World War II, but in Hastings, a seaside town on the south coast of England. The opening confronts the viewer with a series of reversals; it is the 'aliens' with whom we are asked to be concerned, and it is British soldiers and officials who, in actions that reference fictional and documentary images of war and oppression, knock on the door in the night and forcefully separate and imprison the Kramers (it is quite disorientating, if not shocking, to see British soldiers, especially in the Second World War, performing these actions). From the very beginning, the series raised serious questions about both the actions of the British state as well as its people in wartime (and, later, once the series had moved beyond 1945, the Cold War and austerity Britain); in doing so, it represented uncomfortable moral and political dilemmas that resonate today. This is one reason why *Foyle's War* is worthy of critical attention.

Given the origins of the series, 'critical attention' is one of the last things *Foyle's War* seemed destined to attract. It was commissioned at the end of a bidding process instituted by ITV to find a drama series that would replace the critically acclaimed and highly popular *Inspector Morse* (ITV, 1987–2000) and thus fill the much sought-after Sunday night drama slot on UK television. It was one of three, chosen from a pool of 300 submitted ideas, from which pilot series were made. Its creator and main writer Anthony Horowitz is an established novelist and television writer, with episodes of *Agatha Christie's Poirot* (ITV, 1989–2014) and *Midsomer Murders* (ITV, 1997–) to his credit. It was, therefore, the product of a well-tried, ratings-driven process – the Sunday night drama being almost a genre in its own right – designed to reach a large audience in a schedule dominated by police and crime dramas of different types.

Set initially during the early stages of the Second World War, and starring Michael Kitchen as the eponymous Detective Chief Superintendent Christopher Foyle, *Foyle's War* uses the familiar narrative of the 'hero detective' (Turnbull, 2014, p. 16), the lone police investigator as moral agent. Backed by a small team of close collaborators, Detective Sergeant Milner (Anthony Howell) and erstwhile driver, Sam (Honeysuckle Weeks), whose relationships with Foyle (and each other) developed across the series, Foyle takes his place alongside other idiosyncratic detectives (not all policemen) who have peopled the ITV schedule on a Sunday night, and various digital channels thereafter: Jack Frost (David Jason) in *A Touch of Frost* (1992–2010), Hercule Poirot (David Suchet), DCI Tom Barnaby (John Nettles and Neil Dudgeon) in *Midsomer Murders*, the lone female representative, DCI Vera Stanhope (Brenda Blethyn) in *Vera* (2011–), DCI Robbie Lewis (Kevin Whatley) in *Lewis* (2006–) and, of course, Inspector Morse himself (John Thaw).

Foyle's War fulfilled its brief admirably: 'The German Woman' aired on 27 October 2002, gaining an audience of 8.1 million viewers, one third of the potential audience, a figure that rose to 9.4 million by the end of the fourth, and final, episode of the series on 17 November ('Eagle Day') (Gibson, 2002). It won the audience award at the following year's BAFTA Television Awards. Viewing figures remained high throughout the eight series, with individual episodes regularly obtaining audiences in excess of

8 million; series 8, however, saw a falling off, with a season average of around 5 million viewers and the final episode ('Elise', broadcast on 18 January 2015) gaining 4 million – still a significant proportion of the viewing public (Sweney, 2015). In fact, *Foyle's War* was terminated after series 5 (2008) because ITV thought it had run its course: the audience thought otherwise and, after receiving a deluge of letters of complaint, the new ITV Director of Programmes, Peter Fincham, agreed and recommissioned it (Brown, 2010). The final three series took Foyle from the end of the Second World War into a war of a different kind, the Cold War, and the privations of rationing and austerity. Its view of the period has resonated overseas, and *Foyle's War* has sold well around the world, including much of Africa, Australia and the United States where it was shown in the 'Masterpiece Mystery' slot on PBS (see Mary F. Brewer's chapter in this collection).

'Invisible Television' and 'Trojan Horses': What Sort of Crime Drama is *Foyle's War*?

Foyle's War would seem to be a good example of what Brett Mills has termed 'invisible television.' Invisibility is not confined to specific genres or types of programming. 'The definition of invisible television,' Mills argues, 'does not rest on content, for it is a category defined by programme longevity, ratings success and lack of analysis' (Mills, 2010, p. 7). For Mills, a great deal of television that is long-running, popular with audiences and, therefore, of considerable cultural significance, is simply not seen by the critical discourses of television studies because it is neither viewed nor discussed by academics. *Foyle's War* has been largely 'invisible' in these terms, although it has been of interest to historians (Nicholas, 2007). This analysis privileges the power of the audience to decide what is, and what is not, important; it is interesting that *Foyle's War* won the Audience Award at the 2003 BAFTA Television Awards, and not one of the prizes allotted by professional juries, and that it was audience pressure that led to the recommissioning of the last three series. In particular, such television is popular with sectors of the viewing public, whose tastes are often marginalised – older viewers, for example: in 2015, as the last series was drawing to a close, Horowitz noted ruefully that *Foyle's War* was 'everybody's mother's favourite show', though he thought it also had younger fans (Horowitz, 2015).

The notion of invisible television may tell us more about critical debate than it does television programmes, and the categorical challenge posed by *Foyle's War* does not end here. On the one hand, crime drama, though ubiquitous, has highly porous boundaries and individual programmes are, by and large, 'promiscuous hybrids' (Turnbull, 2014, p. 1). Sue Turnbull has noted just how generous and variegated crime drama is, drawing on established genres from literature and popular culture and adapting them for the changing requirements of television. Indeed, some of Foyle's most obvious antecedents are characters adapted from literary crime fiction. In addition to Morse, taken from the novels of Colin Dexter, there is the poet-policeman, Commander Adam Dalgliesh (ITV, 1983–2005), played until 2003 by Roy Marsden (and then by Martin Shaw), from the novels of P. D. James, and Ruth Rendell's Inspector George Wexford (George Baker), the central character in *The Ruth Rendell Mysteries* (ITV, 1987–2000). *Foyle's War*, of course, is not an adaptation, although in many respects, especially in its 'look' and period detail, it seems like one; and Horowitz, as the series' creator and main writer, was promoted as the author in interviews and publicity, allowing something of the kudos of authored television – still powerful in the streamlined world of contemporary television drama – to become attached to the series.

If *Foyle's War* has not received the critical attention it deserves, this is partly because the expectations of this kind of crime drama are low. Indeed, there is an assumption that crime drama *per se* is fundamentally conservative in a multi-channel age, offering reassurance to audiences in an unsettling world. As Lez Cooke has argued, 'as the television companies compete for a diminishing share of the audience, there has been a proliferation of police, detective and crime drama … with endless variations and reworkings of a basic formula in which society is protected and the status quo maintained' (Cooke, 2001, p. 19). More specifically, the format of the series – consisting, like *Morse* and *Poirot*, of narratively distinct, two-hour dramas – promotes each episode as an individual film with a satisfying and comforting resolution.

Foyle's War may be 'invisible', then, because it is thought to be 'formulaic' and overly familiar. Certainly, as Mills argues, television studies scholarship tends to 'focus on the new', which 'might be a problem when it contradicts how audiences make sense of television' (Mills, 2010, p. 6). *Foyle's War* is aligned in the schedules with series that offer the familiar devices of a Sunday night, hero-detective crime drama: a murder established early on, an initial suspect that turns out to be a red herring, a second murder (usually) to ratchet up the tension and complicate the narrative, possible danger for one of the recurring central characters, and a denouement precipitated by the detective, who acts using a combination of intuition and reasoning that both solves the crime and restores the status quo. In the case of *Foyle's War*, the status quo is the narrative premise, the order that pertains between Foyle and his team, and not the wider social order – they are not the same thing. Whatever the claims made for the distinctiveness of *Foyle's War* in this chapter, the series works perfectly well within these well-established conventions, fulfilling the requirement that popular television drama provides novelty within the familiar (Mills, 2010, pp. 6–7). However, the well-oiled smoothness of the murder mystery, though sometimes constricting and predictable, can also be a mechanism for exploring darker subject matter and moral and political ambivalence.

The hero-detective narrative, familiar and functional, places a single character (and, through him or her, a small group of characters) at the centre of the action. The world that the story wishes to explore is seen almost entirely as he or she would see it, and the detective is the viewer's point of access to that world, which is often a highly varied one, given the detective's job. As a policeman, Foyle takes us through virtually every social stratum in Hastings (and beyond), including the armed forces and, in later series, the inner sanctum of the British Secret Intelligence Services. The crime is the mechanism that brings these worlds into collision. This kind of narrative places considerable weight on the shoulders of the detective to interpret and make sense of the worlds he or she encounters, to act as a moral arbiter, making sense out of a compromised and confused world. This is true, not only of Foyle, but also of some of his fellow curmudgeonly and emotionally taciturn Sunday-night detectives – Vera and Morse, for example.

Foyle's War may be thought of as 'quality drama' in the UK context, a term that is both descriptive and uneasily evaluative and which overlays the classification of the series as crime drama. As Charlotte Brunsdon (1990) has noted in an influential account of British quality television drama, accomplished acting is central to ideas of quality (along with relatively generous budgets, literary source material and a conservative idea of 'heritage'). The hero-detective narrative places a great deal of emphasis on a central character, as noted above, and this, when successful, is realised in a commanding central performance. All the ITV Sunday-night detectives are played by experienced actors well known to the viewer: Brenda Blethyn (Vera), John Thaw (Morse) and Kevin Whatley (Lewis). There is little doubt that Michael Kitchen's performance as Christopher Foyle is central to the appeal of *Foyle's War*, and to do justice to it (and the standard of acting in the series generally) would require a separate chapter. Horowitz has recorded his debt to Kitchen, who was 'very much the first name on the list' of actors lined up for the part (Horowitz, 2002). Noting that the first episode was written a year before the other three in series 1, Horowitz said:

> a lot … happened in the year after the first one had been written when Michael had come to the table as it were and brought a great deal of ideas, and thoughts, and approaches with him, and so he was instrumental in making Christopher Foyle, and Christopher Foyle really was fully born after the first episode.
>
> (Horowitz, 2002)

When deciding whether to bring *Foyle's War* into the post-war world, Horowitz consulted Kitchen about the direction the character – and the drama – would take in the new context (Horowitz, 2013). Given that the main actors in long-running series are responsible for maintaining consistency and coherence in changing production teams (see Hewett, 2015), Kitchen's ability to maintain a performance across 8 series and 13 years is to be applauded.

Reviewers were unanimously enthusiastic about Kitchen's performance, even when they did not like the series itself, and judged it in remarkably similar terms. Commending Kitchen's 'genius' as an actor, Jaci Stephen in the *Mail on Sunday* enthused, 'This is an actor who can do no wrong; he does not blink without there being a reason for it … If Michael Kitchen played a corpse, you would still watch him more than anyone else' (Stephen, 2002). Thom Sutcliffe in the *Independent* asked, 'Can any other actor hesitate so speakingly? His pauses and catches of utterance were tactful, pained, reluctant, pensive, tender and searching' (Sutcliffe, 2002). Jonathan Meades in the *Times* echoed this emphasis on what Kitchen's performance leaves unsaid: 'Kitchen's instrument is his face. He has used it to create a gestural language of the utmost suppleness and complexity … His sheer control is awesome. His repertoire causes us to rethink the possibilities of facial musculature' (Meades, 2002).

The reviews indicate what is valued not only in Kitchen's performance but also acting on television generally: understatement and an expressive use of the face to reveal thought and emotional complexity. Television drama relies a great deal on the power of the close-up to carry narrative information and engage the viewer with the character, and Kitchen's facial expressivity – never overt, and often more concerned with conveying what is felt in the act of repressing feeling – is particularly eloquent. Perhaps most important, however, is the actor's taciturn watchfulness: the corollary of *not* speaking is that Kitchen/Foyle is open to the world, a natural observer of events that he does not readily or prematurely judge. This openness, allied to a clear moral compass, makes him a particularly effective hero-detective and is one reason why the series can encompass so many moral and political dilemmas.

'Quality' does not necessarily imply approval, critically speaking; Sarah Cardwell has noted 'a level of discomfort' when academics discuss British quality television, with analyses exhibiting 'not so much a *critical* distance as an *emotional* distance from such programmes' whilst at the same time validating '"realism" and attention to detail' (Cardwell, 2007, p. 22, original italics). As Turnbull has pointed out, realism is also valued in crime drama: 'those series that espouse realism (especially social realism) are routinely more highly regarded than crime dramas that are perceived to be more stylised, formulaic, and entertaining' (Turnbull, 2014, p. 119).

Realism is a famously capacious and complex term, which clearly embraces more than 'correct' period detail or the kind of explicitness in the representation of crimes and violence to the human body that many contemporary-set crime dramas routinely deploy. Realism has an explicitly political dimension in this context, recognising that crime dramas, in following the police/detectives through the office door and out into the streets beyond, have the potential to explore the social and political world at points of crisis and change. Tony Garnett, the executive producer of such key realist crime series as *Between the Lines* (BBC, 1992–1994) and *The Cops* (BBC, 1998–2001), has spoken of his work as 'Trojan horse drama' (Lacey, 2007), meaning that he has used the conventions of a familiar genre to win an audience for difficult subject matter that it would not otherwise choose to consider. Horowitz has spoken of the way that *Foyle's War* engages with pivotal moments in twentieth-century history in similar terms. 'We would never have been able to tell these stories to a mass audience if we were not seen and promoted as a "murder mystery" show' he told the *Daily Telegraph* in 2015, as the final series was drawing to a close;

> [T]he greatest pleasure, for me, has been not the crimes but the way we have been able to explore this extraordinary period in British history. These are stories that deserve to be told and I'm proud that we have told so many of them – often for the first time – in Foyle's War.
>
> (Horowitz, 2015)

Horowitz's Trojan horse, therefore, fulfils one of the primary objectives of realism – to say '*this* is what really happened.'

'A Bloody Mess': How Revisionist is the History in *Foyle's War*?

Foyle's War's period setting places it possibly at the most significant conjuncture in twentieth-century history, the decade 1939–1949, which embraces both the Second World War, the Cold War that rapidly followed it and the austerity that marked the period of economic and social reconstruction. As Siân Nicholas (2007) has argued, 'the television dramatist must … engage with the audience's existing understanding of the past' which 'may exist as stereotypes or popular myths' (p. 204). In short, television representations of history, especially recent history, must 'renegotiate popular memory before it can redraw it' and this is more to do with the 'feel' of a programme rather than its strict adherence to fact:

> This is not just its visual 'look', but the tone and atmosphere of the production as a whole. If the setting is credible and the atmosphere correct, if the production team 'get it right', then the audience is already half won over … For the more recent past, received views may be contested. Here, television drama needs to accommodate both popular and personal memory: cultural myths and remembered realities.
>
> (Nicholas, 2007, pp. 207–8)

Foyle's War establishes a clear relationship to both the 'facts' of the war – including less well-known ones – and its popular mythology. The series was based on research conducted with the support of the Imperial War Museum, with many of its plots coming directly from the archives (see Horowitz, 2009). To take three examples: 'The German Wife', drew on the historical experience of refugees from Nazism, interned from 1940 onwards, and worked a lot of detail concerning the specific regulations into the mechanics of the plot including, for example, how far certain classifications of immigrant were allowed to live from the coast. It also represented the actions of some well-connected members of the local haute-bourgeoisie, who manipulated government procedures to favour their own; the German wife of the title, and also the first murder victim, is married to a local landowner, who connives with his doctor and friendly officials to have her classified as suffering from an acute illness that means she does not have to move inland. 'The Funk Hole' (series 2, episode 4) combines two stories from the archives, the first centring on a group of the well-heeled middle classes who choose to sit out the war in comfort in a country hotel (the funk hole of the title) and, the second, the story of a bureaucratic mistake which led to over 100 victims of the Blitz being abandoned in a London school, without food or drink, and killed during a bombing raid (it is in revenge for this appalling error that the key murder is committed). Finally, the duplicity of some British businessmen when faced with threats to their profits is dramatised in 'War Games' (series 2, episode 3), in which a wealthy food magnate is found to be secretly supplying the German war machine.

This view of the conduct of the Second World War runs counter to much of the popular mythology that has grown up around what is often termed 'the good war'; Londoners enduring the Blitz, pilots barely in their twenties holding back the might of the Luftwaffe during the Battle of Britain, the dramatic rescue of British forces from the beaches of Dunkirk by a flotilla of small boats, the sense that 'we are all in this together' that underpinned civilian resolve. *Foyle's War* often challenges this mythology, whilst at other times accepting, or seeming to peer behind it. Foyle's son Andrew, for example, is a pilot who fought in the Battle of Britain and bears the personal cost of it: in 'Enemy Fire' (series 3, episode 2), an episode that parallels sympathetically the different ways in which combatants buckle under pressure, Andrew suffers a crisis and goes AWOL (absent without leave) and is rescued by a sympathetic commanding officer, who tells Foyle of the terrible pressure that Andrew, and others like him, have been under. The Dunkirk rescue is referenced towards the end of 'The White Feather' (series 1, episode 2), where it is treated as a heroic event; and near the episode's conclusion, Foyle listens to the writer and broadcaster J. B. Priestley's famous radio tribute to the rescuers on the radio.[2]

However, as Nicholas (2007) points out, *Foyle's War*'s view of history is one that would be accepted by many historians, and in this sense is not radically revisionist. There are many historical accounts that document 'panic, looting, class conflict, xenophobia, strikes and absenteeism' (Nicholas, 2007, p. 205), of which the most influential is probably Angus Calder's *The People's War* (1969). Calder uses Mass Observation records and testimonies to provide a detailed and nuanced account of civilian life during the war, with all its daily compromises as well as its pervasive stoicism and occasional heroism. Horowitz (2009) has written of the influence of the book on his writing. *The People's War* is also, politically speaking, radical in its implications, offering a view of the British people at war, consulted and considered to an unprecedented degree. As Nicholas argues, *Foyle's War* offers 'less a "new" perspective on the Second World War, than a modern twist on the original "radical orthodoxy" of 1940: the notion that the war was being fought for and by 'the people' as much as – in fact, far more wholeheartedly than – by those in "authority"' (Nicholas, 2007, p. 213).

It is remarkable how many of the murderers and criminals in *Foyle's War* belong to the upper classes or are in positions of power within the British state and the war machine and, even when they are not actually criminal, the motives of the powerful are often reprehensible. The actions of the landowner in 'The German Wife' described above is a good example, and there are many more; the murderer in 'A Lesson in Murder' (series 1, episode 3) is revealed as a corrupt local judge, trying vainly to cover his tracks; in 'Fifty Ships' (series 2, episode 1), an American businessmen, deemed vital to the war effort (he can provide the 50 ships of the title), is guilty of defrauding his British business partner out of his share of an invention and then murdering him; although not a murderer, an Assistant Police Commissioner in 'A War of Nerves' (series 3, episode 4) demands that Foyle investigate and harass a known socialist activist – a political act that is entwined with personal motivations (the activist is having a relationship with the Commissioner's daughter); and Foyle's son, Andrew, is framed for a crime he did not commit with the connivance of his own superior officers ('Among the Few', series 2, episode 2). Conversely, the series also asks for sympathy for unlikely characters, even the enemy. In 'Fifty Ships', for example, Horowitz draws on a story from the archives concerning a hapless German spy, who was captured almost as soon as he arrived (by U-Boat). In Horowitz's version the spy, Hans Maier (Jonathan Coy), emerges as a sympathetic and honourable man, who is able to help Foyle solve a murder, although he knows he will be hanged and is under no compulsion to assist the police: Foyle agrees to attempt to contact his family in Germany.

A resolution that occurs more than once in *Foyle's War* is that the murderer, when confronted, demands that Foyle weigh the crime against his or her (possible) worth to the war effort; this is the line of argument offered by Michael Turner (Dominic Mafham), a code-breaker, at the denouement of 'The German Wife', for example. Foyle's response is always that one life cannot be judged as having more worth than another, because to take that path would be to make him no better than the enemy. As he says to Turner: 'The war doesn't make any difference at all. She was a human being, she was murdered. Murder is murder. You stop believing that and we might as well not be fighting the war. Because you end up like the Nazis' ('The German Wife', series 1, episode 1). Foyle's moral compass is aligned with the series' politics – indeed, it shapes it – and demonstrates how the hero-detective narrative arc might enable the viewer to see Foyle as 'a light cutting through the darkness' (Horowitz, 2009).

Despite the darkness of individual stories, *Foyle's War* has an inbuilt optimism that has two sources: on the one hand, the genre requires that Foyle will solve the murder and justice will be done; on the other, the audience knows what the characters do not – that Britain will win the war, that it will 'turn out alright' in the end. However, one of the achievements of the series is that it places the characters in the position of *not* knowing, and exploring what would happen as a result. *Foyle's War* is particularly good at capturing the early stages of the war, when it was by no means certain that Britain would not be invaded and that it might well sue for peace. In 'The White Feather' (series 1, episode 2), for example, a group of Nazi sympathisers gathers in a hotel near Hastings, confidently expecting a German invasion which they assume to be imminent. The hotelier, reasoning that during the ensuing chaos a single murder would go unnoticed, kills his wife. *Foyle's War* asks that the audience has a complex relationship to the past, therefore, both repressing and allowing historical memory to be part of the viewing process. It is also, as Horowitz makes clear, aware of the historical situation of its audiences, and part of the appeal of the series is that the present is never too far from the past. This is particularly true of the last two series.

Foyle's 'War on Terror'

The last episode of series 5 of *Foyle's War* was broadcast in 2008. Series 6, the first to be made after the reprieve, appeared in 2010, and was set during the closing moments of the war, June 1945, with Foyle still a policeman. However, the key changes occurred in series 7 and 8, with Foyle out of the police force and drawn into the murky world of espionage and the intelligence services, with the action now in London (though filmed in Dublin) set against the background of austerity and rationing. Horowitz has confessed that he nearly ended the whole project after series 6, but was persuaded by the challenges posed by the new historical context and the prospect of 'opening up' the series; 'this time we're not just dealing with murder' (Horowitz, 2013). Both series 7 and 8 also follow the action, figuratively and literally, out of Britain to, for example, France and Palestine. The research and writing process, however, did not change and the stories, selected for their resonance and representativeness, still came from the archives and a close reading of post-war history. For example, the story of communist-leaning nuclear scientists disclosing secrets to the Soviets ('The Eternity Ring', series 7, episode 1) was inspired by real-life scientists/traitors Klaus Fuchs and Allan Nunn May; and the massacre of British prisoners in France dramatised in 'Sunflower' (series 7, episode 3) was based on actual events.

The political/moral stance of these series reprises that of the earlier ones, with unease about the Cold War, hostility to rationing and a general sense of 'what did we fight the war for?' (as a character in the final episode, 'Elise', says) replacing the uncertainty and confusion of 1940. This period is identifiably closer to that of the audience, however, not only because it is more recent but also because its concerns are more recognisable in a way that brings into focus an important fact about the programme as a whole: *Foyle's War* was first broadcast in October 2002, just over one year after the suicide attacks on the Twin Towers in New York and the Pentagon, the moment of '9/11' and the subsequent 'war on terror.' Although *Foyle's War* cannot represent these events as directly as contemporary US crime series have – for example, *24* (Fox, 2001–10, 2014) – the war on terror was a frame of reference for Horowitz and fellow writers, and it remains one for the viewer.

However, it is not the actions of terrorists – or not only the actions of terrorists – that *Foyle's War* parallels, but also those of Western powers, whose response to terrorist threats is ethically and politically questionable. At a time of metaphorical and covert war, *Foyle's War* dramatises a real one. Noting that 'between 1939 and 1945, 178,000 indictable offences were created for the inhabitants of England and Wales', Horowitz argued that *Foyle's War* drew attention to the actions of a government as concerned to police its citizens as it was to fight the enemy. There is an uncomfortable resonance with Britain after 9/11: 'It's been interesting to watch New Labour [the British Government] cobble together laws to combat the so-called war on terror' he argued, 'laws that have proved equally contentious and unpopular' (2009). The parallels are sometimes more immediate. In 'The Cage' (series 7, episode 2), for example, an MI5 intelligence centre is engaged in ethically dubious activities bordering on torture, 'using methods not that dissimilar to Guantanamo Bay' (Horowitz, 2013). This was based on archival evidence that at least three such centres existed at the time in London.

The connections between *Foyle's War* and the war on terror should not be pushed too far: the series works by inference rather than by direct comparison, permitting the former to provide a prism through which to view the latter. Nonetheless, its view of state power is distinctly more critical than would be found in US crime dramas that take the war on terror as their subject matter. Yvonne Tasker, in an analysis of the representation of war on terror themes in crime dramas such as *24*, *Law & Order* (NBC, 1990–2010), and *Lie to Me* (Fox, 2009–11), notes how the influence of action formats has made state action against its citizens more acceptable: 'As themes of national security and the necessity of combating terror – on occasion via unpalatable techniques – migrate from action formats, whether crime or espionage, they are effectively normalized' (Tasker, 2012, p. 45). The result is that 'Criminals, terrorists, and … asylum seekers are typically constructed as deviant' (p. 64).

It is perhaps through the cumulative effects of recurrent motifs that *Foyle's War* offers its most telling critique: it is sympathetic to immigrants and outsiders (including Germans, Italians and Jews), and this sympathy runs across all series; in exploring the nature of culpability and crime in a war context, it refuses to demonise the enemy; when 'terrorism' threatens, it uses the mechanism of the crime drama to examine why. Along the way, it provides a salutary reminder that the very familiarity of the hero-detective format may permit, rather than constrain, an engagement with history and the contemporary political world.

Notes

1. ARP stands for Air Raid Precaution, and wardens were tasked with supporting and policing the civilian population, especially during air raids, when their main job was to ensure compliance with black-out regulations. For further information see www.bbc.co.uk/history/ww2peopleswar/stories/77/a7714677.shtml.

2. Priestley's tribute to the heroism of the flotilla of small boats was broadcast on 5 June 1940 on the BBC Home Service. It can be heard in the BBC archives at http://www.bbc.co.uk/archive/dunkirk/14310.shtml [Accessed 8 May 2015].

References

Brown, M., 2010. Foyle's War returns in a world of prefabs and rations. *The Guardian*, [online] 10 March. Available at: http://www.theguardian.com/tv-and-radio/2013/mar/10/foyles-war-returns-crime-cold-war [Accessed 10 March 2015].

Brunsdon, C., 1990. Problems with quality. *Screen*, 31(1), pp. 67–90.

Calder, A., 1969. *The People's War: Britain 1939–45*. London, England: Jonathan Cape.

Cardwell, S., 2007. Is quality television any good? Generic distinctions, evaluations and the troubling matter of critical judgement. In: J. McCabe and K. Akass, eds., 2007. *Quality TV: Contemporary American Television and Beyond*. London, England: I. B. Tauris. pp. 19–34.

Cooke, L., 2001. The Police series. In: G. Creeber, ed. 2007. *The Television Genre Book*. London, England: BFI publishing. pp. 19–23.

Gibson, O., 2002. Foyle wins ratings war for ITV. *The Guardian*, [online] 18 November. Available at: http://www.theguardian.com/media/2002/nov/18/overnights [Accessed 10 March 2015].

Hewett, R. 2015. The changing eeterminants of UK television acting. *Critical Studies in Television*, 10(1) pp. 73–90.

Horowitz, A., 2002. Foyle's War. The Michael Kitchen Site. [online] Available at: http://www.nothing-fancy.com/michaelkitchen/interviews/foyle1.htm [Accessed 10 January 2015].

Horowitz, A., 2009. Foyle's War creator on the dark side of the Second World War. *The Telegraph*. [online] Available at: http://www.telegraph.co.uk/history/world-war-two/6017058/Foyles-War-creator-on-the-dark-side-of-the-Second-World-War.html [Accessed 10 January 2015].

Horowitz, A., 2013. Anthony Horowitz: Why this series of Foyle's War will be my last. *Radio Times*, [online] 24 March. Available at: http://www.radiotimes.com/episode/vv69t/foyles-war--the-eternity-ring [Accessed 15 March 2015].

Horowitz, A., 2015. Anthony Horowitz on Foyle's War: 'These are stories that deserve to be told.' *The Telegraph*, [online] 3 January. Available at: http://www. telegraph.co.uk/culture/tvandradio/11304153/Anthony-Horowitz-Foyles-War-ITV.html [Accessed 10 February 2015].

Lacey, S., 2007. *Tony Garnett*. Manchester, England: Manchester University Press.

Meades, J., 2002. Foyle's War – series one reviews. *The Times*, [online] 16 November. Available at: http://www.nothing-fancy.com/foyleswar/media/02mag1.htm [Accessed 15 March 2015].

Mills, B., 2010. Invisible television: The programmes no-one talks about even though lots of people watch them. *Critical Studies in Television*, 5(1), pp. 1–16.

Nicholas, S., 2007. History, revisionism and television drama: *Foyle's War* and the 'myth of 1940.' *Media History*, 13 (2–3), pp. 203–19.

Stephen, J. 2002. Foyle's War – series one reviews. *Mail on Sunday*, [online] 3 November. Available at: http://www.nothing-fancy.com/foyleswar/media/02mag1. htm [Accessed 15 March 2015].

Sutcliffe, T. 2002. Foyle's War – series one reviews: *The Independent*, [online] 18 November. Available at: http://www.nothing-fancy.com/foyleswar/media/02mag1. htm [Accessed 15 March 2015].

Sweney, M., 2015. Call the Midwife pulls in 8 million viewers as BBC1 dominates. *The Guardian*, [online] 19 January. Available at: http://www.theguardian.com/ media/2015/jan/19/call-the-midwife-pulls-in-more-than-8-million-viewers-as-bbc-dominates [Accessed 15 March 2015].

Tasker, Y., 2012. Television crime drama and homeland security: from *Law & Order* to 'Terror TV.' *Cinema Journal*, 51(4), pp. 44–65.

Turnbull, S., 2014. *The TV Crime Drama*. Edinburgh, Scotland: Edinburgh University Press.

8   Cars, Places and Spaces in British Police Drama

Jonathan Bignell

This chapter outlines the significance of cars in British and American police dramas, using brief examples from the 1960s to the present, to show how attention to this topic can link and reconfigure critical approaches to stylistic, formal and institutional aspects of the genre. The chapter cuts into familiar debates in new ways, and is a call for further, more detailed analysis to follow up this provocation. Cars offer a way into the stylistic and generic specificity of police dramas because in different ways the protagonists' surveillance and investigation of the fictional world, and their ability to enforce the law, depend on being able to move in and between places and spaces. These abilities have been increasingly dependent on the use of the car rather than patrolling on foot. Thus, the space of policing is connected with modernity and its associations with mobility and the technologies, like the car and television, which extend mobility in real or virtual space (Morse, 1990). Moreover, television representations of policing adopt a scopic regime to apprehend and control the real. In order to identify crime and to impose justice, television police officers and detectives observe and interpret, attempting (usually successfully) to unveil a truth and put things right (Bignell, 2009). This takes place against an historical background of changing production circumstances for television, which can be summarised as a shift from studio-based programmes to location-based shooting. There are also important distinctions in dramatic tone and emphasis across the genre, such as between character-focused dramas and action-focused ones. These, and other aspects of genre, narrative form, style and historical significance, affect choices of cars in police drama and are expressed in part by them. Cars do some of the work of storytelling, and they are objects whose properties are often deployed very distinctively and effectively.

Aesthetically and industrially, cars in television police series are an aspect of production design, which deals with how a visual style can be created by the ensemble effect of sets and locations, props and costumes, lighting and shot selection.[1] Design falls under the control of the director for aesthetic matters, and the producer for the provision of the production's art department that procures and constructs props and sets. Some cars are specified by the creators of programmes in the production 'Bible' that lays out the format, settings and stylistic approach, and then need to be sourced by production

staff for shooting. The use of cars depends on the ancillary industry of suppliers of vehicles. The British company Action Vehicles,[2] for example, has
been the exclusive supplier of cars to the police dramas *The Bill* (Thames/
Talkback for ITV, 1984–2010), *Midsomer Murders* (Bentley Productions
for ITV1, 1997–), *Inspector Morse* (Zenith/Carlton for ITV, 1987–2000),
Maisie Raine (BBC 1998–99) and *Hamish Macbeth* (BBC 1995–97). The
majority of the cars that feature in police series are the 'ordinary' vehicles
used by secondary characters and in background action with, of course, specialist police vehicles and often a distinctive car driven by the protagonist.
Car suppliers maintain a register of privately owned vehicles available for
hire to productions, and a limited stock of specialist vehicles of earlier periods or with particular liveries (such as police patrol cars). Unusual cars may
also be sourced from published directories of privately owned vintage or
prestige cars whose owners lease or occasionally sell them to productions.
So the procurement and deployment of cars is one of the industrial processes
of television production and although I return to that issue below, I next
consider the textual and aesthetic role of cars in police drama.

Condensation of Time and Extension in Space

The car has a functional significance in police narratives as a means to move
between places, whether to attend a crime scene, meet a witness or locate
a perpetrator. In this role, travel by car is often a brief ellipse between two
connected narrative sequences such as a precinct scene when a new crime
is reported to the protagonist, followed by the detective's arrival at a crime
scene. Therefore, car sequences articulate or hinge segments together. Cars
offer spatial and temporal extension and condensation. In the story-world,
they minimise temporal and spatial delays or intervals by providing a means
for characters to travel from one significant place to another by a mode of
transport that is unremarkable and can therefore be largely passed over in
the narrative. Journeys by car do not take place in real time, but are indicated by moments of departure and arrival, sometimes with short in-car
sequences between them. Cars are associated with temporal ellipsis, and
paradoxically, their presence signifies an interval, a pause in the action and
a shift to a different focus of narrative interest. In the narration, they are
a connective tissue or articulating joint between sequences set in different
times and places.

   The necessity to travel in order to solve crimes has the corollary that
the possibility of travel demonstrates the capability of the police as a state
institution to put into practice the ideologies of law and order by travers-
ing space to deal with social disequilibrium (Clarke, 1992). The structural
conventions of police series narrative include the introduction of an enigma
(a crime) at the beginning of a storyline, and then a focus on process and
progression during an investigation stage that ends in resolution. In relation
to narrative temporality, travelling represents the ordered progression of

detection as the basis of the dramatic structure of storytelling in the television police series. Journeys by car are steps in the larger narrative journey towards order and the end of the narrative. Crime stimulates action, requiring the protagonist to leave his or her base and begin a new narrative segment that both advances the main story, but also represents a deferral or detour of the progress towards resolution. Car journeys seem at one level like the effective minimisation of intervals, so that cars permit the protagonists to get on more quickly with their detective work. As John Fiske and John Hartley (1978, p. 29) have argued, efficiency is a means of demonstrating dramatically that ideologies of law and order are superior to criminality and disorder:

> What the police versus criminal conflict may enact symbolically, then, is the everyday conflict of a competitive society in which efficiency is crucial ... The common concern that television police are becoming more and more like the criminals in their methods and morals means that the few factors that distinguish them take on crucial significance. Of these distinctive features, efficiency is the most marked.

At another level, however, car journeys have the opposite structural role. Delay and spacing-out in police narrative are indications of the narrative's teasing control over the viewer, making him or her anticipate and wait.

The presence of several sequences of car travel facilitates the division of an episode of a police series narrative into groups of storyline segments, or 'acts', with the beginning or end of each one marked by a journey by car (and potentially including further journeys too in some cases). In the US television context (Bignell 2009, pp. 5–6), this suits the division of an hour of television into several segments separated by commercials. In Britain, something similar happens in series made for the commercial networks and, indeed, because of the potential export of BBC programmes to commercial overseas channels, even programmes intended for first-run screening on BBC adopt the same convention. New segments following a commercial break commonly begin with a shot that establishes location. The arrival of the protagonist's car at a location where the subsequent action will take place can bind a conventional establishing long shot of a building to the specificity of the series and its characters by particularising it, via the inclusion of the detective's car in the frame.

The segmentation of narrative and the emphasis on process in the progression from enigma to resolution thus have a direct relationship with spatiality in the police series. However, these structural principles, while fundamental, do not account for the differences in how space relates to action and character. There is frequently a moment of departure, in which the protagonist leaves a room and gets into a car, marking the boundary between a home base and a diffuse surrounding space in which events occur. One space is known and repeatedly represented in the series, while the place visited as part of the investigation may not be known to the protagonist or the viewer. The taken for granted, realist conventions of almost all police narratives will lead the viewer to assume that the space already existed as a location, within an unseen fictional world that extends almost infinitely beyond the borders of the screen frame. For example, in Morse's Oxford, some settings in the city recur, while others (like individual houses) are only called into existence once as a scene of crime. However, in each case, the integration of a setting into an episode narrative always has the potential to change the meaning of the place. A public space like a riverbank, or a private space like a house, changes its significance when it becomes the object of the detective's (and the programme's) attention.

Space is energised, charged with significance by its expected integration into a narrative of detection, problem solving and resolution. The forensic series is a recent development of this trope, epitomised by *CSI: Crime Scene Investigation* (Jerry Bruckheimer/Alliance Atlantis/CBS, 2000–15) in which investigators traverse space so they can arrive at another place that they minutely interrogate. Both on location and back at their laboratory, the use of rapid camera zooms towards and inside body parts or items of evidence (often at extreme magnification), often created using computer generated imagery, develops the common theme in police series that seeing in a special way is the key investigative activity in the genre (Lury, 2005, pp. 44–56). However, whereas the conventional police series develops this by exploring spatial extension, when police extend their spatial purview outwardly, the forensic series works on internal, inward kinds of seeing (Bignell, 2007). One of the pleasures of the police series is for the viewer to anticipate and discover which settings remain neutral locations and which will become crime scenes loaded with important story information, and this pleasure is activated by the arrival of the protagonist, the narrating agency and the camera. Most often, this arrival depends on the use of a car.

Specific examples are helpful in showing how these boundary spaces associated with cars function in different programmes. In the early series of *Midsomer Murders*, Inspector Barnaby (John Nettles) arrived at each week's scene of crime driving a black Rover. The villages of Midsomer are represented as picturesque, conservative and atavistic, and Barnaby's appearance in dark suit and tie, in a well-maintained recent model of rather anonymous fleet car marks a very significant change of tone. There is less distinction between the spaces associated with Inspector Morse (John Thaw) and the spaces to which he arrives in his Jaguar to solve cases in the eponymous ITV series. The conceit of *Life On Mars* (Kudos for BBC, 2006–07) is, in part, that Sam Tyler (John Simm) departs from the space of the contemporary city and arrives in a parallel space that exists in a different time. The coincidence of space and separation in time is represented very concretely by the fact that Tyler drives a Rover in each of them, as I discuss further below.

Exterior/Interior Space: The Car as Studio

The fact that cars can be the vehicles for expression in spatial and temporal terms in such varied and interesting ways, rests ultimately on their function within the fictional world. Cars signify both the reach of policing and the police series as a genre. At any time between the early twentieth century and today, representations of policing in Britain and the United States (and elsewhere in the developed world) will establish a relationship with cars. In a few unusual cases, space and time are expressed by walking, as in *Dixon of Dock Green* (BBC 1955–76) or occasionally *The Bill*, but in fact the sheer size of the area policed by the protagonists effectively disallows drama on foot. Just as Western films take the horse for granted, so police dramas rely on the car. Indeed, in that sense, police cars are usually 'unmarked' in that their necessity is assumed. The failure of a car to transport the characters in a police drama, or the unavailability of car transport in a specific location, becomes a foregrounded storyline point precisely because the routine presence of journeys by car is not remarked on most of the time. For example, the premise of the US police series *McCloud* (Universal for NBC, 1970–77), in which the eponymous rural police detective from New Mexico (Dennis Weaver) goes to work in New York, is signified rapidly and in a visually striking way in the credit sequence of each episode, where McCloud is represented riding his horse down an urban street. The key elements of format and tone are announced by a recognition and simultaneous repudiation of the car as an icon of the police series.

The great majority of American police drama is set and shot in Los Angeles where, as Rayner Banham's (1971, p. 23) groundbreaking study of the ecology of its built environment argued, 'the language of design, architecture and urbanism … is the language of movement … I learnt to drive in order to read Los Angeles in the original.' Therefore, police series have routinely included numerous scenes set in cars because this recognises the quotidian necessity of travel within many US cities, of which Los Angeles is a paradigmatic example. It is very notable, for example, how many scenes in the realist police procedural series *Dragnet* (Mark VII for NBC, 1951–59, Universal for NBC, 1967–70), which is set in Los Angeles, begin and end with journeys taken by the detective protagonists to relatively anonymous locations in the city. Moreover, this consideration of format and storyline leads to the opening up of stylistic choices about where character interactions can be set. The car can function as a place for drama as much as a functional object within the fictional world. A journey by car can form a narrative segment in itself, and here the car functions as a kind of mobile TV studio, in which conversations and character-based action are constrained spatially and, thus, can gain dramatic intensity.

In Britain, the conception of the uniformed police as a motorised force was introduced prominently in *Z Cars* (BBC, 1962–78), and some subsequent dramas have used the car as a performance space in ways that recall US examples because of the duration of their in-car sequences and the aesthetic of urban space that they assume. Police patrol cars in *Z Cars* were designated by their call signs, Z-Victor 1 and Z-Victor 2, referring to the alphabetic call signs of the real Lancashire police and not to the Ford Z series cars (the Zephyr and Zodiac) that featured in it. These cars, equipped with radios, were designed to police conurbations much larger than the beat of a police officer on foot. In television drama, they designated the modernity of post-imperial Britain and introduced the problem of how to understand and control extensive spaces by technological means, as well as by local interpersonal knowledge. The spatial identity of the conurbation of Newtown in *Z Cars*, as a dispersed collection of former villages connected by belts of housing and industrial districts, represented a departure from the traditional urban geography of British police series towards one that referenced the United States, and especially Los Angeles. The Zephyr, and especially the Zodiac, referenced American Ford designs (in their wide bench seats, rear fins and extensive use of chrome, for example). The series is often cited for its relationship with the gritty, Northern, working class realism of British cinema of the period (Laing, 1991). But spatially it recalls Banham's (1971, p. 36) claim that the distinctive thing about Los Angeles,

> this giant city, which has grown almost simultaneously all over, is that all its parts are equal and equally accessible from all other parts at once. Everyday commuting tends less and less to move by the classic systole and diastole in and out of downtown, more and more to move by an almost random or Brownian motion over the whole area.

To know Newtown, the police of *Z Cars* need to spend much of their time travelling, with and against flows of movement undertaken by the city's population. The corollary of this aesthetic and representational form is that the protagonists spend a lot of screen time in patrol cars.

The great majority of each *Z Cars* episode was shot live in its early years, including the sequences set in patrol cars. Although exterior filming was important to the series' realist tone, film cameras and sound recording equipment were too cumbersome to use for dialogue scenes in cars, and in-car scenes were shot on live video in the studio with back-projected street scenes running behind them. Extended dialogue scenes, where the officers were driving, could explore their relationships with each other and signify the mobility and scope of the narrative action made possible by in-car radio. Spatial extension was matched dramatically by spatial restriction. This motif persists in contemporary police dramas centred on character interaction, or which feature an ensemble of protagonists rather than one or two central characters. In the US series *Hill Street Blues* (MTM for NBC, 1981–87), the relationship between the uniformed patrolmen Bobby Hill and Andy Renko (Michael Warren and Charles Haid) was developed in lengthy in-car sequences, and long takes in cars explored the interactions between the detectives of *Homicide: Life on the Street* (Baltimore Pictures for NBC, 1993–99). Location shooting, with film cameras attached to cars, made a focus on action and spatial extension routine in US police series, as discussed below. But the variations on the two-shot possible in in-car sequences, especially frontal shots and alternating three-quarter shots, exploit the centripetal characteristics of the car as a symmetrical, windowed enclosure. The camera can look into it, while the characters look out.

Cars on Film: Action Vehicles

In the broad historical movement from studio-based shooting to location shooting, developing in the 1960s and 1970s, cars gradually took on a changed narrative role in British police series. They became the focus of action sequences in real space, taking place within the iconography and functional possibilities afforded by specific choices of setting. There are very few cars in the studio-shot video interiors of *Dixon of Dock Green* (BBC, 1955–76) in which epistemological problems of how knowledge of spaces could be acquired were solved narratively by the local knowledge of the foot patrol officer. By the 1970s, 16 mm cameras were light and robust enough to fit onto rigs on car doors, as in *The Sweeney* (Euston Films for ITV, 1975–78), where all-film production integrates the car's interior space with the ways that its exterior can be deployed within a contiguous and continuous exterior space. Shooting on film in soundstages, in exterior locations and for in-car sequences made on location blurred the boundaries between physical action and character dialogue, and reduced distinctions between public and private space. The Flying Squad officers of *The Sweeney* struggled to assert the law's mobility, over and against the mobility of organised and violent crime, and their ability to know and control different kinds of space was expressed by the use of film to shoot each of them.

In the United States, police series have been made on film since the 1950s, when television drama production shifted from New York to Hollywood. Because of its Hollywood base, the cinema industry's techniques for filming cars, and filming in and from them, had already been developing since the 1920s. In the Keystone Cops films, for example, the city of Los Angeles, still partly under construction at the time, works as a setting and production base for numerous films featuring car chases. There is, of course, a long lineage of action cinema, often in the detective and thriller genres, in which car chases in urban settings exploit cinema's association with mobility, speed and the mobile point of view created by tracking within the shot and rapid cutting between shots (Tasker, 2015, p. 25). Technologies for stabilising cameras, recording sound on location and staging stunts, for example, were developed initially for cinema and consequently have been available for filmed television police series. In major television production centres of the developed world, there are established relationships between car makers and film and television production companies, so that multiple action vehicles can be supplied. For example, in *Starsky and Hutch* (Spelling-Goldberg for ABC,

1975–79), the Ford Motor Company's Studio-TV Car Loan Program was the contracted supplier of vehicles to the series' production company, providing two red Gran Torino cars that were modified for their role as David Starsky's (Paul Michael Glaser) own car.[3] In series that have extended car chase sequences, like *Starsky and Hutch*, the choice of a distinctive vehicle for the protagonists, or means of making vehicles distinctive by the choice of colour or customised features, facilitate storytelling by clarifying the identities of the regular characters' cars versus those of the non-recurring characters by whom they are chased, or who they chase. Indeed, towards the end of the second season, the episode 'Starsky and Hutch are Guilty' (1977) exploited this trope by reversing it. Two criminals masquerade as the two detectives, in a lookalike Gran Torino, to blacken Starsky's and Hutch's reputations so that their evidence in a forthcoming trial will be discredited.

Action sequences involving police in cars are much more common in the open urban settings of US series, than in British police drama. The chase normally occurs in the third quarter of the drama as a prelude to the capture of the criminal. The series that adopted the trope most self-consciously, however, was *Miami Vice* (Michael Mann/Universal for NBC, 1984–89) representing the city as a place associated with mobility and conspicuous consumption. Because of the illegal cash economy of the drug trade, the mobile and anonymous suspects pursued by the protagonists were very often in luxury cars, yachts and speedboats used for smuggling and other kinds of crime. Plainclothes police and detectives of television fiction need to merge with the locality where their missions are conducted, and work semi-independently of the hierarchy of the police institution. In *Miami Vice*, the plainclothes detectives Sonny Crockett and Rico Tubbs (Don Johnson and Philip Michael Thomas) go undercover and simulate the behaviour of the criminals they are seeking. Appearances are deceptive in a similar way to the aesthetic and narrative premises of the *films noir* of classical Hollywood (Butler, 1985). Sonny Crockett drove Ferrari Daytona and Testarossa sports cars, leading to frequent and lengthy car chase sequences shot on Miami's freeways, cut to rhythmic and exciting pop music, in which one exotic supercar pursued another.[4] Episode narratives had to work to establish that despite the apparent indistinguishability of the detectives and the criminals, each of whom drove luxury sports cars, the police are fundamentally supporters of normality and justice, whereas the criminals are forces of violence, disorder and destruction.

There are examples of police dramas that barely use cars. Scenes in the British precinct drama *The Cops* (World Productions for BBC, 1998–2001) were shot with a single camera, always following the uniformed police characters into action on foot. A single camera was used, often hand-held, moving with the police as they moved through the corridors of the police station, through the streets and into houses, rather than establishing an outside location before their arrival. The effect was to embed the characters more fully into the settings of the police station culture and into the wider community that they policed. This also minimised the senses of temporal interval and spatial separation discussed above. *The Cops* aimed to give the impression of unrehearsed action occurring in real time, adopting conventions used in television documentary to appear to follow action as it occurred. At the time, television police drama conventions were being reassessed just as the legal and political role of policing was being debated in the public sphere (Brunsdon, 1998). The structural and formal qualities of *The Cops* work together to both signal genre conventions but also to blur them, and the avoidance of sequences of car travel and the focus on uniformed officers walking, rather than detectives driving, was a key part of this.

Sign Vehicles: Car Iconography

A car is an iconographic resource, whether static or moving, and its role is carved out in relationships with characters and settings. An iconographic role is, by definition, important for any car on screen, since the distinctiveness of a car may be significant but so too might a car's self-effacement as part of a group of signifiers of ordinariness. For instance, in 1997 when *Midsomer Murders* began, its protagonist Inspector Barnaby drove a Rover Sterling, but following Rover's takeover by BMW, he acquired a Rover 75. The car was chosen to indicate his managerial status in the police and his solid, dependable character. The specific model (the Connoisseur) had Rover's 'Xenon Pack' optional fittings, which included alloy wheels, headlamp washers, cruise control, rain-sensing windscreen wipers, rear parking sensors, climate control, electric windows and electrically adjustable side mirrors.[5] However, the administrators appointed to deal with Rover's debts reclaimed the Rovers loaned to ITV for the series. John Nettles requested an older Rover to replace it, the CoupA of 1970, but that model was associated with organised crime, so instead Barnaby was given a Jaguar X-Type in order to retain the British flavour in a luxury saloon (Laws, 2005). What mattered was not so much the specific cars chosen for the character, but the continuity of their iconographic meaning when the cars had to be changed.

Inspector Morse's Jaguar Mark II matched the character's upper-middle class tastes for opera, real ale and cryptic crosswords, and contrasted with the Ford Sierra driven by his working class subordinate Lewis (Kevin Whately). The Jaguar Mark II was launched in 1959 with the advertising strapline 'Space, Grace and Pace.' Compared to the previous model, it had larger glass area, giving a feeling of openness and space to the interior, and was equipped with a 3.8 litre engine that could take it from rest to 60 mph in less than 9 seconds. This made the Mark II the fastest saloon car in the world, yet also a luxurious status symbol, with a real wood and leather interior. In Colin Dexter's Inspector Morse novels, on which much of the television series was based, Morse drove a Lancia. But his Britishness, and links with Oxford as an historic location with aspirational class associations, were expressed in the Regency Red 1960 version of the Mark II, retained throughout the series' seven seasons.

Similarly, the Channel Island tax haven settings of *Bergerac* (BBC, 1981–91) made the classic Triumph Roadster (featured in the series from 1985 onwards) seem less quirky when driven by John Nettles as the lead character. The car was a distinctive product of the British company in the early years following the Second World War, and was, in its time, a fashionable and aspirational vehicle similar to the Jaguars of the period. However, the 1948 model driven by Bergerac would have had only a three-speed gearbox and a top speed of 77 mph (though the actual car used had been slightly upgraded before being sold to the BBC).[6] To signal a more powerful and sophisticated vehicle, the sound of a Jaguar was substituted for the Triumph's engine in post-production. As with all the cars in police series, the automotive history of the marque may be relevant to some viewers but the semiotic significance of a car within a paradigm of types and styles of car is much more important to producers and probably to most viewers. Brenda Blethyn as the eponymous *Vera* (ITV/Company Pictures for ITV1, 2011–), daughter of a farmer, drives a shabby Land Rover that matches her own dishevelled appearance and the series' setting in a bleak, mainly rural Northumbria.

Figure 8.1 The Land Rover in *Vera's* rural setting.

Choices of vehicle are especially interesting in dramas set in the past, where cars function as indices of class, taste and gender identity but also to indicate period. In *Inspector George Gently* (Company for BBC, 2007–), Gently (Martin Shaw) drove a Rover P5 and then a P6, solid, white-collar vehicles that signifies the 1960s setting carefully recreated in the series. But they belie Gently's progressive outlook, one that is contrasted with his sidekick John Bacchus's (Lee Ingleby) lack of the expected youthful liberalism that appeared to be signified by his MG sports car in the first series. The tweed-suited ex-soldier Gently is in many ways more au fait with the 'Swinging Sixties' than Bacchus, despite the latter's Beatle haircut and fashionable suits. The cars are a ruse that viewers learn to see through.

Figure 8.2 A Rover P6 in *Inspector George Gently.*

Sam Tyler arrives at a crime scene in the first episode of *Life on Mars* in a modern Rover. When Tyler wakes up in 1973, the first thing he sees is another Rover, a 2000TC, and the substituted car links and separates the chronological periods. The car marks the change of epoch as much as Tyler's clothes. His 1973 boss Gene Hunt (Philip Glenister) demonstrates his machismo through his top of the range Ford Cortina Mark III GXL, and the comparison between the cars works as a complementary mechanism to other systems of comparison in the mise en scène of the series, such as costume and the actors' use of expressive physical gesture and posture. In the 1980s-set sequel to *Life on Mars*, *Ashes to Ashes* (Kudos for BBC, 2008–10), Hunt's character reappears and, befitting the later date, he drives an Audi Quattro. Again, the car is highly significant as an indicator of period and a specific form of masculine identity. The Quattro is identified with the brash Tory 1980s, when its extraordinary engine power made it a very difficult and dangerous 'hot hatch' to control despite its four-wheel drive.

It was advertised to, and appealed to, the socially ascendant 'yuppies' of the period, and did this so effectively that it appeared, in April 2010, on election posters for both the Conservative and Labour parties (Nikhah, 2010). These posters debated the legacy of the 1980s, contesting the decade's meanings via Hunt's character as signified by his totemic car. Labour's poster showed the Conservative opposition leader David Cameron posing on the bonnet of a red Audi Quattro, with the caption 'Don't let him take Britain back to the 1980s.' In response, Conservative campaigners produced an online poster with the same image of Cameron beneath a new slogan: 'PM Dave Cameron. He's gonna sort Britain out. Conservatives, fixing broken Britain.' In association with the Quattro, each advertisement represents the 1980s as a time of capitalist excess and portrays Cameron as a leader with laddish bravado. But, of course, the value of the sign is reversed from one poster to the other, demonstrating the instability of its component meanings. While not such a direct allusion to police drama, the Conservative Home organisation's blog ran another poster alluding to *Life on Mars*, captioned 'Back to debt, decline and the 1970s with Gordon Brown.' The central image for signifying the era was another car, whose connotations are more or less opposite to those of the Audi Quattro. It was a mustard-coloured Austin Maxi, with Prime Minister Gordon Brown perched on its bonnet, dressed in a 1970s beige safari suit with a pile of uncollected rubbish and strikers' placards behind him.

Cars in police drama are much more significant than they might initially seem, and in this chapter I have suggested some routes for further work that can use cars as a way to reconsider the genre from several points of view at the same time. Cars signify performatively, and I have argued that they do important work to contribute to programmes' form, meaning and distinctive identity.[7] They are things that come to have a life of their own within the fictional world of a television police series. This point alludes to Marx's (1867) explanation of the commodity in capitalist society, where he argued that the effect of industrial capitalism on people was to turn them into objects deployed to service a profit-driven economic system. Conversely, objects (like cars) are endowed with apparent agency, character and personality that conceal their nature as products of human labour. In this chapter, I have suggested that the significance of cars in television police drama is also dependent on an industrial history in which changing production circumstances affect how cars can appear on screen. Studio-based programmes, programmes using filmed inserts of car action in combination with studio drama, then filmed or digitally recorded programmes, deploy cars differently because of what can be achieved with available cameras and technologies of sound recording. Within the police genre, there are differences between character-focused dramas versus action-focused ones that affect how often, and in what ways, cars appear in programmes. But in each case, cars are narrative vehicles and drive the narrative, at the same time as they are relatively passive components of setting. Cars are an aspect of aesthetic style, and contribute to its rapid definition early in a programme as a marker of the programme's distinctive identity. In association with the protagonists, and because of the car's continuity through an episode across sequences and across commercial breaks, cars specific to a series are important to its brand identity. Structurally, car sequences work as a kind of glue, linking places in the fictional world and linking segments of storyline. In as much as they are a tool for, and extension of, the police protagonist, the police's cars signify the ideological function of law enforcement and its ability to control physical space. Tracing the different roles of cars in police series is a way into the textual, historical and cultural work of television as well as the police genre specifically.

Notes

1. The topic is little studied academically, though Britton and Barker's (2003) study of 1960s British television fantasy series has begun to chart its significance.
2. See the Action Vehicles' company website at: http://actionvehicles.com.
3. For full details of the modifications and eventual replacement of the original cars by later models, see: http://en.wikipedia.org/wiki/Starsky_%26_Hutch.
4. These frequent chase and stunt sequences meant that lookalike vehicles substituted for the Ferraris, ironically repeating the programme's tropes of simulation and deceptive appearance (see: http://en.wikipedia.org/wiki/Cars_in_Miami_Vice).
5. Advertisement for sale posted on 3 August 2012 by 'Rabett Rover' on the Rover 75 and Rover ZT owners' club webpage, available at: http://www.the75andzt-club.co.uk/forum/showthread.php?t=121141.
6. This information derives from a description of the car when auctioned by Bonhams in 2013, available at: https://www.bonhams.com/auctions/20933/lot/425.
7. I have made a related argument about the 'performances' by puppets and models in children's science fiction series including *Stingray*, *Thunderbirds* and *Captain Scarlet and the Mysterons* (Bignell, 2014).

References

Banham, R., 1971. *Los Angeles: The Architecture of Four Ecologies*. Harmondsworth, England: Penguin.

Bignell, J., 2007. Seeing and knowing: reflexivity and quality. In: J. McCabe and K. Akass, eds., 2007. *Quality TV: Contemporary American Television and Beyond*. London, England: I.B. Tauris. pp. 158–70.

Bignell, J., 2009. The police series. In: J. Gibbs and D. Pye, eds., 2009. *Close-Up 03*. London, England: Wallflower. pp. 1–66.

Bignell, J., 29 November 2014. Space and performance: Gerry and Sylvia Anderson's 1960s science fiction. *CST online*. [online] Available at: http://cstonline.tv/space-and-performance-gerry-and-sylvia-andersons-science-fiction.

Britton, P. and Barker, S. 2003. *Reading Between Designs: Visual Imagery and the Generation of Meaning in The Avengers, The Prisoner, and Doctor Who*. Austin, TX: University of Texas Press.

Brunsdon, C., 1998. Structure of anxiety: recent British television crime fiction. *Screen*, 39(3), pp. 223–43.

Butler, J., 1985. *Miami Vice* and the legacy of film noir. *Journal of Popular Film and Television*, 13(3), pp. 127–38.

Buxton, D., 1990. *From The Avengers to Miami Vice: Form and Ideology in Television Series*. Manchester, England: Manchester University Press.

Clarke, A., 1992. 'You're nicked!': Television police series and the fictional representation of law and order. In: D. Strinati and S. Wagg, eds., 1992. *Come on*

Down?: Popular Media Culture in Post-War Britain. London, England: Routledge. pp. 232–53.

Fiske J. and Hartley, J., 1978. *Reading Television*. London, England: Methuen.

Laing, S., 1991. Banging in some reality: the original 'Z Cars'. In: J. Corner, ed. 1991. *Popular Television in Britain: Studies in Cultural History*. London, England: BFI. pp. 124–34.

Laws, R., 10 July 2005. TV cop ordered to hand back Rover; administrators swoop on star's prized car. *Sunday Mercury*. [online] Available at: http://www. thefreelibrary.com/TV+cop+ordered+to+hand+back+Rover+ADMINISTRATORS+ SWOOP+ON+STAR'S...-a0133898212.

Lury, K., 2005. *Interpreting Television*. London, England: Hodder Arnold.

Marx, K., 1867. *Capital, vol. 1: A Critique of Political Economy*. Translated by B. Fowkes., 1992. Harmondsworth, England: Penguin.

Morse, M., 1990. An ontology of everyday distraction: the freeway, the mall, and television. In: P. Mellencamp, ed. 1990. *Logics of Television: Essays in Cultural Criticism*. Bloomington, IN: Indiana University Press. pp. 193–221.

Nikhah, R., 3 April 2010. Labour poster attack on Tories backfires. *Daily Telegraph*. [online] Available at: http://www.telegraph.co.uk/news/election-2010/7549078/ Labour-poster-attack-on-Tories-backfires.html.

Tasker, Y., 2015. *The Hollywood Action and Adventure Film*. New York, NY: John Wiley.

Part III
Exporting and Adapting Crime

9 Crime Drama and Channel Branding
ITV and *Broadchurch*

Ross P. Garner

Introduction

Writing in relation to the prominence of crime dramas on US television throughout the 1980s and 1990s, Jonathan Nichols-Pethick (2012, p. 46) concludes his overview of production in the period by stating:

> Genre is a *tool* used by producers and programmers alike to anchor programming decisions – to provide some security and certainty while simultaneously trying something new in the ongoing effort to reach as large and valuable an audience as possible … the ways in which the police genre was activated (and re-activated) across a range of programming strategies points to both the ordinariness of the form and to its openness.

The crime drama, he notes, was employed by the major American networks (ABC, CBS and NBC) as both a secure base from which mainstream appeal could occur, whilst also functioning as a malleable form that was highly adaptable to the increasing aim of niche-targeting commercially salient audiences. Whilst exploring overlapping ideas concerning the TV crime genre, this chapter considers a different national context and area of production by analysing how the UK broadcaster, ITV – a network which 'has often been marginalised or neglected' (Johnson and Turnock, 2005, p. 1) in British TV Studies – discursively uses the crime drama for its contemporaneous channel branding purposes. Responding to Jason Mittell's (2004, p. 14) calls for examining genre categories 'from the bottom up, by collecting micro-instances of generic discourses in historically-specific moments', the chapter analyses two examples of material used to brand the ITV channel. These are ITV's Winter 2013 drama trailer, which is one iteration of the channel's continuing 'Where Drama Lives' campaign, and a widely disseminated poster image promoting the first series of *Broadchurch* (ITV, 2013–), ITV's critically acclaimed crime drama which debuted in March 2013. By analysing this promotional material, two core arguments arise: firstly, ITV consistently gives high visibility to crime dramas but this publicity material continuously negotiates ongoing value judgements between celebrated 'realist' and disparaged 'melodramatic' discourses when marketing the channel to different imagined audiences. Secondly, ITV's construction of crime dramas within its channel branding demonstrates what I have named 'self-reflexive anxieties' concerning both the genre's cultural status and ITV's contributions to its heritage. Whilst crime series are consistently employed as signifiers of the channel's mainstream appeal, genre-specific meanings are always enhanced through being layered with appeals to additional audience segments.

ITV: Context and Branding

Before commencing the analysis, some contextualising statements concerning ITV's programming output, the approach to branding that this chapter employs and ITV's current channel brand values are required for purposes of clarification and locating readers who are unfamiliar with the broadcaster. ITV currently has a strong association with crime dramas. Alongside *Broadchurch*, it produces and commissions annually returning series such as *Vera* (ITV, 2011–), *DCI Banks* (ITV, 2010–), and *Lewis* (ITV, 2006–) as well as limited-episode serials including *Code of a Killer* (ITV, 2015), *Safe House* (ITV, 2015) and *Black Work* (ITV, 2015). The channel does not solely specialise in crime dramas, though. Rather, as an overhang of its initial public service remit, ITV provides a mixed schedule which encompasses myriad popular forms including light entertainment, reality-based game show formats, news and current affairs and dramas, including soap operas and period pieces, alongside its crime output. Branding subsequently presents a challenge for ITV as it necessitates bringing coherence to the channel's range of content. As Catherine Johnson (2012) explains, 'within the public service context of the mixed programme schedule ... brands function to connect together different products and services within one set of values' (p. 125).

However, in terms of understanding this chapter's approach to channel branding, two significant points can be extrapolated from Johnson's argument. Recognising the range of content that is used to build the channel brand, Johnson suggests that brands are always semiotic creations (Danesi, 2006, p. 25). Within the context of television, this means recognising that any programming material that has been selected for communicating the channel brand has not been utilised because of any 'intrinsic property' (Mittell, 2004, p. 7) locatable within those examples. Instead, clips, shots and images are used 'in a manner that suits ... institutional needs' (Altman, 1999, p. 48). In the case of ITV, the channel's marketing personnel insert the chosen material into institutionally defined discourses for the purpose of communicating effectively its intended brand identity, both to the public and interested parties such as advertisers. An understanding of the channel's core brand values is therefore essential for comprehending how and why (crime) programmes are made to mean when constructing ITV's channel brand.

ITV plc – the wider corporation of which the ITV channel is part – currently insists that all of its services (including niche, digital channels such as youth-orientated ITV2 and online platforms like itv.com and ITVPlayer) should occupy a position at 'the heart of popular culture' (Radcliffe in Sweney, 2012). This core corporate brand value was instituted in January 2013 as part of an extensive rebranding exercise and translates to the ITV channel via positioning it as 'the largest commercial channel in the UK' (ITV plc, 2015, p. 6). ITV programming therefore strives to attract 'a *coalition* of audiences' (Johnson, 2005, p. 130; original emphasis) comprised of myriad demographics to maximise viewing figures and commercial returns. This goal is reflected in ITV plc's understanding of the broadcaster's role as exemplified in its 2014 Annual Report (p. 6) which identifies the channel's ability to 'consistently ... deliver peak audiences of more than five million' as a strategic advantage. Yet, despite having a brand identity that aims for cross-demographic appeal, research undertaken by UK communications regulator OFCOM (2012) indicates that the channel's audience consistently skews towards female viewers in their mid-thirties and upwards. OFCOM's audience profiling data is important to note as it suggests a gap between the intended brand identity for the ITV channel and empirical audience data relating to the channel. As shall become evident, negotiation between these discursive constructions of its audience informs how ITV's crime dramas are positioned in different forms of publicity for the channel.

The sources discussed in this chapter coincided with ITV plc's major rebranding exercise. For the purposes of this discussion, this interpretive frame is of varying significance to the materials analysed. Elsewhere, I have examined the complex set of circumstances motivating ITV's rebrand (Garner, 2015) but the examples discussed below bear differing relations to this historical-institutional context. The 'Where Drama Lives' trailer works across the time period as it was instigated prior to rebrand and so, despite undergoing some minor reconfigurations (e.g., incorporating the new ITV logo), provides continuity between 'old' and 'new' incarnations of ITV's channel brand. In contrast, *Broadchurch* represented a 'new' series for ITV in early 2013, and its marketing and promotion deserves to be read in light of such rebranding discourses because of how it combines crime drama iconography with appeals to audience groups that ITV has previously overlooked, like cult TV fans. Consequently, whilst the rebrand context is occasionally invoked to assist in better understanding ITV's promotional strategies, the ensuing analysis' primary aim is to account for the meanings that ITV assigns to its crime dramas for channel branding purposes.

Crime Drama, Cultural Meanings and ITV

Academic commentaries discussing ITV crime series, both historical and contemporary, regularly devalue the broadcaster's contributions by aligning these with negatively evaluated discourses [although Lacey's discussion of *Foyle's War* (ITV 2002–15) in this volume complicates this understanding]. Whilst the crime series represents 'one of the oldest and most recognisable genres on television' (Nichols-Pethick, 2012, p. 26), ITV's contributions in sustaining the genre's popularity are continually overlooked as a result of the dominant discourses framing their interpretation.

For example, Charlotte Brunsdon (2013) observes that ITV crime dramas are 'not, in any way, difficult television' and that the channel has a 'long tradition of "nice crime"' (p. 382). Brunsdon's evaluations can be illuminated by recognising that generic 'texts operate culturally and historically, activating larger circulating discourses and meanings' (Mittell, 2004, p. 123) which work to fix the meaning of individual programmes at specific historical moments. By positioning ITV crime dramas as 'nice' and 'easy', Brunsdon is drawing upon what Nichols-Pethick (2012) names as the 'fundamental contradiction' underpinning crime fictions (whether televisual or otherwise) where 'its realist aesthetic (practical location shooting, handled cameras, naturalistic lighting, etc.) is constantly undermined by the conventions of melodrama' (p. 2). This tension traces back to the earliest examples of mediating deviance from the nineteenth century as public appetite for detailed reports of crime and its punishment were frequently communicated through exaggerated rhetoric. Early reports and restagings of infamous crimes established 'a matrix of narrative and stylistic possibilities that the creators of television crime drama were able to draw upon' (Turnbull, 2014, p. 20) and negotiation of this internal tension is ongoing. Academic analysis of *The Wire* (HBO 2002–08) demonstrates how discursive work leads to value judgements of individual series as this programme has been consecrated through being read as gritty and 'realist' and thereby distanced from 'melodramatic' associations (Klein, 2009). Nevertheless, demonstrating the discursive and relational use of melodrama as a discourse for devaluing (ITV) crime series, what constitutes the 'melodramatic' shifts across historical contexts and interpretive communities? Within an academic context, some scholars read serialised narratives and 'an engagement with the personal lives of the serving men and women' (Turnbull, 2014, p. 76) as evidence of the genre's melodramatic capabilities whereas others highlight that 'the distinction is based primarily on formal qualities such as acting, psychological motivation and *mise-en-scène*: the surface indicators of verisimilitude' (Nichols-Pethick, 2012, p. 109). Recurrent across these discussions is melodrama's historical status as a dramatic mode which works against perceived codes of 'realism' circulating during different periods (Frank, 2013, p. 538). Interpreting ITV's crime series as 'nice' and 'safe' positions them away from valued realist readings, instead aligning them with disparaged discourses of melodrama.

Further proof of how melodramatic discourses combine with additional, culturally gendered interpretations and encourage further devaluations of ITV crime dramas can be evidenced through examining academic analyses of *Inspector Morse* (ITV, 1997–2000). For many years, *Inspector Morse* constituted ITV's flagship crime drama in branding campaigns (Johnson, 2012, p. 73). Nevertheless, academic engagements with the series have been less than favourable: Robin Nelson (2007a, p. 176) describes

Inspector Morse as an example of 'quality popular' programming which offers anodyne pleasure to viewers 'through negotiating a story with some small surprises but no major ones.' Elsewhere, despite being occasionally read as offering narratives that posit challenging questions about British social structures (Barker, 1994), the programme's dominant image has either foregrounded its heritage aspects or located its appeal in culturally feminised terms. These include the appeal of lead actor John Thaw and/or the character's melodramatic undercurrents as a virtuous hero confronting an increasingly morally bankrupt world (Thomas, 2002). Such gendered readings have now arguably been self-consciously appropriated by *Endeavour* (ITV, 2012–), ITV's current prequel series which charts Morse (Shaun Evans) in his early years as a detective constable, by episodically demonstrating the character's chaste and chivalrous nature.

ITV's heritage within British television crime drama is significant as it also points towards how its output is repeatedly read through discourses of the 'mainstream' which further denigrate its contributions. Products understood as mainstream are frequently culturally feminised (Baker, 2013, p. 14) and, echoing both Brunsdon and Nelson's comments, additionally tainted through being associated with hegemonic perspectives and/or established formulas. As Alison Huber (2013) elaborates, 'the spectre of negativity haunts the mainstream' (p. 11) as it is a metaphor that is constructed 'as all-encompassing, homogenous and homogenizing.' The 'mainstream' therefore constitutes a cultural space where products 'lose their "identity", "purity", "originality" and "authenticity"' (ibid.). Such an understanding seems easily applicable to how ITV's crime dramas have been discussed academically, but Turnbull's (2014) comments on long-running series *Midsomer Murders* (ITV, 1997–) provide yet another iteration of this perspective:

> The appeal of *Midsomer Murders* may depend upon a nostalgia for the idealised, less ethnically diverse version of 'Great Britain' as imagined in the pages of the classical detective story at the start of the twentieth century: a place where crime may be committed but where the perpetrator would be brought to justice. (p. 26)

This is not to argue that ITV has not produced more gritty, and therefore valued, examples: academic analyses of *Prime Suspect* (ITV, 1991–2006) have celebrated this series for both its gender representations and its unflinching depictions of police work (Brunsdon, 1998, 2013; Creeber, 2004; Hallam, 2011; Jermyn, 2003) whilst, despite infrequent melodrama-indebted readings of the series (Turnbull, 2014, pp. 142–3), *Cracker* (ITV, 1993–2006) has similarly been praised through realist discourses (Blandford, 2013, pp. 41–53). Contemporary ITV crime dramas such as the short-lived *Chasing Shadows* (ITV, 2014) arguably represent a continuation of this gritty trend. Yet, the dominant perception of ITV's crime dramas hinges upon their implicitly negative interpretation as 'mainstream', melodramatic fare which primarily appeals to female audiences. Given these characterisations, why does crime drama recur across ITV's channel branding material, and how are discourses circulating around these series negotiated to provide distinction? The next sections engage with these questions, beginning by arguing that ITV embraces but recodes its approach to the genre in promotional trailers summarising the channel's drama output.

'Quality Melodrama': The Winter 2013 Drama Trailer

ITV's Winter 2013 drama trailer is a 60-second clip that consists of 35 short sequences. Crime dramas including returning series such as *Scott & Bailey* (ITV, 2011–) and new programmes like *Broadchurch* make up over two-thirds of the included segments. The trailer is part of ITV's ongoing 'Drama Lives' branding – a campaign initiated before the 2013 rebrand. However, coinciding with the exercise, subtle readjustments occurred as the tagline shifted from 'Drama Lives on ITV' to 'ITV: Where Drama Lives' and its aesthetics changed to incorporate the new ITV logo. The campaign is ongoing at the time of writing, and subsequent on-air and online clips promoting the channel's 2014 and 2015 drama seasons have employed similar strategies to those discussed here, meaning that the campaign has provided continuity between different incarnations of the channel brand.

Crime drama's generic meanings and signifiers are continually housed in this branding campaign within a discourse of melodrama. Set to the moving track 'Explosions' by Ellie Goulding (Goulding and Fortis, 2012), which discusses a failing relationship, the clip firstly, and continuously, constructs its discourse via cultural associations of melodrama as 'excess and sentimentality' (Frank, 2013, p. 540) featuring multiple medium close-ups of recognisable actors looking troubled and off-camera. Most prominent of these is *Broadchurch*'s DS Miller (Olivia Colman) who is seen three times: early in the clip, Miller is seen in a medium shot looking concerned as she approaches the body on the beach; she then appears half-way through the trailer, crying whilst framed in close-up and side profile (see Figure 9.1), before being seen again in the penultimate sequence whilst crying and hugging her husband, and perpetrator, Joe (Matthew Gravelle). Through employing these strategies, and using music to amplify emotion, ITV positions its forthcoming drama output (whether crime-based or otherwise) as intense and affect-heavy. These associations also extend to two of the three instances when crime drama is explicitly denoted: a sequence from *Broadchurch*'s first episode where Beth (Jodie Whitaker) is restrained by uniformed officers whilst attempting to view the corpse of her (at this point, unbeknownst) deceased son is included alongside a shot from *The Ice Cream Girls* (ITV, 2013) which features one of the titular characters (played by Georgina Campbell) being released from a prison cell. Whereas the *Broadchurch* sequence codes the series' themes of the loss of a child in emotional terms, the latter suggests melodrama's opposing of 'person and institution' (Bratton, Cook and Gledhill, 1994, p. 2) by connoting that the event constitutes a loss of innocence.

*Figure 9.*1 *Broadchurch*-as-melodrama in ITV's Winter 2013 drama trailer. (*Source:* ITV.)

Melodramatic discourses are also constructed through foregrounding moments of high tension. Short sequences, such as DC Scott (Lesley Sharp) from *Scott & Bailey* having a drink thrown over her and Mr. Selfridge (Jeremy Piven) throwing a male character on a table, are positioned towards the trailer's end and are skilfully combined with the track's lyrical content discussing figurative explosions. Intertextual connections across different genres and programmes are thus made by defining drama primarily as confrontation. These resonate with melodrama's 'capacities to amplify effect (as well as affect)' (Frank, 2013, p. 539) by offering a series of tableau-like flash-points which cumulatively suggest heightened emotion as a key feature of ITV and its (crime) drama output.

If read solely through the literature on channel branding, the clip's strategies (and its successors) may seem normative. In line with John Ellis' argument (2011, p. 67), the clip functions as a 'super-trailer … defin[ing] the whole channel experience.' By generating 'vectors of significance' (ibid., p. 66) for viewers via identifying core programmes and stars, but containing these within a melodramatic mode that provides coherence across disparate examples, ITV's identity as a mainstream brand favouring a primarily female audience is reaffirmed. Of greater significance, however, is the role that crime dramas play in constructing ITV's brand identity. Firstly, the trailer reflexively embraces the ubiquity of the crime drama to ITV, and its subsequent connotations of mainstream appeal, to signify these core channel brand values to its audience(s). Secondly, although the trailer's strategies may initially appear to reinstate negative associations concerning the channel's

favouring of melodramatic examples over gritty fare, this reading oversim-
plifies the tensions arising from how crime series are made to mean throughout. This is because the trailer uses discourses of 'quality' television at the
same time as positioning these examples as affect-heavy. Writing in relation
to discourses of 'quality' television in the UK, Charlotte Brunsdon (1997,
p. 143) has argued that 'quality' historically has been defined in accord-
ance with 'upper-middle-class taste codes', which includes '[t]he presence
of name theatrical actresses and actors add[ing] the international dimension of British theatre to the programmes' (ibid., p. 142). The acting talent attached to ITV's crime dramas in the trailer conforms to these values:
David Tennant's star identity incorporates theatrical associations via his
stage work in Shakespeare (Hills, 2010, pp. 159–65) and Suranne Jones,
whose appearance in the trailer as DS Bailey from *Scott & Bailey* employs
the same melodramatic aesthetic of expressing emotionality via close-up,
brings similar associations. Moreover, Olivia Colman and Paddy Con-
sidine (seen as Mr. Whicher from period crime series *The Suspicions of
Mr. Whicher* (ITV, 2011–)) connect with alternative inflections of 'quality'
discourse due to their associations with the politically charged and highly
respected British social realist movement (Cooke, 2003, pp. 66–9). Through
foregrounding the stars appearing in ITV's forthcoming crime dramas, the
trailer suggests that, although its crime dramas will be melodramatic, they
will feature esteemed acting talent and so the affective content should be
read through the appreciation of performance over other meanings. ITV's
Winter 2013 drama trailer therefore suggests that its crime dramas should
be read as 'quality melodrama' in that negative connotations arising from
its particular take on the genre are off-set through aligning the series with
non-genre-specific discourses concerning 'quality' television.

This idea of quality melodrama also extends to the instances where the
crime drama is explicitly invoked within the trailer. The sequence from
Broadchurch, for example, is directly lifted from the first episode where
it appears in slow-motion, as is the case in the trailer. Although potentially readable as excessive, the stylistic techniques nevertheless utilise the
established generic mode for exploring the emotional impact of losing a
child (Nichols-Pethick, 2012, pp. 113–14). Through being readable as an
appropriate way of exploring these themes, further intertextual connections with 'quality' discourses arise; as Robin Nelson argues, '[t]he quality
of … dramas needs to be judged in terms of aesthetic and production values appropriate to the dramatic mode' (2007b, p. 47). The trailer engages
these ideas by aligning *Broadchurch* with a sense of aesthetic coherence
(Cardwell, 2013, p. 37) as the elements included – the slowing of narrative
time, the emotion of the performances – appear appropriate to *Broadchurch*'s subject matter. Moreover, when enhanced in this context by the
Goulding song, further matching between audio and visual elements arise
that permit reading the strategies demonstrated as 'tasteful' (Wheatley,
2004, pp. 329–30): a point that also applies to the sequence included

from *The Ice Cream Girls* as the song's lyrics, discussing reassurance in the face of anxiety and uncertainty, accompany the shot of the character being released from a prison cell. Whether considered in terms either of its encoding of performance, or its aesthetics, ITV's Winter 2013 drama trailer therefore uses melodramatic readings of crime dramas to assert both its mainstream status and culturally feminised brand identity but enhances this by drawing upon 'quality' discourses. As such, it constructs its emblematic crime dramas, and therefore its channel brand, as 'quality melodrama.'

Mainstream/Quality/Cult: Publicising *Broadchurch*

From its first series onwards, *Broadchurch* has been heavily publicised by ITV and arguably functions as (one of) the channel's current flagship drama series. Multiple press images were produced and distributed in the marketing of series 1. Whilst these would demonstrate occasional variations, such as including more of the cast and so constructing the series as an ensemble piece, recurrent across all of these images was *Broadchurch*'s beach location and its stars – Tennant and Colman. Most prominent of all the images produced for marketing series 1 was that seen in Figure 9.2. This provided the anchor for *Broadchurch*'s off-air publicity as it was used to promote the series on large billboards prior to the first episode airing (Pirrie, 2013). The image makes explicit reference to *Broadchurch*'s status as a crime drama through the presence of the blue and white police tape and further generic readings are encouraged by Tennant and Colman's characters jointly holding the tape in a nod to the police series' buddy convention. Connotations of the detective narrative also arise from the stylised manner in which the tape flows from Tennant and Colman's characters to encircle and bind the entire town. Writing in relation to 'classic' detective literature such as Agatha Christie novels, Lawrence M. Friedmann and Issachar Rosen-Zvi (2001, p. 1416) argue that '[t]he detective story plays on ... themes of false identity and hidden motives' with the detective characters being particularly 'adept at untying knots' (ibid., p. 1417). *Broadchurch*'s main press image therefore 'sets up, begins and frames many of the interactions that [audiences] will have' (Gray, 2010, p. 48) with the series by intertextually referencing this generic trope and suggesting that the whole town will be investigated and long-buried mysteries will gradually be revealed. This preferred reading of *Broadchurch* as detective drama is then further reinforced through its tag-line of 'A Town Wrapped in Secrets.'

ITV's employment of crime drama discourses is interesting, however, as the image positions *Broadchurch* ambiguously in relation to the melodrama/realism binary. Whilst academic commentary upon *Broadchurch* discussed the series' complex relationship with the melodramatic mode (Geraghty, 2013), allusions to such elements as its affect-saturated locations (Ellis, 2013) are not immediately denoted in the publicity image. This does not

Figure 9.2 Publicity image for publicising *Broadchurch*'s first series.

mean that the *Broadchurch* image eschews melodramatic readings: the anguished and emotional expressions demonstrated by Tennant and Colman's characters may connote such readings whilst its rural and seaside locations might, when read in combination with the ITV logo, activate similarities between *Broadchurch* and other rural ITV crime dramas such as the much-maligned, yet hugely popular, *Midsomer Murders*. However, these positions exist alongside other 'quality'-inflected readings: the dishevelled and unkempt look of DI Alec Hardy (David Tennant) connotes a more downtrodden character instead of his narrative coding as a melodramatic hero (Garner, 2013). Moreover, the image's muted colour palette of light blues, greys and faded yellows implies the kind of 'washed-out daylight exteriors' (Turnbull, 2014, p. 182) which connote 'a bleak present in which society itself seems to be the crime' (ibid.), in the vein of imported crime dramas such as *The Killing* (DR 2007–12) which have been celebrated for their engagement with contemporary geo-political issues (Peacock, 2011). By forging these associations, the poster encourages reading *Broadchurch* as 'quality' television as a result of having a distinctive aesthetic style (Cardwell, 2007, p. 26) and suggesting that the series will feature a 'realist' engagement with its narrative themes.

The publicity image therefore articulates a complex relationship with the cultural meanings of crime drama at both generic and channel-specific levels. On the one hand, corresponding with strategies used for the

'Where Drama Lives' campaign, the crime drama's iconography is used to signify ITV's mainstream appeal. *Broadchurch*'s status as a crime drama is foregrounded for publicising both the series and the ITV channel, meaning that the genre is employed to restate the channel's core brand values concerning its centrality to its viewers' lives. However, as this image was widely used to publicise not only *Broadchurch* but also ITV's new channel brand aesthetic and logo, its recourse to a crime series for these purposes can be read as fulfilling additional functions. Rebranding exercises 'carr[y] a high level of reputation risk' (Muzellec and Lambkin, 2006, p. 803) by potentially displacing established brand equity for the organisation. ITV's use of *Broadchurch* as its flagship drama arguably eases such audience uncertainties, as the crime drama suggests continuity and an ongoing mainstream focus for the channel. The image's activation of the mystery genre also becomes significant here, as these signifiers locate *Broadchurch* alongside ITV's generic lineage of crime dramas by connoting preceding popular murder-mysteries. Yet, the image's mainstream associations are complicated through being layered with 'quality' discourses through the image's aesthetics and its use of characters and actors. This ambiguity towards ITV crime dramas' mainstream associations is, then, furthered by recognising that the image also makes intertextual connections with forms of 'cult' television.

These intertexts are activated in two ways: firstly, the polysemy of the two leads encourages such associations. Jonathan Gray (2010) argues that recognisable actors operate within paratexts 'as an intertext of all their past roles and their public performance' (p. 53). Whilst both Colman and Tennant embody connections to 'quality', they can also be read through cult discourses via their appearances in *Peep Show* (Channel 4, 2003–) and *Doctor Who* (BBC One, 2005–), respectively. Additionally, *Broadchurch*'s 'A Town Wrapped in Secrets' tagline intersects with 'cult' discourses by amalgamating two iconic lines of dialogue from early-1990s series *Twin Peaks* (ABC, 1990–91; Bianculli, 2010, p. 303). When taken together, the strategies employed in the poster suggest ITV's ambiguity towards the crime drama's role in its (re)brand(ed) identity. On the one hand, the genre is used to signify the channel's mainstream appeal and subtly suggests continuity between its previous and current brand images. However, these appeals are layered with attempts at attracting hitherto absent audiences to the network such as 'knowing' (and primarily masculine) 'cult' TV fans (Jancovich and Hunt, 2004, pp. 28–30) alongside 'quality' demographics. Nonetheless, whilst *Broadchurch*'s promotional strategies can be read through these imagined audience profiles, empirical audience data questions the success of these appeals. An OFCOM report (2014) on adult viewing trends in 2013 saw *Broadchurch* rank in the top 20 most-watched programmes for 45–64 and 65 plus age-groups (ranked eighth and fourteenth, respectively) but not be listed for 16–24 or 25–44 year-olds (demographics which are industrially linked to either valued ABC1 demographics or 'cult' profiles). Thus, whilst *Broadchurch*'s marketing demonstrates a complex and ambiguous relationship to the crime drama genre by attempting to attract new niches to ITV, the series' viewing audience appears resolutely rooted in less sought-after demographics.

Conclusions

Two main arguments arise from this chapter's analysis of ITV's use of the crime drama for constructing its current brand identity. Firstly, ITV consistently positions the genre as a base from which the channel's brand values, as a cornerstone of British television culture, can be communicated. This echoes Nichols-Pethick's (2012, pp. 25–47) argument that the crime series was used as a tool by American TV producers during a period of institutional change and transition. However, variance in terms of what the crime drama is made to mean is evident suggesting that it is used as a flexible sign which has additional discursive and intertextual frames built on to it depending on the intended imagined audience for the publicity campaign. ITV's internally facing trailers, which air primarily as part of the channel's programming flows, bring together disparate examples of crime programming and unite these within a discourse of melodrama to provide a coherent brand identity that reassures their core female audience about the tone of its drama output. Yet, to provide distinction, negative connotations concerning the channel and its approach to the genre are downplayed by forging intertexual connections with 'quality' discourses which reconfigure ITV's (crime) dramas by positioning them as 'quality melodrama.' In comparison, externally facing publicity material used for off-air marketing, namely *Broadchurch*'s promotional poster, discourages melodramatic readings by layering the series with 'cult' and/or 'quality' intertexts in an attempt to attract new audiences (back) to the channel. Thus, by examining how ITV uses the crime series for constructing its channel brand, at both channel-wide and programme-specific levels, it can be demonstrated that the genre is used consistently as a signifier of its status as a mainstream broadcaster, but flexibly to address different markets.

However, the fact that ITV continually positions the crime series as a base that is in need of further enhancement to provide distinction to its channel brand is suggestive of a set of self-reflexive anxieties circulating around both the genre itself and the channel's contributions towards it. As Mittell (2004) argues:

> discursive practices can be broken down into three basic types by how they work to constitute genres: *definition* (for instance, 'this show is a sitcom because it has a laugh track'), *interpretation* ('sitcoms reflect and reinforce the status quo'), and *evaluation* ('sitcoms are better entertainment than soap operas'). These discursive utterances may seem to reflect on an already established genre, but they are themselves constitutive of that genre; they are the practices that define genres, delimit their meanings, and posit their cultural value. (p. 16)

ITV adopts a self-conscious, evaluative attitude towards the crime drama genre as is evident from how the marketing materials analysed in this chapter layer the genre with additional meanings and intertexts. Whilst this could be understood commonsensically as necessary, given that ITV is not a genre-specific channel and therefore needs to bring coherence to the diversity of its output, this reading overlooks the nuances of what the crime drama means in ITV's promotional material. By either embracing its melodramatic reputation and then complicating this through additional 'quality' intertexts or else by treating the genre ambiguously as with *Broadchurch*, there is a sense that ITV is aware of negatively weighted discourses circulating outside of its channel brand. Consequently, the meanings that the channel assigns to its crime series are reconfigured to negate these associations. Whilst ITV regularly uses the crime drama as a marker of distinction for its current channel brand, its mainstream approach to the genre generates anxieties that need to be managed and downplayed.

References

Altman, R., 1999. *Film/Genre*. London, England: BFI.

Baker, S., 2013. Teenybop and the extraordinary particularities of mainstream practice. In: S. Baker, A. Bennett and J. Taylor, eds., 2013. *Redefining Mainstream Popular Music*. London, England: Routledge. pp. 14–24.

Barker, S., 1994. 'Period' detective drama and the limits of contemporary nostalgia: *Inspector Morse* and the strange case of a lost England. *Critical Survey*, 6(2), pp. 234–43.

Blandford, S., 2013. *Jimmy McGovern*. Manchester, England: Manchester University Press.

Bianculli, D., 2010. *Twin Peaks*. In: D. Lavery, ed. 2010. *The Essential Cult TV Reader*. Lexington, KY: University Press of Kentucky. pp. 299–306.

Bratton, J., Cook, J. and Gledhill, C., 1994. Introduction. In: J. Bratton, J. Cook and C. Gledhill, eds., 1994. *Melodrama: Stage, Picture, Screen*. London, England: BFI. pp. 1–8.

Brunsdon, C., 1997. *Screen Tastes: Soap Opera to Satellite Dishes*. London, England: Routledge.

Brunsdon, C., 1998. Structure of anxiety: recent British television crime fiction. *Screen*, 39(3), pp. 223–43.

Brunsdon, C., 2013. Television crime series, women police, and fuddy-duddy feminism. *Feminist Media Studies*, 13(3), pp. 375–94.

Cardwell, S., 2007. Is quality television any good? Generic distinctions, evaluations and the troubling matter of critical judgement. In: J. McCabe and K. Akass, eds., 2007. *Quality TV: Contemporary American Television and Beyond*. London, England: I.B. Tauris. pp. 19–34.

Cardwell, S., 2013. Television aesthetics: Stylistic analysis and beyond. In: J. Jacobs and S. Peacock, eds., 2013. *Television Aesthetics and Style*. London, England: Bloomsbury. pp. 23–44.

Cooke, L., 2003. *British Television Drama: A History*. London, England: BFI.

Creeber, G., 2004. *Prime Suspect*. In: G. Creeber, ed. 2004. *Fifty Key Television Programmes*. London, England: Bloomsbury. pp. 159–63.

Danesi, M., 2006. *Brands*. Abingdon, England: Routledge.

Ellis, J., 2011. Interstitials: how the 'Bits in Between' define the programmes. In: P. Grainge, ed. 2011. *Ephemeral Media: Transitory Screen Culture from Television to YouTube*. London, England: BFI. pp. 59–69.

Ellis, J., 2013. The *Broadchurch* case. *Critical Studies in Television Online*, [blog] 26 April. Available at: http://cstonline.tv/broadchurch-case [Accessed 05 May 2013].

Frank, M., 2013. At the intersections of mode, genre and media: a dossier of essays on melodrama. *Criticism*, 55(4), pp. 535–45.

Friedmann, L. M. and Rosen-Zvi, I., 2001. Illegal fictions: mystery novels and the popular image of crime. *University of California at Los Angeles Law Review*, 48, pp. 1411–30.

Garner, R. P., 2013. Renaissance or otherwise?: Broadchurch, ITV's rebranding and imagined audiences. *On/Off Screen: A Communal Academic Blog On International Screen Media*, [blog] 03 May. Available at: https://onoffscreen.wordpress.com/2013/05/03/renaissance-or-otherwise-broadchurch-itvs-rebranding-and-imagined-audiences/ [Accessed 08 April 2015].

Garner, R. P., 2015. Brand reconciliation? A case study of ITV's 2013 rebrand. *Critical Studies in Television: The International Journal of Television Studies*, 10(1), pp. 3–23.

Geraghty, C., 2013. Broadchurch – the pleasures of ordinary television. *Critical Studies in Television Online*, [blog] 10 May. Available at: http://cstonline.tv/broadchurch-pleasures [Accessed 17 May 2013].

Goulding, E. and Fortis, J., 2012. Explosions. Recorded by Ellie Goulding. *Halcyon*. [CD] London, England: Polydor Records.

Gray, J., 2010. *Show Sold Separately: Promos, Spoilers, and Other Media Paratexts*. New York, NY: New York University Press.

Hallam, J., 2011. *Lynda La Plante*. Manchester, England: Manchester University Press.

Hills, M., 2010. *Triumph of a Time Lord: Regenerating Doctor Who in the Twenty-first Century*. London, England: I.B. Tauris.

Huber, A., 2013. Mainstream as metaphor: imagining dominant culture. In: S. Baker, A. Bennett and J. Taylor, eds., 2013. *Redefining Mainstream Popular Music*. London, England: Routledge. pp. 4–13.

ITV plc, 2015. Annual reports and results 2014. [online] Available at: http://www.itvplc.com/investors/reports-and-results [Accessed 08 April 2013].

Jancovich, M. and Hunt, N., 2004. The mainstream, distinction and cult TV. In S. Gwenllian-Jones and R. E. Pearson, eds., 2004. *Cult Television*. Minneapolis. MN: University of Minnesota Press. pp. 27–44.

Jermyn, D., 2003. Women with a mission: Lynda La Plante, DCI Jane Tennison and the reconfiguration of TV crime drama. *International Journal of Cultural Studies*, 6(1), pp. 46–63.

Johnson, C., 2005. *Telefantasy*. London, England: BFI.

Johnson, C., 2012. *Branding Television*. London, England: Routledge.

Johnson, C. and Turnock, R., 2005a. Introduction: approaching the histories of ITV. In: C. Johnson and R. Turnock, eds., 2005. *ITV Cultures: Independent Television Over Fifty Years*. Maidenhead, England: Open University Press. pp. 1–12.

Klein, A. A., 2009. 'The Dickensian aspect': melodrama, viewer engagement and the socially conscious text. In: T. Potter and C. W. Marshall, eds., 2009. *The Wire: Urban Decay and American Television*. New York, NY: Continuum. pp. 177–89.

Mittell, J., 2004. *Genre and Television: From Cop Shows to Cartoons in American Culture*. London, England: Routledge.

Muzellec, L., and Lambkin, M., 2006. Corporate rebranding: destroying, transferring or creating brand equity? *European Journal of Marketing*, 40(7/8), pp. 803–24.

Nelson, R., 2007a. *State of Play: Contemporary 'High-End' TV Drama*. Manchester, England: Manchester University Press.

Nelson, R., 2007b. Quality TV drama: estimations and influences through time and space. In: J. McCabe and K. Akass, eds., 2007. *Quality TV: Contemporary American Television and Beyond*. London, England: I.B. Tauris. pp. 38–51.

Nichols-Pethick, J., 2012. *TV Cops: The Contemporary American Television Police Drama*. London, England: Routledge.

OFCOM, 2012. *OFCOM – Channel Demographics*. [online] Available at: http://stakeholders.ofcom.org.uk/market-data-research/market-data/communications-market-reports/cmr13/tv-audio-visual/uk-2.78 [Accessed 17 December 2014].

OFCOM, 2014. *UK Adults' Media Use and Attitudes: Annex*. [online] Available at: http://stakeholders.ofcom.org.uk/binaries/research/media-literacy/adults-2014/Annex_to_Adults_report_2014.pdf [Accessed 01 July 2015].

Peacock, S., 2011. The impossibility of isolation in *Wallander*. *Critical Studies in Television*, 6(2), pp. 37–46.

Pirrie, J., 2013. *Broadchurch* trailer and billboards. *Pickle Foley*, [blog] 15 February. Available at: http://www.picklefoley.com/tag/broadchurch/ [Accessed 05 May 2013].

Sweney, M., 2012. ITV launches major brand overhaul. *The Guardian*, [online] 16 November. Available at: http://www.guardian.co.uk/media/2012/nov/16/itv-launches-major-brand-overhaul [Accessed 14 June 2013].

Turnbull, S., 2014. *The TV Crime Drama*. Edinburgh, Scotland: Edinburgh University Press.

Thomas, L., 2002. *Fans, Feminisms and 'Quality' Media*. London, England: Routledge.

Wheatley, H., 2004. The limits of television? Natural history programming and the transformation of public service broadcasting. *European Journal of Cultural Studies*, 7(3), pp. 325–39.

10 Bodies of Evidence

European Crime Series, BBC Four and Translating (Global) (In)Justice into (National) Public Service Television Culture

Janet McCabe

'Nothing says "It's Saturday night, it's BBC 4" like the discovery of a muti-lated European teenager', wrote TV critic John Robinson (2011). Foreign language television has not always found sustained distribution in the United Kingdom, but this niche scheduling of subtitled Euro-crime dramas has not only served as a way of recruiting viewers and differentiating the minority digital public service channel within the British TV landscape, but has also offered a particular approach to representing character and the social world in relation to local (in)justice and crime that transcends geographical perim-eters of nation-state borders. Starting with the French police/legal drama *Spiral* (*Engrenages*, 2005–) in 2006 and followed in 2009 by the Swedish *Wallander* (2005–13) starring Krister Henriksson,[1] the Saturday primetime Euro-crime strand quietly consolidated its alternative reputation with the first series of the Danish thriller, *The Killing* (*Forbrydelsen*, 2007), in January 2011. Its success heralded a generic invasion of the type of show that is now 'as integral to the British TV drama landscape as *EastEnders* or *Miss Marple*' (Midgley, 2014). In 2012, Italian *Inspector Montelbano* (*Il commissario Montalbano*, 1999–) and Swedish-Danish co-production, *The Bridge* (*Bron/Broen*, 2011–) arrived on British public service television, after which came the Swedish five-part series *Arne Dahl* (2011, 2015). The year 2014 saw further imports with Belgian thriller serial *Salamander* (2012), Italian period sleuther *Inspector De Luca* (*Il commissario De Luca*, 2008) and Swedish period classic whodunnit *Crimes of Passion* (*Mördaren ljuger inte ensam*, 2013), based on the popular crime novels of Maria Lang; to say nothing of those shows that have come from further afield like the Israeli thriller series, *Hostages* (2013), and Australian political thriller *The Code* (2014). In their own unique way, each crime series has added to the portrayal of what former BBC Four Controller Richard Klein called, 'a social hinterland through the prism of the day-to-day of police investigation' (Seale, 2013).

Locations as captivating as the plots are intricate. Disfigured corpses that speak acutely of an individual's status in the social network. World-weary, deeply flawed heroes/heroines formed by finely drawn environments – in explicit as well as implicit and allegorical ways. Where the search for a serial killer reveals the deep fissures and social dislocation ailing contemporary Western democracies and where resolutions are 'tinged with regret, collat-eral damage and moral compromise' (Robinson, 2011). These characteristics loosely define this group of crime dramas selected to fill the Saturday night primetime BBC Four schedule; and it is a focus on the importance of this sub-genre of police procedurals in European motion in the formation of the BBC as a cultural public sphere that forms the core of my contribution. In looking at how the European crime wave has been used to build the reputation of the minority digital public service channel, I consider how this corpus of TV drama, designed to travel, translates into a repertoire of shared images at the BBC used to intervene into nation-specific debates about jurisdiction and justice within the contemporary age of inter-connected global markets and transnational cultural consumption. This chapter is essentially concerned with *representation*, not only in terms of *social* belonging – *who* is (and is not) represented in the community – but also in relation to *cultural* capital and affinities defining the role of contemporary British public service broadcasting.

Trading Stories/Cultural Flows: Euro-Crime at BBC Four

Any attempt to interpret why these European crime dramas have found such a particular cultural niche on UK public service television must first recognise how these stories speak openly to the ever-increasing interconnectedness of the world. Often set at a border (social, territorial, jurisdictional) and told from a periphery, these narratives entwine pervasive social unease (class and economic inequities) with the new challenges (migration and trafficking, trade and finance, ethnic and racial segregation, pollution and environmental damage) that confront supposedly stable Western democracies as a result of neoliberal, transnational market forces and global communication systems. Familiarity and a sense of proximity related to cross-border generic themes and values are cultivated at the BBC where, as Joseph Straubhaar describes, 'Cultural affinities create forms of cultural capital that inform cultural proximity' (2007, p. 206).

Underlying the cultural rise of the European crime imports is the fact that it might not have happened at all if Sky had not purchased all UK broadcasting rights to US shows produced by AMC, HBO and Showtime. BBC Four, as a consequence, lost *Mad Men* (2007–15) in 2010 after being outbid by the satellite broadcaster, which paid four times as much as the corporation had done previously. 'We're in the process of looking for other things that would sit in that same mould', was Klein's response to the deal (Conlan, 2010). As astounding as is the spending capacity of BSkyB, with Sky Atlantic holding sway over the transmission of HBO originals like *Boardwalk Empire* (2009–14), *Game of Thrones* (2011–) and *Girls* (2012–), BBC Four has also conceived of itself as another kind of exclusive cultural domain. Granted, this is out of commercial necessity; but this sense of institutional self is also prompted by former Conservative Culture Minister Jeremy Hunt, who expressed deep reservations about BBC Four's very existence, saying how it cost 'nearly £100m … to run, but with very, very small audiences' (quoted in Conlan, 2010). As a precarious cultural field, vulnerable to the vicissitudes of governmental intervention and commercial pressures shaping the future of the BBC as a national broadcaster, BBC Four's exclusivity nonetheless appeals directly to a restricted taste culture and to viewers with particular cultural sensibilities. 'It may also be that there's an element of snobbery and slight pretension in our appetite for the Euro cop drama', surmises TV critic Robinson. 'The person entering into a pact with 20 hours of subtitled television hopes to say something about their highbrow nature that someone with a hard drive full of *Midsomer Murders* might not' (2011).[2] What Robinson highlights is what Pierre Bourdieu describes as a restricted field of cultural production, in which a group of individuals shares a set of common assumptions, values and taste preference necessary for identifying particular objects as art; but 'what enables one to distinguish between works of art and simple, ordinary things' (1993, p. 254)? The answer for Bourdieu lies not in the intrinsic worth of an object, but the social field that produces and nurtures belief in its exalted value. 'The art object', he explains, 'is an artifact whose foundation can only be found in an *artworld*, that is, in a social universe that confers upon it the status of a candidate for aesthetic appreciation' (ibid).

In opposition to the premium subscription service held by private corporate power offering a form of gated community based on subscription and the free-market forces of competition, the public service philosophy of the BBC grants open access to a restricted field of cultural production grounded in the very same high (or at least higher) vernacular forms such as international (primarily European) art cinema and literature. In a period of what Georgina Born and Tony Prosser define as 'voracious competition' and 'pronounced entrepreneurialism' (2001, p. 668), this kind of free-to-air minority programming at the BBC heavily invests in, as it reimagines, core Reithian values 'of serving and stimulating the audience, justifying the licence fee, and quality and integrity of output' (2001, p. 669). In this case 'public' is set against the 'private', where culture has become progressively commercialized and collapsed into the market. If, as ex-Liberal Democrat culture spokesman Don Foster said, 'BBC4 is the BBC at its best, supporting riskier, lesser known projects that would otherwise struggle to find airtime' (Conlan, 2010), then the way in which the channel has been able to bring to the fore little known, or so-called 'marginal' television from the global media landscape and give it a primetime visibility – Saturday evenings at 9pm – speaks directly to how channel identity is *legitimised* through being accountable to a *national* public rather than *global* capital. In these conditions, the cultural and institutional power of the corporation reverses dominant (American) media flows and speaks instead to a new regional media cartography. Another way to thus see the cultural proximity involved in the circulation of these police procedurals from the various corners of Europe is what the BBC believes it is delivering with these series; namely, a democratizing cultural experience involving global media flows as a form of cultural capital, taste preference and public debate.

'Passion, purpose and proposition' proved Richard Klein's programming mantra on his arrival at BBC Four in December 2008. As a minority digital channel, BBC Four is positioned to pursue innovation in a way that the main channels will not. 'We do big subjects in a niche or authored way', declared Klein. 'There's a popular subject that you would expect on BBC1 or ITV. BBC4 could do it but I think we'd do it in a very distinctive way, and I think it could be as controversial or provocative ...' (Rushton, 2009, p. 28). Early in 2011, for example, the channel programmed a themed season on justice. 'Asking what is justice in the 21st-century, everything from the criminal sense of justice through to asking what is a just world, almost a "big society", if you like' (Klein in Conlan, 2010). This sense of debating the ethics of an issue that does not stop at the borders of territorial state, yet formulated within a national media, motivated by a sense of service to the public, recalls contemporary public-sphere theory (Habermas, 1989, 1996; Fraser, 2014; Couldry, 2014). Enclosed within a national broadcasting infrastructure aiming to enrich the fabric of public debate at a local level sees BBC Four reframing European series like *Inspector Montalbano*, *Salamander* and *Crimes of Passion* to *re-form*, in the words of Nick Couldry, 'national and local citizens into a larger group of actors with a sensitivity to transnational processes and demands' (2014, p. 53).

Look, for example, at how Richard Klein talks about his approach to programming at the digital channel: 'We are different from virtually every other digital channel because we don't strip and strand. *We curate moments and seasons and ideas.* We apply a lens to a subject matter, and through that lens you will see subject matter in a different way' (Rushton, 2009, p. 28; emphasis mine). More than scheduling, Klein champions the idea of BBC Four as a curator of culture and public intellectual life, open to alternative approaches and staging pertinent debates for our time. Talking about curating 'moments and seasons and ideas' immediately implies a particular kind of cultural sensibility, which defines the relationship between audience and the broadcaster. It speaks to a way in which the television 'curator' intervenes and compiles a package of programming that actively facilitates, what Laura Marks describes as an 'interaction between works and the audience to unfold' (2004, p. 38). BBC Four has not conceived of any new markers for defining public debate and doubtless has not discovered any new ones. But it has, nevertheless, initiated new ways of thinking about and comprehending what a national public service delivery might look and 'feel' like at the BBC at a time when the corporation has increasingly been forced to redefine its role and purpose, 'adjusting old policies for new market-based solutions and consumer-oriented thinking' (Born, 2005, p. 68).

Such thinking helps to elucidate further how the asymmetrical cultural flows and contemporary power relations between public service and commercial television are being articulated at the site of culture, cultural legitimisation and the pursuit of innovation. BBC Four as a cultural intermediary, and supported by a network of critics, public intellectuals and scholars, is validated through these intraregional cultural flows. This happens not only in terms of selecting and buying generic pieces of television from relatively new (or at least traditionally unfamiliar) TV territories as a means of adjusting, what former BBC Four Editor Cassian Harrison called, 'the pitch, tone and content from business as usual' (Kanter, 2014); but also legitimisation is revealed in and through the corporate affiliations and entwined values shared with other European public service broadcasters. Choosing a range of police procedurals, a familiar genre but resituated within different European locations, further emphasises the way in which this type of television engages actively in public debate about the nation and what it stands for as a society, global progress and what that means for rights and representation at the local level. What BBC Four presents in its curated schedule is a de-centring and reforming of a popular generic form characterised by social commentary. Othered by linguistic difference (with subtitles) and a strong sense of place and rootedness, these series are presented as offering different approaches to the same questions about criminal justice and the law, but existing in a shared public sphere determined to advance debate, namely: BBC Four.

This idea of how we think about society, so central to series like *The Killing*, *The Bridge* and *Spiral*, dialogues to a large extent with how the BBC makes sense of its public service enterprise. With the 'Martin Beck' series, created in 1965 by two Swedish crime writers from the political left, Maj Sjöwall and Per Wahlöö, the police procedural has long been associated with social critique as the form explores the moral dimension of democratic politics. How this sub-genre entwines realism with its political agenda has subsequently made it an ideal form for public service broadcasters charged with speaking to, and on behalf of, the nation.[3] Just as the *Wallander* stories (both the Swedish series with Henriksson and the original set of TV films featuring Rolf Lassgård) deliver a nation-specific response to shifts in Swedish society and its commitment to democratic principles, social welfare and human rights in relation to cultures of globalisation and neo-liberal market forces, similar forces are at work within the social, political and ethical character of the BBC. What is activated in and through the purchase and scheduling/curating of this sub-genre in European motion is a set of assumptions, attitudes, ideas, values and judgements about the cultural importance of BBC Four as a public body. Concealed in a tenacious rhetoric about the universality of culture, modern citizenship and importance of serving the nation, and in and through the *local* encounter with 'new' *global* stories, BBC Four uses these European dramas, not only in terms of what Bourdieu calls *symbolic* capital as prestige accumulates around the acquisitions, but also as a form of knowledge to legitimise its cultural role in that process.

(In)Justice in a Borderless World

Generic Public Stories/In-between Spaces and Identities

These generic stories from around Europe more often than not deal with the in-between-ness of identities, affiliations and experiences *behind* and *beyond* borders as a condition of living in an increasingly globalised, trans-border and transnational world. Yet the way in which these various investigative tales of crime and punishment (or not) are curated on BBC Four affects both how those stories are received, but also how they mediate a bigger picture in which local, national, intraregional and global questions of legality will inevitably be weighed. With illegality and justice negotiated at specific national levels – France, Sweden, Denmark, Belgium or Italy – the in-between-ness between these different nation-specific approaches to law and order adds fresh perspectives and additional moral and ethical dimensions for the sub-genre circulating on British public service television. It is plausible to speak of international, perhaps global stories based on widely shared beliefs and commitment to human rights and democratic values, but where the contestation of those experiences in terms of social *belonging* and other affiliations (family and community obligations), who gets representation and who is denied its possibility, are played out in delimited territories and among nation-specific social and local cultural groupings. The different legal zones represented in the BBC Four Euro-crime strand are revealed as similar enough, where nuance rather than profound difference emerges. This curated schedule uses the sub-genre to intervene into public opinion, to challenge and provoke a broader debate about national and international law and human rights – or as David Held describes it, 'the space between domestic law which regulates the relationship between a state and its citizens, and traditional international law which applies primarily to states and interstate relations' (2008, p. 159).

Conceptualisations of cultural proximity and shareability take on supplementary meaning when we consider how these police procedurals from Europe often deal with states of statelessness – stateless individuals (itinerant workers, asylum seekers, refugees), terrorism (cyber, religious, economic), environmentalism and the state of the planet, and criminal gangs and international smugglers, supranational agencies and transnational corporations with interests far beyond the national perimeter. What lurks in the dark shadows of a global, neo-liberal ambition for a 'world without borders' is what Homi K. Bhabha insightfully describes as 'a complex and contradictory mode of being or surviving somewhere in between legality and incivility' (2008, p. 39). These 'no-man's land' stories of crime and punishment (often evaded) are ones routinely traded across territorial borders. In recognising the new transnationalism of crime, and with a brief to address 'all kinds of heavy-cross-border criminality', the *Arne Dahl* series, for example, literally moves its Swedish detectives out of the nation-bounded police precinct and into the Europol headquarters in The Hague, to create what Kerstin Bergman calls 'a truly European crime series' (2014, p. 21). Where *Arne Dahl* departs from the other series like *Wallander* or *Inspector Montalbano* is in how this series, like the books, 'favors a more civic sense of European identity.' This is literally embodied in the Opcop team, composed of detectives from across Europe, as they investigate an international paedophile ring ('To The Top of the Mountain', Parts One and Two) or the Italian Mafia

('Europa Blue', Parts One and Two), and untangle webs of corruption that stretch far beyond the European continent.

The Euro-crime sub-genre in motion often explores the implications for national law enforcement agencies when a supranational organisation, like an international peace or security alliance, becomes entangled in local crime. Season 2 of *The Killing*, for example, begins with the brutal murder of lawyer Anne Dragsholm (Sarah Gottlieb). Working as a passport officer in the southernmost Danish seaport of Gedser on the Baltic, which services various European routes, and with her reputation for stepping across various jurisdictions, DCI Sarah Lund (Sofie Gråbøl), in her raggedy knitwear, is recalled to Copenhagen to investigate. Politics, society and the law become deeply entangled and profoundly structure a narrative that demands moral resolution for victims and witnesses, but also openly questions the ability (or not) of a so-called stable Western nation to uphold its commitment to democratic principles at a time when affiliations and reputation extend beyond borders. As Lund investigates, her inquiries parallel those of Thomas Buch (Nicolas Bro), the newly appointed Minister of Justice, who suspects his predecessor of covering-up an international war crime. Lund eventually travels to Helmand, where she uncovers the truth about the indiscriminate slaughter of innocent Afghan women and children by a unit of Danish soldiers under rogue command and the subsequent suppression by a government desperate to protect its military funding and international reputation as a peace-keeping force. Ambivalence and ethical thinking are introduced as the series explores how the very foundations of a fair, humane and decent society are compromised *internally*, because of the failures of assimilation and multicultural policies, and *externally*, as a result of the international 'war on terror' and the backlash it has sparked.

Claims for recognition of a crime, and the subsequent conspiracies of silence, emerge as key generic elements of these dramas, staging and resolving contests of representation, namely: who belongs *inside* power and who does not, who defines who gets justice and who does not. The main instigator of the barbarism in Afghanistan is none other than Lund's partner and would-be lover, Detective Inspector Ulrik Strange (Mikael Birkkjær). But with the reputation of an entire nation at stake, no formal action will be taken. Revealed is how these Euro-crime series wrestle with the role of narrative in ethical thinking; how to tell stories of barbaric acts where power is safeguarded and the struggle for a democratic culture involves universal principles of liberty, human rights and the rule of law with the constitutional obligation to protect the rights and freedoms of its own citizens. Is the brutal slaughter of innocent, but unknown, women and children from somewhere else in the world the collateral for preserving the foundations of a fair, equal and humane society at home, especially if there is an election on the horizon? If the true price of social democracy is silence (Buch takes up his new position in government as the price for his), then the narrative charges Lund with the task of dispensing a moral justice, alone and at night.

'I've got away with worse', Strange tells her as he discharges bullets into her body. Seemingly to rise from the dead Lund inflicts retributive violence, firing not once, but a magazine of ammunition into his body. Justice may be done, but 'officially' Strange has got away with his heinous crimes and Lund is left to wander into the dark night alone.

Similar issues are at play in the Belgian thriller, *Salamander*. Old-school detective Paul Gerardi (Filip Peeters) is charged with investigating the theft of 66 private safety deposit boxes, only to uncover a cabal consisting of the country's leading judicial, industrial, financial and political figures whose collective secrets could undermine the social project of the nation. As with Lund, Gerardi pays a high personal price for demanding recognition and seeking retribution for crimes involving power that cannot be adequately grasped, and leaking across some other kind of border (social, political, geographical) with respect to justice. The ethical role of the investigator is to expose hypocrisies of power and hold it to account (however terrifying), while at the same time deprived of the possibility of a justice that eludes both formal domestic and international legal systems. Such a narrative mechanism has the effect of destablising power and questioning the democratic values of Western nations shaped by a commitment to other principles that routinely overflow its borders – and therefore prompts us to change the way we think about the law and social justice.

This gesture of narrative ambivalence extends to stories about global crime, questions of jurisdiction and how to patrol imaginary, often borderless spaces. It features strongly in these European crime series as a way of exploring how national economies are often subject to transnational corporations and supranational agencies, like the European Central Bank, beyond the reach of individual state democracies. Some acts of injustice carried out in a globalised world are inherently non-territorial in nature. These crimes are committed in borderless spaces beyond the legal jurisdiction of any one, single constitutional democracy, but at the same time are deeply implicated in the structural control and organisation of national economies now subject to transnational corporations and global financial markets. In the third, and final, instalment of *The Killing* the kidnap of Emilie Zeuthen (Kaya Fjeldsted), the child of billionaire business tycoon Robert Zeuthen (Anders W. Berthelsen), forms the dramatic centre of a story about an international financial corporation entwined with a national government dealing with an economic crisis. *Global* neo-liberal market impulses have *national* ethical implications, contributing to a vocabulary of these series that specifically defines who is the victim – who is the true casualty of crime – and who does (and does not) get *representation* and justice.

Questions of protection, citizenship and civic participation and how to police the insider/outsider status of itinerant labour and immigrants, both legal and illegal, is another common generic feature of these police procedures from Europe. Characters, strongly marked by ethnicity and racial difference, profoundly define the ethical thinking and morality of their respective communities, and are often most vulnerable *to* and *in* the law. Stories involving local minorities or global migrants address local claims to freedom, equality and rights to justice, as evocatively described by Bhabha, 'connected with cultural differences and social discrimination – the problems of inclusion and exclusion, dignity and humiliation, respect and repudiation' (2004, p. xvii). Put another way, the function of characters that occupy 'the space of flows' is to test social democratic principles of integration and citizenship. In series 4 of *Spiral*, for example, lawyer Joséphine Karlsson (Audrey Fleurot) finds herself in perilous waters when she takes up the case of undocumented immigrants. Earlier in series 2, the team, led by Captain Laure Berthaud (Caroline Proust), gets embroiled in drug trafficking and gang culture in the Parisian *banlieue*, following the death of a dealer. North African Samy (Samir Boitard) arrives from Special Branch to aid the investigation into the Larbi crime family (also of North African descent), only to find his own identity compromised.

Neither at the centre of the narrative nor at the periphery, these ethnically defined characters speak in the midst of unresolved debates regarding minorities and social membership, civic participation and national citizenry. A sense of divided loyalties and deeper affiliations (religious, cultural, community) hovering in the European social imagination is translated by the genre into a narrative precarity, rendering these characters prone to suspicion and vulnerable to what Nancy Fraser describes as, 'disputes about *who* should count as a member and *which* is the relevant community' (2013, p. 192). Whereas each of the Euro-crime series touch in one way or another on issues of migratory movements and social belonging, tolerance and racism (particularly Islamophobia) lurking in the collective secular psyche of Western European democracies, a good example can found be in the first season of *The Killing* involving Rahman 'Rama' Al-Kemal (Farshad Kholghi), a suspect in the murder of Nanna Birk Larsen (Julie R. Ølgaard) and her teacher at Frederiksholm College. Suspicion falls on him when he cannot explain his whereabouts on the night of her disappearance. However, local politicians seize on this apparent 'guilt' for the purposes of winning a local mayoral election. Danish, but a Muslim from an immigrant background, Rama is one of Troels Hartmann's (played by Lars Mikkelsen) community role models. The scheme is an important plank in Hartmann's social integration policy, central to his mayoral campaign and political ambitions. Pressure is placed on Troels to distance himself from Rama once the media get hold of the story. 'Any press material on immigrants will be recalled', Hartmann is advised (series 1, episode 6). The evidence may be circumstantial, but the *mis*framing of Rama serves to perpetuate pervasive social anxieties about criminality, immigrants and the failure of social integration policies. Political rival Poul Bremer (Bent Mejding) wastes no time in making political capital during a TV debate with Hartmann. He may claim that his 'role models' are making a real difference in reducing crime amongst immigrants, but the argument is lost with the media-friendly sound-bite from his opponent: 'a thief catching a thief' (series 1, episode 6). Political machinations of power *mis*frame Rama, removing him from visible bourgeois spaces (classroom) and into the unseen urban periphery (underground car parks, dark and rain-sodden dockyards). It *mis*represents him as his status slips far too easily from respectable teacher to fugitive, a symptom of Denmark's broken borders and fractured communities. The final *mis*framing is captured briefly on the TV news, as a report on his guilt segues into the announcer saying, 'Now to Iraq.' Paralleling the politics is the investigation, which finds Lund and her partner Jan Meyer (Søren Malling) questioning a local imam (Kadim Faraj). Casual racism (Meyer's comment about Lund wearing a burka) and cursory ignorance (a failure to remove shoes) define the uneasy encounter. Slight, where no offence is acknowledged, speaks to the textual grammar determining injustice as both cultural and social. Such framing of Rama and assumptions of guilt result in Theis Birk Larsen (Bjarne Henriksen) taking matters into his own hands; and Theis, along with Vagn Skærbæk (Nicolaj Koperniku), who is the real culprit, brutally assault Rama until interrupted by the police. Theis is arrested, but Rama decides not to press charges despite sustaining horrific injuries. In such a case, juridical resolution – Rama's decision not to take the matter further and go to court – raises the uneasy spectre of discrimination within the territorial state.

Rama is eventually cleared after his 'accomplice' Mustafa Akkah (Jali Kazim) confirms his alibi. Still, not before language, miscommunication and misrecognition lead to further confusion over which claims to justice and representation matter most. 'She was ill and could hardly walk', Mustafa admits in Arabic, his words translated by a female wearing a headscarf, but also in the subtitles for the English-speaking audience. It quickly becomes apparent that the 'she' to whom Mustafa refers is not Nanna at all, but a young Muslim girl called Leyla, who Jamal Rama is helping to flee an arranged marriage. So fixated on what has happened to Nanna that the fate of this other woman, sensing she had no other option than to be ferried silently out of her close community, remains largely hidden from view. Her disquieting decision speaks to how societies draw boundaries around representation and justice in such a way as to make some people more vulnerable and beyond the rule of law. Systems of alliance shaping *mis*representation, from the familial (a girl 'feeling' forced into marriage/a girl 'belonging' to a religious community) to the overtly political, are themes running through *The Killing*, but also explored in other series like *The Bridge* and *Wallander*.

Sexuality, and the politics of the female body *as* victim, emerge within this sub-genre, reframing feminist debate and altering how we might argue about gender and sexual politics in our continued age of troubled emancipation (McCabe, 2015, pp. 29–43). Common to crime fiction from this region of northern Europe[4] is how narratives shift from a detailed account of a lone male abusing a woman (often violently) into arenas where institutions and the state perpetuate, or even support, insidious abuses against women. In the course of an investigation, and in particular how the narrative unfurls at such a slow and steady pace, Euro-crime TV drama inherits this textual strategy and finds a generic grammar for exploring social justice and how this theme more often than not gets mapped across a female body. The first series of *Spiral*, for example, begins with the gruesome discovery of a young woman's body discarded on a Parisian rubbish dump. Her face is eradicated: as the cogs of the French justice system grind into gear, her Romanian identity and past life are slowly uncovered. Coiled around this investigation is a wider network of corruption, which is revealed to touch the lives of all those uncovering the truth about what has happened to this woman. Violence is a collective, as well as an individual act, and these series set out to directly address how society is implicated. How violence stems from structural injustice, but also how it sustains those inequalities as well as the response to the contemporary challenges of it.

The Bridge is probably the best example of what I mean here. It starts with a female corpse placed precisely in the middle of the Øresund Bridge, on the border connecting the Swedish industrial city of Malmö (and regional centre of Skåne) with the Danish capital of Copenhagen, where two jurisdictions run 'directly through the fabric of the female body. It is the (ob)scene of the border, disconnecting and disconcerting, engaging with intimate geographies of female bodies' (McCabe, 2015a, p. 37). It quickly emerges that the body is not one, but two, with the recognisable top half belonging to a prominent and respected (Swedish) politician matched with the unidentified legs of a (Danish) prostitute. Series 1 may draw political spaces and territorial lines of justice quite literally through the female body, but the sexual politics of series like *Wallander*, *Arne Dahl* and *Spiral* with their diverse settings time and again reveal the reproductive function of the female body *as* representation makes visible an entire catalogue of social justice – poverty, drug addiction, homelessness, human trafficking and prostitution. A new and uneasy sense of vulnerability starts to emerge, with gendered and sexual inequalities subject to new flows that show little or no regard for borders, through smuggling and international trade, cyber-technologies and global communications.

The TV detective has long proved a highly potent national symbol. Traditionally they have been primarily a local affair, emblems of an individual state territory and differentiating broadcasting nations of the world. How the detective is rooted within borders of local jurisdiction has become intensified in recent times, where landscapes of social belonging (or not) entwine with a strong sense of place. Sicilian-based detective stories featuring Inspector Salvo Montalbano (Luca Zingaretti) are set in an ancient rural landscape of gnarled olive trees and dry-stone walls, located between the fictional town of Vigàta, with its honey-coloured sandstone buildings and Baroque palazzos, and the azure of the Mediterranean. This vivid sense of location has prompted a wave of British tourism to places like Punta Secca and the seafront of Cafalu in Sicily, rural regions such as Bergslagen (*Crimes of Passion*) or cities like Ystad (*Wallander*) and Malmö (*The*

Bridge) in Sweden, lured by the promise of these fictional worlds. Global stories are prompting global travel, but imagined spaces no longer have to be imagined but instead experienced; and this walking in the footsteps of fictional characters, physically mapping out of the public's spaces of crime and punishment, and seeing it for ourselves, contributes further to questions of cultural proximity and shareability that reformulates our sense of the fabric of transnational spaces and local public spheres. Extending Steven Peacock's remark about Ystad as 'no longer on the outskirts of something, but everywhere is now part of a global hinterland' (2014, p. 112), this sense of being here and there has become a central appeal of these European crime series at the BBC.

Concluding Remarks

This chapter in many ways responds to Nick Couldry's (2014) call for how 'we can investigate, first, how transnationalizing pressures might be more adequately addressed in public spheres on every level (including local and national), and second, whether an eventual "transnational public sphere" might be better understood not as a single thing, but as the networked result-ant of transformation at multiple levels' (2014, p. 45). For one thing, the trend for these travelling narratives has prompted further movement. The specificity of the televisual form – its stories, narrative structure and generic form, for example, is designed for contemporary media flows, not only for distribution in television markets around the world, but also for circulation through formatting and the format trade. Crimes committed on the Øresund Bridge have been rerouted onto the Bridge of the Americas that serves as the crossing between El Paso, in Texas, and Ciudad Juárez, Chihuahua in the US version of *The Bridge* (2013–), as well as into the Euro Tunnel link-ing northern France with Kent in southern Britain in *The Tunnel* (2013–). As for *Wallander*, the BBC has its own version of the maverick detective, with Kenneth Branagh taking the lead role in the BBC One primetime series (2008–), which exists alongside both the Swedish versions, one starring Kris-ter Henriksson and the other Rolf Lassgård, within the UK media ecology. Each text compliments the next, stripped across different BBC platforms as these different *Wallanders* make important statements about the UK national broadcaster as a purveyor of public culture (McCabe, 2015b). Yet, in how these various versions talk to each other facilitates a rethink for a globalised world of increased complexity as the buying and scheduling of these dramas from here and there reformulate public opinion of such matters.

Of course, the police procedural vernacular of this sub-genre is one with which British television is already familiar. Dramas like *Inspector Morse* (1987–2000) and *Foyle's War* (2002–15) share with their European counter-parts an intense local sense of place and social justice where the killer often originates from inside the local community. Yet what the European crime dramas add is an alternative perspective thanks to a heightened awareness of transnational issues – trade and finance, human rights and trafficking, migration and the environment; and how issues that transcend traditional state borders cannot help but trouble and reframe the 'how' and the 'who' of the law and social justice, with implications for democratic societies where justice is (or not) dispensed at a local level.

Let me conclude by reiterating how this sub-genre of the police procedural has been curated at BBC Four. The decision to include subtitled series from Europe was no doubt in response to the changing UK television landscape in the late-2000s, in which, as Georgina Born highlights, 'neo-liberal economic reforms ... swept over the British media and Britain's public sector institutions – including the BBC' (2006, p. 691). Still, the choice of subtitling, rather than dubbing, proves instructive, in that these series retain the audible trace of their country of origin. Public debate about law and order is conducted in the national language with English translation. Insofar as language has the potential to compromise clarity, this multilingual public sphere speaks to the promise of transnationalising the national. What results is no singular shared linguistic medium of communication, but with the two languages (local and translated) operating in tandem, these European dramas in motion speak directly to the increased complicity that conditions public debate in the transnational age.

Notes

1. Although *Wallander* aired regularly from July 2009, the first UK broadcast was Saturday 6 December 2008, at 10pm.
2. Continuing, Robinson notes: 'Though, interestingly, the converse may be true abroad, where – retitled *Barnaby* –*Midsomer* is syndicated to a vast worldwide audience' (2011). The point is well made in terms of how television texts are culturally reclaimed and reimagined as a show moves from one territory to another and it is an issue which Mary F. Brewer considers in this volume in her analysis of the appeal of *Poirot* (1989–2013) to viewers in the United States.
3. Recently, the BBC adapted the series for radio under the rubric of *The Martin Beck Killings* (2012–13).
4. Examples include Stieg Larsson's *Millennium* trilogy and *Miss Smilla's Feeling for Snow* (Høeg, 1993).

References

BBC Trust. 2011. *Delivering Quality First Proposal* [online]. Available at: http://downloads.bbc.co.uk/aboutthebbc/reports/pdf/dqf_detailedproposals.pdf. [Accessed March 9, 2015].

Bergman, K., 2014. Beyond national allegory: Europeanization in Swedish crime writer Arne Dahl's *Viskleken*. *Clues*, 32(2), Fall, pp. 20–9.

Bhabha, H. K., 1994. *The Location of Culture*. 2004. New York, NY: Routledge Classics.

Bhabha, H. K., 2008. Notes on globalisation and ambivalence. In: D. Held and H. L. Moore, eds., 2008. *Cultural Politics in a Global Age: Uncertainty, Solidarity, and Innovation*, Oxford, England: Oneworld Publications. Ch. 3.

Born, G., 2008. Trying to intervene: British media research and the framing of policy debate. *International Journal of Communication*, 2, pp. 691–98.

Born, G., 2004. *Uncertain Vision: Birt, Dyke and the Reinvention of the BBC*. 2005. London, England: Vintage.

Born, G. and Prosser. T., 2001. Culture and consumerism: citizenship, public service broadcasting and the BBC's fair trading obligations. *The Modern Law Review*, 64(2), September, pp. 657–87.

Bourdieu, P., 1993. *The Field of Cultural Production: Essays on Art and Literature*. London, England: Polity Press.

Bourdieu, P., 1984. *Distinction: A Social Critique of the Judgement of Taste*. Translated by Richard Nice. Cambridge, MA: Harvard University Press.

Conlan, T., 2010. Richard Klein on why BBC4 is the corporation's best-loved channel. *The Guardian*, [online] 11 October. Available at: http://www.theguardian.com/media/2010/oct/11/richard-klein-bbc4-controller [Accessed 12 May 2015].

Couldry, N. 2014. What and where is the transnationalized public sphere? In: K. Nash, ed., 2014. *Transnationalizing the Public Sphere*. Cambridge, England: Polity. Ch. 2.

Fraser, N., 2013. *Fortunes of Feminism: From State-Managed Capitalism to Neoliberal Crisis*. London, England: Verso.

Fraser, N., 2014. Transnationalizing the public sphere: on the legitimacy and efficacy of public opinion in a post-Westphalian world. In: K. Nash, ed., 2014. *Transnationalizing the Public Sphere*. Cambridge, England: Polity. Ch. 1.

Habermas, J., 1989. *The Structural Transformation of the Public Sphere: An Inquiry into a Category of Bourgeois Society*. Translated by Thomas Burger with Frederick Lawrence. Cambridge, England: Polity.

Habermas, J., 1996. *Between Facts and Norms: Contributions to a Discourse Theory of Law and Democracy*. Translated by William Rehg. Cambridge, England: Polity.

Held, D., 2008. Cultural diversity, cosmopolitan principles and the limits of sovereignty. In: D. Held and H. L. Moore, eds., 2008. *Cultural Politics in a Global Age: Uncertainty, Solidarity, and Innovation*. Oxford, England: Oneworld Publications. Ch. 16.

Høeg, P., 1993. *Miss Smilla's Feeling for Snow*. Translated by Felicity David. London, England: The Harvill Press.

Kanter, J.2014. Cassian Harrison, BBC 4. The Broadcast Interview. *Broadcast*, 13 March 2014.

McCabe, J., 2015a. Disconnected heroines, icy intelligence: reframing feminism(s) and feminist identities at the borders involving the isolated female TV detective in Scandinavian noir. In: L. Mulvey and A. Backman Rogers, eds., 2015. *Feminisms: Diversity, Difference and Multiplicity in Contemporary Film Cultures*. Amsterdam, the Netherlands: Amsterdam University Press. Ch. 1.

McCabe, J., 2015b. Appreciating *Wallander* at the BBC: producing culture and performing the glocal in the UK and Swedish *Wallanders* for British public service television. *Continuum: Journal of Media and Cultural Studies*, 29(5), pp. 755–768.

Marks, L., 2004. The ethical presenter: or how to have good arguments over dinner. *The Moving Image*, 4(2) Spring, pp. 34–47.

Midgley, N., 2014. How British television fell under the spell of Nordic noir. *The Telegraph*, [online] 28 March. Available at: http://www.telegraph.co.uk/culture/tvandradio/tv-and-radio-reviews/10724864/

How-British-television-fell-under-the-spell-of-Nordic-noirThe-Tu.html [Accessed 30 April 2015].

Peacock, S., 2014. *Swedish Crime Fiction: Novel, Film, Television*. Manchester, England: Manchester University Press.

Robinson, J., 2011. Will *Spiral* become your new favourite Saturday night Euro cop drama? *The Guardian*, [online] 1 April. Available at: http://www.theguardian.com/tv-and-radio/2011/apr/01/spiral-the-killing-bbc4 [Accessed 27 April 2015].

Rushton, K., 2009. Culture, class, controversy. The broadcast interview. *Broadcast*, 21 Aug., pp. 28–9.

Seale, J., 2013. BBC4 buys new Swedish and Italian dramas. *Radio Times*, [online] 11 March. Available at: http://www.radiotimes.com/news/2013-03-11/bbc4-buys-new-swedish-and-italian-dramas [Accessed 27 April 2015].

Strauhbaar, J., 2007. *World Television: From Global to Local*. Los Angeles, CA: Sage Publications.

11 Exporting Englishness
ITV's *Poirot*

Mary F. Brewer

Introduction

Former Director of Global Distribution at ITV Studios, Tobi de Graaf describes *Poirot* as just the kind of programme international buyers want because it represents a 'safe bet' (Fry, 2009). This chapter explores why *Poirot* represents a 'safe bet' for programmers in Britain and its biggest export market, the United States. In tandem with analyses of key themes in a selection of episodes, and the style in which Christie's stories have been adapted, I explore *Poirot* within the context of the English Heritage industry. I consider how the programme's success relates to the export of a nostalgic brand of Englishness and what this reveals about shared values between England and America in a cultural and ideological sense. Although much recent critical attention (including in this volume) focuses on novel treatments of the crime genre, *Poirot* exemplifies how some of the most popular and profitable examples are mainstream and fit within the conservative period mystery genre.

'Ratings Warhorse'

In 2012 Elizabeth Jensen, in *The New York Times*, declared: 'America is having a love affair with British drama and mystery' – an assertion based on the popularity of the Public Broadcasting System's (PBS) *Masterpiece* series (1971–), the longest running prime-time drama series on American TV, which offers a range of British productions.[1] As part of its *Mystery!* franchise, *Poirot* is screened in conjunction with other ITV productions including *Endeavour* (2013–), *Foyle's War* (2002–15), *Lewis* (2006–) and *Marple* (2004–13).

Agatha Christie's Poirot[2] premiered on 8 January 1989, and it has enjoyed remarkable longevity, ending its 24 year run on 13 November 2013 when *Curtain: Poirot's Last Case* was screened.[3] Its 70 episodes, divided into 13 series, exhausted Christie's catalogue of short stories and novels featuring the Belgian sleuth in a mixture of 50-minute and feature-length episodes. In March 2011, though, it appeared that *Poirot* had reached its end, when ITV announced its cancellation as part of a cost-cutting exercise (Holmwood, 2011). Production costs were considerable; IMDb estimates the budget for one feature length episode, *Death on the Nile* (2004, season 9, episode 3), at 2 million pounds (2004). Nevertheless, the decision was unusual given *Poirot*'s consistent ratings success and the home advertising revenue and foreign sales that it regularly generated. In the domestic market, well into its second decade, *Poirot* remained able to dominate the ratings in an increasingly competitive multichannel market. In 2003, Gareth McLean described the show as a 'ratings warhorse', commenting on the timeliness of its return in *Five Little Pigs* (2003, season 9, episode 1) given the overall failure of ITV1's contemporary drama season.

By November 2011, *Poirot* had won a reprieve: ITV reversed its decision to 'bump off' its most famous detective, and instead commissioned feature-length adaptations of the five Christie novels yet to be filmed (*Radio Times*, 2011). The show's domestic success cannot be discounted here. In January 2006, *The Mystery of the Blue Train* (season 10, episode 1) out-performed the BBC's Oscar-winning *Chicago*, attracting 7.4 million viewers (Tryhorn, 2006). In 2009, the series was one of two ITV3 programmes to draw audiences of over 1 million (ITV, 2009). However, overseas profits might have counted even more strongly in its favour. As Ruth McElroy's 'Introduction' to this collection records, exports figure as UK commercial television's largest income stream, with crime/mystery drama counting among the most lucrative of finished television exports. However, Simone Knox explains, in some cases British drama is not 'simply being exported', but being 'produced to be exported and exportable in a global marketplace' (2012, p. 43). Hence, the kind of programmes British television can produce, particularly ITV which relies so heavily upon exports, is increasingly influenced by what American networks in particular will buy and, in the case of PBS, what its corporate sponsors are willing to subsidise.

Since its inception, *Poirot* has proven one of the most successful of UK export products. It helped ITV open new territory in Europe when it was sold to an Italian network, thus 'breaking the unwritten rule that Italy is a territory which won't buy UK period drama' (Broadcast, 2003a). *Poirot*, alongside *Marple*, was the lead draw in Granada International's sales to ABC Asia in 2004 (Broadcast, 2004). Indeed, it seemed that anywhere the little Belgian detective travelled, tall profits were sure to follow. In 2003, *Poirot* was sold throughout the Middle East, including to Bahraini, Iranian, and Saudi TV (Broadcast, 2003b). In 2005, 'Chinese broadcasters' appetite for classic UK drama ... helped Granada International secure five new deals in the territory' (Broadcast, 2005). Christie's undoubted enormous readership has made her writing a particular favourite for adaptation to TV and film,[4] but the success of ITV's adaptations has created a reciprocal commercial relationship, one whereby the adaptations are now feeding the success of Christie's originals. Harper Collins, which produces a series of Christie novels designed to be used in English language teaching, attributes their huge appeal partly to the TV adaptations (Garner, 2012).

By 2009, *Poirot* was pre-eminent among UK exports, with Noel Hedges, head of drama at ITV Global Entertainment, reporting sales to more than '180 territories' (Hurrell, 2009). However, the United States remains the single largest market (Broadcast, 2006b), where *Poirot* has been shown on the Arts and Entertainment Network (A&E), a cable and satellite channel established in 1984 as a commercial counterpart to public television. By the mid-1990s, A&E reached '69.5 million subscribers in the U.S. and Canada, representing close to 66% penetration in the U.S.' (A&E, 1996), giving *Poirot* exposure to a substantial segment of the pay TV market. However, *Poirot* has gained its largest share of American viewers through its screening by PBS and its over 350 affiliate stations across the country, where the show has been a flagship title since 1990. Henry Chu cites average audiences of 5 million and a 'national rating about 80 per cent higher than the public network's prime-time average' (2013). PBS receives limited congressional funds and thus relies heavily on viewer donations to purchase rights to expensive UK programmes. *Poirot* has been core to PBS's 'pledge schedule', attracting high levels of revenue from private donors (Sefton, 2014), and though PBS is commercial free, its programmes are underwritten by corporations who seek to increase the value of their own brand by associating it with another quality brand. *Poirot* was among the catalogue of British programmes that enabled Acorn Media to defy the downward trend for home video sales in the United States (Jensen, 2012). Recognising its commercial value, in 2012, Acorn acquired 64 per cent of the Christie literary estate, making it the majority owner of her novels, plays, and their TV adaptations (Wagner, 2012). In 2014, the company exercised its exclusive option to bar PBS from screening the final three episodes of *Poirot*, which could be seen only on Acorn TV, the first service to offer streaming of the series in North America (RLJ Entertainment, 2014).

Stylish Whodunnits: *Poirot* as Incarnation of Edwardian England

One element that makes ITV's *Poirot* stand out from other adaptations is the series' heightened degree of fidelity to Christie's vision of the central character and his world.[5] Throughout its run, Poirot was played by David Suchet, who recounts reading every story and novel featuring the character in preparation for the role. Suchet records his goal of portraying 'Poirot exactly as Christie wrote of him, right down to the smallest detail' (Dillin, 1992). He describes resisting attempts over the years by scriptwriters who wanted to do 'new things' with the character. 'I am very firmly Agatha Christie's Poirot and I won't allow him out of the box in which she put him', he stated (Thomas, 2012).

There is a current trend for updating iconic detectives on British TV. Most notably, Conan Doyle's Sherlock Holmes has been given a radical facelift in Mark Gatiss and Steven Moffat's adaptation for the BBC (2010–). Even the spinster Miss Marple is sexed-up in the opening episode of ITV's *Marple*, featuring Geraldine McEwan, whom we watch bid goodbye to her married lover as he boards a train bound for the trenches. In contrast, John Voorhees notes, *Poirot*'s 'formula is familiar' and predictable (2013). *Poirot* bucks the trend of refreshing crime writing for a contemporary audience, and its static nature raises the question of why audiences remain keen to watch it, especially American viewers who have an almost countless array of innovative alternative detective programmes available.

Poirot's ability to attract viewers and revenue is buttressed by its high production values. Winner of four BAFTAs, and an Edgar Award in the United States, *Poirot* has earned critical kudos for its well-crafted scripts and strong acting on both sides of the Atlantic. Christine Spines argues that 'anyone who's seen previous iterations of … Christie-inspired policiers developed for British TV knows that these are considered to be the acme adaptations and among the only ones to reliably pass muster with even the most discerning of Brit mystery buffs' (2011). Even though Christie's novels belong to a genre – detective fiction – that is associated with popular culture rather than the privileged category of literature, and as such denigrated by some, critical accolades for *Poirot* place it firmly within the sphere of quality programming, underscored by the fact of its presence on PBS – the undisputed hub for quality TV. Knox defines PBS' *Masterpiece* as synonymous with a very particular type of heritage quality drama in the United States (2012, p. 31). Worth noting is the distinction between what counts as quality TV among many in the British industry, however, as Knox recognises when she quotes Channel 4's former programme director Jeremy Isaacs, who asserts that *Masterpiece* represents the 'worst of what we do' – 'simple, safe costume dramas' (2012, p. 45).

Knox's assessment gestures toward the ideological import of the *Poirot* stories, which are deeply embedded in the partly imagined values of Edwardian England. Susan Rowland suggests that Poirot himself represents an English anti-type, labelling him 'an affront to English masculinity in his neatness, fussiness, demands for fine food and central heating', and because he can be critical of English habits (2001, p. 63). Poirot is remarkably different from the type of detective developed by most classic writers of the genre during the inter-war years in Britain. Ngaio Marsh's Roderick Alleyn belongs to the English gentry, and Dorothy Sayer's Lord Peter Wimsey is a wealthy aristocrat. They are members of the established order, for whom investigating crimes is a hobby. To the contrary, Poirot is a former Belgian policeman whose comfortable standard of living depends on attracting wealthy clients.

Christie was outspoken about her love-hate relationship with her character. Earl F. Bargainnier quotes her speaking about Poirot in 1938: 'There are moments when I have felt: "Why, why, why did I ever invent this detestable, bombastic, tiresome little creature?" … eternally straightening things, eternally boasting, eternally twirling his moustache, eternally tilting his egg-shaped head' (2005, p. 45). And yet, Poirot cuts a dapper figure in upper-class circles, within which he moves with ease. Despite the slight whiff of labour about him, there is nothing in Poirot's character to detract from either his social respectability, or his relation to the traditional view of the British justice system as compassionate and paternal. Indeed, his outsider status, a common trope of the detective genre, enables him to act as a benign critical friend of the English establishment. Structurally, his good-natured criticisms of English food and love of outdoor pursuits afford a gently ironic perspective on English identity.

As a Belgian repeatedly mistaken for French, Poirot possesses a façade of foreign mannerisms, but his many quirks, which so annoyed his creator, paradoxically align him more closely with other classic British detectives by placing him in the tradition of English eccentrics. Historically, personal eccentricity has been not merely tolerated in English society, but positively valued as a specific incarnation of Englishness. David Long's *English Country House Eccentrics* (2011) demonstrates the close connection between eccentricity and social respectability by mapping the peculiarities of the gentry; whereas Edith Sitwell's classic *English Eccentrics* (1933) asserts that: 'Eccentricity exists particularly in the English, and partly, I think because of that peculiar and satisfactory knowledge of infallibility that is the hallmark and birthright of the British nation. This eccentricity, this rigidity, takes many forms' (p. 16). Thus, Poirot's heightened individualism, combined with his ability to solve the most baffling crimes, places him in the very best of English company and serves to endear him to the reader/viewer.

Christie's framing of Poirot recalls the England of Empire. She gives the character a birth date at some point in the mid-nineteenth century, and places him as a war refugee in 1916 England where readers first encounter him in *The Mysterious Affair at Styles* (1916). Though in the midst of the First World War, the nation remained a global power, with a far-reaching cultural influence, and in the course of solving mysteries, Poirot ventures across Britain's colonial territories. Yet, wherever we encounter him, we find ourselves, like Rupert Brooke's eponymous soldier, in a place that is 'forever England.' Thus, it is fitting that most of Christie's Poirot stories are set in England, specifically the Home Counties, and frequently in country houses, for beneath the mask of foreignness, Poirot functions to validate English nationalist sentiment.

Detective novels are generally perceived as structurally conservative. They follow a tight set of generic rules, something especially true for the puzzle-fiction that Christie helped invent. Similarly, they are viewed as ideologically conservative. Critics are divided about the politics of Christie's fiction, with some viewing her work as conservative and even reactionary, whereas others suggest she challenges established values at least as often as she confirms them. Stephen Knight identifies Christie's original readership as the English property-owning class, and mainly women who shared a background of socially formative experiences with her (1980, p. 107). Christie's 1977 (posthumously published) autobiography makes clear her longing for imperial England. As a retrospective on Christie's work in *The New Yorker* makes clear, her fictional world mirrored the society in which she felt at home:

> Her people are upper middle class, or … upper class. They gaze with astonished disgust at housing developments and supermarkets. They complain bitterly about how heavily they are taxed and how they can no longer afford to maintain the grand houses they saw as their birthright. Eventually, they sell these huge piles to the nouveau riche.
>
> (Anon., 2010)

Christie's autobiography contains wistful accounts of her childhood in the seaside resort of Torquay, Devon. Before her father's financial difficulties, she recalls how he would spend his days at his club, return home in a cab for lunch, and go back to the club for an afternoon of whist, returning home in time to dress for dinner. Christie's mother, free of mundane domestic chores, spent her time writing poetry and dabbling in esoteric interests ranging from Theosophy to Zoroastrianism (1977, p. 13; p. 23) Christie's novels nostalgically evoke the kind of Englishness represented by affluent members of her parents' generation. One need not read far to see how her fiction is driven by a sense of melancholy loss for a presumed authentic Englishness – an identity she believed had been eroded by the cultural forces unleashed in two world wars.

Christie's conservatism is replicated in ITV's highly faithful adaptations. The England presented to viewers represents a social idyll, one that is defined by archaic class hierarchies that represent continuity and security for the upper-classes. Poirot himself displays values that English nationalist discourse designates as peculiar to Englishness: a devotion to fair play and justice being chief among them. Significantly, his allegiance is to a trans-historical system of 'natural justice' rather than any statutory framework that might be polluted by post-war liberal values. He works independently to solve crimes, with the result that 'good' is seen to prevail over 'evil' through locating the guilty individual and the restoration of the status quo. Poirot's ordinary background seems to contrast with his extraordinary traits, and his sense of duty with his independence, but in fact, they accord with a popular literary trend that followed the First World War, which Gill Plain defines as an attempt to validate and restore the individual in the aftermath of the excesses of death that characterised the Great War (2001, p. 34).

Christie helped usher in the golden age of detective fiction during the modernist period. Whereas modernist writers responded to the devastation of the Great War and the social changes that followed by rejecting established stylistic forms and abandoning faith in traditional beliefs and institutions, Christie eschewed such innovations. Preferring traditional narrative forms, she also maintained allegiance to pre-War social conventions. Her conservatism appealed to a large section of the reading public, for whom radical social change was disorienting and frightening. Christie's fiction could enable readers imaginatively to neutralise social changes. Similarly, *Poirot* appeals to viewers because it offers a comfortable experience, where the greatest challenge one faces is guessing 'whodunnit.' On a deeper level, it feeds into a contemporary longing among some segments of English society for a bygone and largely mythical England.

This sense of nostalgia marks the series from its beginning. Consider Clive Exton's adaptation of 'The Dream' (1937) – episode 10, series 1. Christie writes:

> Hercule Poirot gave the house a steady appraising glance. His eyes wandered a moment to its surrounding, the shops, the big factory building on the right, the blocks of cheap mansion flats opposite.
>
> Then once more his eyes returned to Northway House, relic of an earlier age – an age of space and leisure, when free fields had surrounded its well-bred arrogance. Now it was an anachronism, submerged and forgotten in the hectic sea of modern London. (2011, p. 623)

The mournful tone of this passage is reproduced on screen through dialogue between Poirot and Hastings, as well as the use of colour and sound to suggest that the landscape has been irremediably tarnished by modernity. The men arrive at Northway House on a chilly evening. Darkness shrouds the still grand manor, but which now abuts a pie factory. The destruction of the rural beauty that once surrounded it is punctuated by a loud hiss of steam emitted by the factory's smokestacks, which startles the men and provokes Hastings to observe that the owner 'lives above the shop.' The fact that Northway House is now owned by the untitled Mr. Farley, whose wealth comes from making large numbers of horrible pies, clearly underscores the sense of deterioration of the English social fabric. As Janice Doane and Devon Hodges (1987) suggest, nostalgia takes its emotional energy from this kind of opposition between an idealised past and a ruined present.

Setting is not the only means through which *Poirot* fuels a sense of longing for an age of greater certainty. How Poirot solves and sometimes prevents crimes, as well as the nature of the crimes, is another way to mythologise and signal the metaphorical restoration of an English golden age. In 'The Kidnapped Prime Minister' (1990, season 2, episode 8), Poirot foils a plot to kidnap Mr. David McAdam, who is described by Christie as 'more than England's Prime Minister – he *was* England, and to have removed him from his sphere of influence would have been a crushing and paralyzing blow to Britain' (2011, p. 95). By saving McAdam, Poirot ensures much more than the safety of an individual. He guarantees also the perpetuation of a set of dominant political and social conventions that, in reality, were already in the descendant when the story was published in 1923.

At a time when British national sovereignty has been the subject of fierce debate, especially with regards to its membership of the European Union,

Poirot offers the contemporary British viewer a chance to share imaginatively in a world where threats to social stability are easily identifiable and foiled. This kind of comfort-viewing stands in contrast to other ironic iterations of period mystery drama, most notably ITV's *Midsomer Murders* (1997–). Whereas *Midsomer* also deliberately evokes the style and social structure of 'Golden Age' detective fiction, Tiffany Bergin illustrates how it does so as an act of 'intentional pantomime': it is structured and filmed in a way designed to call attention to its own artificiality (2012, p. 87). *Midsomer's* violence, gore, profanity, and postcoital dialogue also stands in marked contrast to the straight-laced gentility of *Poirot*, which is designed to lure the viewer away from unpleasant aspects of contemporary daily reality.

Jake Wallis Simmons compares *Poirot* to the pleasures of a gentleman's club – 'a reassuringly fixed point, the echo of a civilised English way of living, a place where people still prefer a silver salt cellar that doesn't pour to a plastic one which does.'[6]

> There have been minor cosmetic changes over the years … but essentially Poirot is Poirot, and watching it makes one feel that all is right with the world.
>
> Far fetched it may be, but here's the thing: we need this stuff. Unlike with modern police dramas, Poirot keeps us at all times several steps removed from reality, and that is really the whole point. When the final episode airs next month, Britain will doubtless become a slightly less colourful and reassuring place. (2013)

Simmons' review resonates with Raymond Williams' construction of a 'culture of feeling' (1961, p. 64) – a shared set of perspectives and values that characterise a generation or era and that are observable in cultural forms, including literary and visual ones. *Poirot* is unusually faithful to the 'culture of feeling' that informs Christie's fiction, marked by her Edwardian political worldview. Her biographer, Laura Thompson, relates how, as a child, Christie was 'protected by structure and certainty' (p. 20), and as an adult she 'lived in an enclosure, that of the upper-middle class into which she was born' (p. 145). A recurrent indicator of this is the racial exclusiveness of *Poirot's* world. One connection Christie shares with modernists like Pound and Eliot is an 'unfortunate egregious racism' (Birns and Birns, 1990, p. 124). The prominent figure of the social outsider in her fiction ties into the kind of caricature of the alien 'other' that is a feature also of British tabloid journalism and less salubrious right-wing political propaganda.

Threatening foreign characters abound in *Poirot*, reinforcing the idea of unbridgeable difference between 'us' – the English – and 'them' – everyone else, and which underpins much current public discourse about the dangers of immigration. A prime example is found in Christie's *Cards on the Table* (1936), adapted as a feature-length episode, (2006, season 10, episode 2). Firstly, there is uncertainty about the dark-skinned, effeminate

Mr. Shaitana's origins: 'Whether [he] was an Argentine or a Portuguese or a Greek, or some other nationality, rightly despised by the insular Briton, nobody knew' (Christie, 1969, p. 10), but there is no uncertainty regarding his illegitimate presence in England. Hence, Mr. Shaitana is duly dispatched by one of his many blackmail victims.

In narrative terms, the removal of Shaitana, alien in terms of his racial, sexual and national difference, allows for the reaffirmation of conservative values and patterns of division between groups in English society that stem from its imperial history. According to Roland Robertson, one 'of the major features of modernity which has had a particularly powerful impact with respect to nostalgia is undoubtedly the homogenizing requirements of the modern nation state through much of the twentieth century in the face of ethnic and cultural diversity' (1992, p. 153). Outside the box, so to speak, the series' nostalgic elements could serve as palliative for viewers who are concerned about foreign threats to a traditional understanding of English identity and culture, that is, by virtue of offering a congealed Englishness. In short, *Poirot* defines Englishness as superior to an ultimately containable 'other,' thus helping allay anxiety about the spread of multiculturalism that began with post-Second World War immigration.

Poirot in America: Nostalgia and Consumerism

Poirot's nostalgic appeal is not limited to a national audience, but rather has a global resonance. The model of national identity exported in *Poirot* resembles what Stephen Haseler describes as 'theme-park Englishness' (1996, p. 57). This is the 'English product' that is sold around the world and is favoured especially by American audiences. The idea that such a contrived replica of English political and social mores resonates with contemporary American viewers appears aberrant when this brand of conservatism is compared to the values that allegedly uphold the American way of life – democratic and egalitarian. However, it looks less unusual if, following Haseler, one understands Englishness within the context of the televisual heritage industry as being principally about lifestyle and status (1996, p. 57). The fictional English heritage of natural Toryism fits snugly with American consumer capitalism, and the ever-present desire to demonstrate social superiority, and indeed the quintessence of Americanness, by means of acquiring a certain type of material lifestyle. Middle-class Americans may buy many, if not all, the accoutrements of Englishness displayed in *Poirot*. For those lacking the capital for mimicry, the series allows a vicarious taste of a glamorous, aristocratic world of leisure.

Images of the series' 1930s Art Deco surrounds are commonplace in its advertising, whether press releases, network websites, or promotional materials for DVDs and streaming services. When *Poirot* was first broadcast in the United States, *The New York Times* applauded its arrival in a review that emphasises the series' faithful recreation of period England: 'Once again the British producers bring into play a boutique's worth of togs and furnishings from the 1930s, along with the odd vintage car' (Goodman, 1990) – items that rarely have a narrative function. Paul Kerr assesses the function of props in classic serials, where they are 'employed specifically as signifiers of the past ... Such ambitions of authenticity function to factify the fiction, literally to prop it up, performing a positivist role as the tangible trace of a lost era' (1982, p. 13). *Poirot* is crafted to evoke a sense of pleasure in the display of heritage artefacts. Poirot's flat and the houses he visits are filmed to show in detail their upmarket Art Deco settings, and he is frequently filmed in his dressing room taking meticulous care over his period costumes. In this way, *Poirot* may be compared to other instances of heritage drama, such as *Upstairs Downstairs* (LWT, 1971–75). Discussing the iconic 1970s series, Helen Wheatley describes how the room functions as television's definitive space: the television studio is a room in which another room is created, which is then broadcast into the viewer's room (2005, p. 145), with the fictional spaces reflecting and/or influencing how viewers design their real life spaces.

Poirot's boutique style is a key factor in its phenomenal international success, illustrated by comparison to the relative lack of success of contemporary British programmes abroad. In 1999, a report for The Department of Culture, Media and Sport, Broadcasting Policy Division concluded that the style and content of the majority of British programming, and the nation's image portrayed therein, is unattractive to foreign audiences.[7] In 2008, BBC One's *Spooks* and *Hustle* were 'going great guns' – but according to Hedges these were 'the exceptions rather than the rule' (quoted in Shepherd, 2008). Shows such as *Eastenders* are perceived as filled with distasteful characters and storylines that 'show ... a relatively poor, down at heel place, which does not inspire interest' (quoted in Carson and Llewellyn-Jones, 2001, p. 9). This remains the case, as evidenced by a recent PACT report on UK exports, which cites overly domestic content as an obstacle to programme sales (TRP Research, 2014, p. 3). American viewers, who are most sought after by commercial networks and advertisers, do not want to watch unvarnished portrayals of poverty and social failure being experienced by an unglamorous working class, but rather they seek to engage with images that play into the consumerist aspirations of American capitalism.

Linda Hutcheon refers to the 'commercialization of nostalgia' in the mass media, citing advertising campaigns for Ralph Lauren's fragrance *Safari* as typical of media that invites the viewer to miss things that he or she never lost and experience 'armchair nostalgia' for a time never experienced (pp. 254–55). Like Lauren's advertising narratives for *Safari*, *Poirot* enables the viewer to consume the nostalgic style of an ostensibly less problematic imperial era, at most for the cost of a DVD, but certainly without any tangible social costs. The successful commercialization of nostalgia is associated with technological advances; as Hutcheon notes, nostalgia no longer relies on individual memory or desire, but rather technology enables quick access to an 'infinitely recyclable past' (pp. 250–51). Ultimately, corporate sponsors and brand advertisers support the entertainment industry's capability to furnish the public with a storehouse of nostalgic images on film and TV that may be recycled because marketing research suggests that nostalgic products 'create or recall positive affective responses,' especially among 'baby-boom' and senior citizen markets (Haylena and Holak, 1991) – two key demographic groups for *Poirot*.

Poirot's popularity is not entirely due to the charm of its luxurious lifestyle, though; it also carries ideological resonances for American viewers comparable to those of British ones, a theory buttressed by similarities in audience demographics. Drawing upon Nielsen data, PBS reports that 'over the course of a year, nearly 90% of all U.S. television households – and 217 million people – watch PBS. The breakdown of PBS's full-day audience reflects the overall population with respect to race/ethnicity, education and income' (Anon., 2014). However, if we break these statistics down according to programming type, socio-economic differences between audiences for particular series become clear. Charlotte Brunsdon uses the term 'sociology of taste' to describe the 'demonstrable links between social origins/position/trajectory and taste sets' in television viewing (1990, p. 74). *Poirot's* American followers represent such a niche demographic. They share similar social biographies with those who prefer the heritage variety of mystery drama in the United Kingdom, tending to be upmarket, older (outside the 16–34 age bracket), and, like Christie's original readership, primarily female.[8]

Having inherited the role of the great imperial power from Britain, John McGovern argues that Americans' Anglophilia lies in US expansionist impulses. He uses the James Bond franchise as a case study to show what British cultural exports reveal about Anglo-American relations. He argues:

> The pleasures of the empire are experienced through Bond. The promises of capitalism are embodied in the lifestyle of Bond; travel to exotic locations across the globe, sex with beautiful women, luxurious accommodations, high-end cuisine and expensive booze.
>
> (McGovern, 2012)

Not all of these characteristics are shared with *Poirot*, but there are enough commonalities to render McGovern's comments applicable to this exemplar of heritage TV. Besides, *Poirot's* upmarket audience can more likely afford a taste of grandeur, evidenced by the lucrative corporate sponsorship from Exxon Mobil and luxury brands Viking River Cruises and Ralph Lauren that the show has helped PBS to access.

America's status as a global power, however, does not preclude the nation's susceptibility to fears about the potential for its power to be diminished by a host of internal and external threats. The 'War on Terror' represents an incessant reminder of the nation-states' vulnerability and the possibility of being drawn into costly and seemingly unending foreign conflicts. Like their British counterparts, Americans experience anxiety about a range of identity issues. Increasing immigration from Central America, conjoined with extra-legal border crossings from Mexico, calls for illegal immigration amnesties, and concomitant 'culture wars' are perceived as threats to the privileged status that white, Anglo-Saxon Protestants have held tradition- ally as *the* distinctively American social grouping. Further, Americans must contend with their fears about the loss of a traditional American way of life without the help of stabilising grand narratives of bourgeois progressivism or religion that were available to previous generations.

Heta Pyrhönen asserts that the typical settings for, and even the conun- drums in, Christie's novels reflected her classes' sense of confidence about being able to control their world, a world in which individualism is care- fully balanced with collectivism, wealth rightly accompanies morality, and notions of duty because freely chosen safeguard a system of living that promises the respectable classes continued enjoyment of the lifestyle they have earned (1994, pp. 100–101). The ideological field upon which *Poirot* is structured enables it, albeit partially, to anaesthetise one to the discon- certing effects of the postmodern condition – for a brief moment it can return the viewer to a mythical premodern age where traditional narratives go unquestioned, society coheres, and where no threat, foreign or domes- tic, can disturb the order of things for long. For Robertson, the accelerated speed and attendant cultural complexities of globalisation amplify the need for nostalgic forms of a secure world order (1992, p. 146; p. 162), making nostalgia just as much an issue of post-modernity as modernity. The success of *Poirot*, as exemplar of UK heritage programming, suggests that television adaptations of the English mystery genre represent an important cultural space for accessing the kind of nostalgic experience many contemporary British and American viewers seek.

Notes

1. Since 2008 under the umbrella titles *Masterpiece Classic*, *Contemporary* and *Mystery!*.
2. The abbreviated title *Poirot* will be used throughout the rest of the chapter.
3. New episodes were not filmed on a yearly basis, with repeats being shown when there was a production hiatus.
4. The variety of sources that estimate Christie's sales offer figures that vary from 2 million to 4 billion units sold, with translations into 45–50 languages, with books remaining in print in over 90 countries.
5. For example, in contrast to CBS Entertainment's *Thirteen at Dinner* (1985) and Warner Brothers' *Murder in Three Acts* (1986).
6. Simmons quoting Anthony Lejeune's *The Gentleman's Clubs of London*.
7. Report titled: *Building a Global Audience: British Television in Overseas Markets*.
8. See Chozick, 2012. This is also true of UK viewers; see Rogers, 2008.

References

A&E, 1996. *A&E Television Networks*. [pdf] [online] Available at: http://www.loc. gov/film/pdfs/tva&e.pdf [Accessed 5 August 2014].

Agatha Christie: Poirot – The Definitive Collection (Series 1–13). 2013. [DVD] London, England: ITV Studios Home Entertainment.

Anon., 2010. Queen of crime: How Agatha Christie created the modern murder mystery. *The New Yorker*. [online] Available at: http://tinyurl.com/on5eo4o [Accessed 5 August 2014].

Anon., 2014. PBS Overview. [online] Available at: http://www.pbs.org/about/ background/ [Accessed 14 August 2014].

Bargainnier, E. F., 2005. *The Gentle Art of Murder: The Detective Fiction of Agatha Christie*. Bowling Green, OH: Bowling Green State University Popular Press.

Birns, N. and Birns, M. Boe, 1990. Agatha Christie: modern and modernist. In: R.G. Wagner & J. M. Frazer, eds., 1990. *The Cunning Craft: Original Essays on Detective Fiction and Contemporary Literary Theory*. Macomb, IL: Western Illinois University. pp. 120–34.

Broadcast, 2003a. Trade talk – wheeler-dealer. [online] Available at: http://www. broadcastnow.co.uk/trade-talk-wheeler-dealer/1120846.article [Accessed 4 August 2014].

Broadcast, 2003b. Granada ships period drama to Middle East. [online] Available at: http://tinyurl.com/o88vacp [Accessed 4 August 2014].

Broadcast, 2004. Granada International success in Asia. [online] Available at: http:// tinyurl.com/m4wt4tu [Accessed 4 August 2014].

Broadcast, 2005. Granada Int leads charge into China. [online] Available at: http:// tinyurl.com/jwtxweo [Accessed 4 August 2014].

Broadcast, 2006a. Granada Int sells shows into South Korea. [online] Available at: http://tinyurl.com/l6bee8c [Accessed 15 August 2014].

Broadcast, 2006b. UK programme exports hit new high. [online] Available at: http:// tinyurl.com/p3lh9nk [Accessed 15 August 2014.].

Bergin, T., 2012. Identity and nostalgia in a globalised world: Investigating the international popularity of *Midsomer Murders*. *Crime Media Culture*, 9(1), pp. 83–99.

Brunsdon, C., 1990. Problems with quality. *Screen*, 31(1), pp. 67–90.

Carson, B. and Llewellyn-Jones, M., 2001. *Frames and Fictions on Television: The Politics of Identity within Drama*. Chicago, IL: University of Chicago Press.

Chozick, A., 2012. PBS takes on the premium channels. *The New York Times*. [online] Available at: http://tinyurl.com/7dbvamq [Accessed 14 August 2014].

Christie, A., 1923. The kidnapped prime minister. In: *The Complete Short Stories: Hercule Poirot*. 2011. London, England: Harper Collins. pp. 94–109.

Christie, A., 1937. The dream. In: *The Complete Short Stories: Hercule Poirot*. 2011. London, England: Harper Collins. pp. 623–43.

Christie, A., 1969. *Cards on the Table*. London, England: Fontana Books.

Christie, A., 2001. *Agatha Christie: An Autobiography*. New ed. London, England: Harper Collins.

Chu, H., 2013. David Suchet bids farewell to Agatha Christie's *Poirot*. *Los Angeles Times* [online] Available at: http://tinyurl.com/ppqayq5 [Accessed 5 August 2014].

Dillin, J., 1992. The actor behind popular 'Poirot.' *The Christian Science Monitor*. [online] Available at: http://www.csmonitor.com/1992/0325/25141.html [Accessed 6 August 2014].

Doane, J. and Hodges, D., 1987. *Nostalgia and Sexual Difference: The Resistance of Contemporary Feminism*. London, England: Methuen.

Fry, A., 2009. Overview: distributors weather the storm. *Broadcast*. [online] Available at: http://tinyurl.com/nxampfn [Accessed 8 August 2014].

Garner, R., 2012. The mysterious affair of how Agatha Christie is teaching foreigners English. *The Independent* [online] Available at: http://tinyurl.com/7yfrzg8 [Accessed 3 February 2015].

Goodman, W., 1990. Review/television; enter Poirot, ever the natty narcissist. *The New York Times*. [online] Available at: http://tinyurl.com/o9pzvxb [Accessed 13 August 2014].

Haseler, S., 1996. *The English Tribe: Identity, Nation and Europe*. Basingstoke, England: Palgrave Macmillan.

Havlena, W.J. and Holak, S.L., 1991. "'The Good Old Days': observations on nostalgia and its role in consumer behavior". *Advances in Consumer Research* 18, pp. 323–29. [online] Available at: http://www.acrwebsite.org/search/view-conference-proceedings.aspx?Id=7180 [Accessed 21 Dec. 2015].

Holmwood, L., 2011. TV Poirot is bumped off. *The Sun*. [online] Available at: http://tinyurl.com/njm6ywf [Accessed 14 February 2013].

Hurrell, W., 2009. ITV Global scores bumper US drama sale. *Broadcast*. [online] Available at: http://tinyurl.com/la7hket [Accessed 5 August 2014].

Hutcheon, L., 2009. Irony, nostalgia and the postmodern. In: M. Hughes-Warrington, ed., *The History on Film Reader*. London, England: Routledge. pp. 249–59.

IMDb, 2004. *Agatha Christie: Poirot*. Season 9, episode 3. [online] Available at: http://www.imdb.com/title/tt0406516/business?ref_=tt_dt_bus [Accessed 4 August 2014].

ITV, 2009. Half-yearly report: ITV plc interims results 2010. [online] Available at: www.itvplc.com/investors/announcements/half-yearly-report-0 [Accessed 16 August 2014].

Jensen, E., 2012. Home video company cashing in on British revivals. *The New York Times*. [online] Available at: http://tinyurl.com/lw978er [Accessed 31 July 2014].

Knight, S., 1980. *Form and Ideology in Crime Fiction*. Basingstoke, England: Palgrave Macmillan.

Kerr, P., 1982. Classic serials: to be continued. *Screen*, 23(1), pp. 6–19.

Knox, S., 2012. Masterpiece Theatre and British drama imports on US television: discourses of tension. *Critical Studies in Television*, 7(1), pp. 29–48.

Long, D., 2011. *English Country House Eccentrics*. Stroud, Gloucestershire: The History Press.

McGovern, J., 2012. Skyfall: Anglophilia in the age of globalization. *Highbrow Magazine*. [online] Available at: http://tinyurl.com/oan9t2l [Accessed 15 August 2014].

McLean, G., 2003. *Poirot: Five Little Pigs* (ITV1). *Broadcast*. [online] Available at: http://tinyurl.com/k5adgmx [Accessed 4 August 2014].

Plain, G., 2001. *Twentieth-Century Crime Fiction: Gender, Sexuality and the Body*. Edinburgh, Scotland: Edinburgh University Press.

Pyrhönen, H., 1994. *Murder from an Academic Angle: An Introduction to the Study of the Detective Novel*. Columbia, SC: Camden House.

Radio Times, 2011. *Poirot* and *Miss Marple* to return to ITV. [online] Available at http://tinyurl.com/m65s8w9 [Accessed 14 February 2013].

RLJ Entertainment, 2014. Agatha Christie's Poirot final three mysteries only on Acorn TV. [press release] 21 July 2014. Available at: http://www.rljcompanies. com/phpages/wp-content/uploads/2014/07/RLJ-Entertainment-Announces-Agatha-Christies-Poirot-Final-Three-Mysteries-Only-on-Acorn-TV.pdf [Accessed 5 August 2014].

Robertson R., 1992. *Globalization: Social Theory and Global Culture.* London, England: SAGE.

Rogers, J., 2008. Ratings focus: Poirot and Tess. *Broadcast.* [online] Available at: http://tinyurl.com/lx9meqz [Accessed 14 August 2014].

Rowland, S., 2001. *From Agatha Christie to Ruth Rendell: British Women Writers in Detective and Crime Fiction.* Basingstoke, England: Palgrave Macmillan.

Sefton, D., 2014. PBS to track behavior of viewers pledging to core-schedule programs. Current.org. [online] Available at: http://tinyurl.com/kpplwyz [Accessed 5 August 2014].

Shepherd, R., 2008. Hot topic: International distribution. *Broadcast.* [online] Available at: http://tinyurl.com/nvxsa8z [Accessed 15 August 2014].

Simmons, J.W., 2013. Agatha Christie's Poirot: The big four, ITV, review. *The Telegraph* [online] Available at: http://tinyurl.com/ojgw6ps [Accessed 14 August 2014].

Sitwell, E., 1933. *English Eccentrics: A Gallery of Weird and Wonderful Men and Women.* 1971. Harmondsworth, England: Penguin.

Spines, C., 2011. A double dose of Agatha Christie: PBS Masterpiece serves up a new batch of Hercule Poirot and Miss Marple episodes. *word&film.* [online] Available at: http://tinyurl.com/nfbcpu2 [Accessed 6 August 2014].

Thomas, C., 2012. Hanging up his moustache: Suchet confirms next series of Poirot will be his last. *The Daily Mail.* [online] Available at: http://tinyurl.com/pycfq9u [Accessed 6 August 2014].

Thompson, L., 2007. *An English Mystery: Agatha Christie.* London, England: Headline Publishing.

TRP Research (2014). *UK Television Exports FY 2013/2014.* [pdf] [online] Available at: http://www.thecreativeindustries.co.uk/media/354136/tv-exports-survey-fy-13-14-1-.pdf [Accessed 4 February 2014].

Tryhorn, C., 2006. ITV slays rivals with *Poirot* film. *The Guardian.* [online] Available at: http://tinyurl.com/ljg6k3p [Accessed 4 August 2014].

Voorhees, J., 2013. Many challenges confront Poirot in new '*Mystery!*'. *The Seattle Times.* [online] Available at: http://tinyurl.com/qatmzdx [Accessed 6 August 2014].

Wagner, C., 2012. Acorn Media takes control of Agatha Christie estate. *Redeye.* [online] Available at: http://tinyurl.com/p6ypcqn [Accessed 5 August 2014].

Wheatley, H., 2005. Rooms within rooms: Upstairs Downstairs and the studio costume drama of the 1970s. In: C. Johnson and R. Turnock, eds. *ITV Cultures: Independent Television Over Fifty Years.* Maidenhead, England: Open University Press. pp. 143–58.

Williams, R., 1961. *The Long Revolution.* 2011. London, England: Vintage.

12 Lost in Translation – TV Remakes, Transatlantic Determinants and the Failure of *Prime Suspect USA*

Deborah Jermyn

TV montage or clip shows have become a cheap and common staple in contemporary television schedules; these magazine-style 'lists' are generally held together by a handful of soundbites from celebrity commentators, then padded out with clips, often taken from nostalgia-inducing old favourites. In September 2001, Channel 4's *Top Ten TV* series broadcast a show dedicated to 'Cops' with David Soul of *Starsky and Hutch* fame (ABC, 1975–79) at the helm. Reaching the end of the countdown, suspense was accompanied by some apparent surprise as it was revealed: 'Yes – our number one TV cop is a woman!' Ten years after its ITV debut, *Prime Suspect*'s Jane Tennison (ITV, 1991–2006) – the lone woman Detective Chief Inspector compellingly played by Helen Mirren, who so memorably battled within and against the systemically misogynistic police service to convict a serial killer – had taken the prime position in this TV poll. It is difficult to imagine today that this result would be divulged in quite this way, where, implicitly, the foregrounding of Tennison's gender marks it/her as still something of a novelty for the genre. Women protagonists now populate the genre with ubiquity, unquestionably in large part due to the success of *Prime Suspect*. But equally, the poll result evidenced popular recognition of just how widely esteemed, and how landmark, *Prime Suspect* had already become in the history of TV crime drama by this time. The show would eventually number seven 'mini-series' broadcast with some irregularity, but always met with huge anticipation, over a period of 15 years (Jermyn, 2009). Along the way, as Gray Cavender and Nancy Jurik note, it 'aired in seventy-eight countries and worldwide audiences for some episodes [approached] two hundred million viewers' (2012, p. 3). The show was held to be a triumph for British TV – critically and commercially, nationally and internationally – from the outset. This chapter sets out to explore how it is, then, that against the backdrop of such an accomplished history, in 2011 *Prime Suspect* was adapted into a US remake only to be swiftly dropped from schedules after just a single season.

But the story begins in the United Kingdom, in 1991. First broadcast that April in two, 2-hour episodes shown on consecutive evenings, the original *Prime Suspect* was truly an 'overnight sensation.' As *The Sunday Times* review put it, 'Prime Suspect was the programme people talked about on Monday morning, and even more of Tuesday morning ... It was, simply, one of the grittiest and most gripping dramas of recent memory' (Anon., 1991). The first of its awards soon followed, including BAFTAs in 1992 for Best Drama Serial and Best Actress, and an Edgar Allen Poe Award for writer Lynda La Plante in 1993. The series also quickly gained worldwide distribution, being broadcast in the United States from its inception on public television as part of the prestigious *Masterpiece Theatre* series. Unsurprisingly given all this, speculation soon began to circulate that the show would be picked up for a remake. In 1993, as *Prime Suspect 2* scooped the first of its Primetime Emmys (for Outstanding Mini-Series) a US remake started to seem increasingly probable, with conjecture particularly centring on whether Mirren would be cast again as DCI Jane Tennison. There were rumours that the series would be made into a film, but that producers would want a better-known star than Mirren was at that time to take the lead. As Lorrie Lynch's syndicated 'Who's News' column pondered in 1993, 'It's true she has not been asked ... Hollywood reports suggest the producers want a big name, like Jodie Foster' (Lynch, 1993), Foster being an obvious proposition given her Oscar-winning turn as FBI investigator Clarice Starling two years earlier in *The Silence of the Lambs* (directed by Demme, 1991). But despite much seeming enthusiasm for the project in an era where textured, determined female detectives were pushing back generic boundaries like never before, the film never materialised.

As the series continued though, remake speculation never entirely subsided. Finally, in 2009 the old rumours became reality as US network NBC at last greenlit the new *Prime Suspect* (distinguished here as *Prime Suspect USA*). By 2011, however, following a 13-episode run commencing that September, it was all over; almost before it had really started, it seemed, the series was cancelled after one season, having garnered an average audience of not quite 5 million viewers an episode by that November (Goldberg, 2011). So what went wrong? How is it that one of the most influential and highly regarded TV police series of all time failed to 'make it' in its transatlantic translation? This is the curious question I seek to answer in what follows, primarily through examining the newspaper reception of the show (largely drawn from the United States), and supported by textual analysis of the remake and existing critical work on transnational remakes. Reviewers, of course, cannot lay claim to speak for 'regular viewers' (if such a thing can be said to exist at all) but their work does constitute a useful archive in terms of accessing prevalent discourses circulating in the history of a text at any one time. With its seemingly established US fan-base, apparently solid commercial potential, and after years of anticipation, why did *Prime Suspect USA* bomb? We are currently in an era in which TV crime drama and crime fiction literature seemingly travel internationally more visibly and fluidly than ever before. As early as 2007, Robin Nelson observed of 'TV fiction exchange' that, 'More than ever, a product successful in one context is likely to be taken up in another' (2007, p. 4). This is a position that has seemingly been bolstered further still of late in particular respect of TV crime drama, following a series of much heralded transnational exports and remakes of 'Scandi-crime' including *Wallander* (Sweden, 2005–; remade BBC, UK, 2008–) and *Forbrydelsen* (DR1, Denmark, 2005–12; first broadcast BBC4, 2011; remade as *The Killing* (AMC, US, 2011–)) (see Janet McCabe's chapter in this collection). The high-profile cancellation of *Prime Suspect USA* was certainly not without precedent.[1] But given its long 'back story', the failed transnationalisation of this crime drama stands out as a notable instance of the challenging path tread by remakes, and commentators were left all the more curious to understand how the series had been 'lost in translation.'

While in what follows there is insufficient space to interrogate the enduringly thorny question of television 'authorship', I want instead to explore how a number of other key interrelated generic, institutional and (inter)national contexts come into play here. These were connected, firstly, to the inability of the 'reinvented' series to brand itself sufficiently and distinctively in relation to an 'old' series – and, crucially, a British one at that – as well as within a marketplace by now saturated with crime drama; and, secondly, to the notion that in a post-*Prime Suspect* TV landscape, the 'novelty' of a woman detective leading a show can no longer in itself function sufficiently as a primary selling-point. There are of course many factors that can contribute to the success or failure of a series, from the degree and nature of marketing, to scheduling, to the status of the current 'competition', and it is only possible to focus here on a handful of the most evidently prevalent themes that emerged in the series' reception. Nevertheless, this process provides a rich opportunity too, to address a neglected arena in television studies, where until recently discussion of international television formats has traditionally centred on 'how American (Hollywood) programs are rebroadcast or remade in other markets', pursuing 'concerns about cultural imperialism', while 'British-to-American remakes [have] been largely unexplored' (Lavigne and Marovitch, 2011, p. x). Indeed, in the same vein, in his study of fans' Internet discussion boards about the US remake of *Life on Mars*, Brett Mills found that many commentators were preoccupied with 'America's perceived domination of the global cultural sphere', while never considering the remake as possibly constituting 'cultural imperialism *from* Britain *to* America' (2012, p. 137). British and American TV drama are to be more fully understood not in isolation but in relation to each other, situated both 'culturally and historically'[2] and as 'outcomes of a long tradition of mutual exchange, observation and collaboration', as Elke Weissman observes (2012, p. 3). What does the failure of *Prime Suspect USA* begin to suggest, then, about the recent operation of UK-US transatlantic remakes and the criteria for carving out or exchanging success across national borders in the competitive landscape of contemporary crime TV?

Prime Suspect USA: Reinvention, Remake or Reboot?

It wasn't until 2009, some three years after *Prime Suspect: The Final Act* was broadcast, that news of NBC's deal with ITV was confirmed. On 2 September, *Variety* reported that 'NBC is developing a new take on the groundbreaking UK drama series "Prime Suspect"', slated to be 'the first output in a multiproject pact sealed by NBC and ITV Studios.' This was just the latest recent partnership between ITV and NBC, however, since 'in a reverse of this pact, ITV earlier signed on to produce and air a UK version of long-running Peacock procedural "Law and Order"' (Schneider, 2009) which had launched in the United Kingdom earlier in 2009. In the same article NBC Primetime Entertainment President Angela Bromstad was cited as stating, 'We want to carefully choose a couple of iconic titles this year to reinvent, and our intention is to create another classic television show from this brilliant original format ... we are incredibly excited about this modern vision for the show' (ibid). The new deal was particularly important for ITV because it constituted a return to a high profile drama deal in the United States. In the 1990s, as Granada America, ITV had adapted a number of popular UK series for US networks, albeit with disappointing results in the case of short-lived titles such as *Cracker* (ITV, 1993–96; ABC, 1997–98) and *Cold Feet* (ITV, 1997–2003; NBC, 1999–2000). More recently, however, ITV's transatlantic deals had centred on selling reality TV formats to US networks, including *Hell's Kitchen*; *I'm A Celebrity, Get Me Out of Here!* and *Celebrity Fit Club* (Irvine, 2009), while other UK broadcasters had intermittently managed to sell culturally esteemed 'scripted' formats that had gone on to covetable lasting success in the United States, including *The Office* (BBC, 2001–03; NBC, 2005–13) and *Shameless* (Channel 4, 2004–; Showtime, 2011–). Talent shows, quiz formats and 'factual entertainment' rather than drama have predominated in these deals; a context which made the *Prime Suspect* deal all the more significant, constituting a 'major leap back into the U.S. scripted game' for ITV (Schneider, 2009).

Albert Moran has designated this process of creating US TV remakes from UK originals as falling under 'the cultural practice of format franchising' (2011, p. 37). He goes on:

> Television program format franchising has become a major component of the international television industry since the 1990s as program producers seek insurance against failure in an increasingly fragmented and diverse television marketplace. The format program remake represents an attempt by producers and broadcasters to repeat in a second market the success achieved in an original market.
>
> (Moran, 2011, p. 38)

It is in the light of such strategic safeguarding 'against failure' that Sarah Hughes in *The Independent* was want to remark, 'On paper, the new version should have worked', noting the pedigree of Executive Producer Peter Berg

as 'the man behind the award-winning *Friday Night Lights*' and the participation of 'its creator Lynda La Plante' (Hughes, 2012) as further evidence
of such strategising. In this same vein, the US's NPR (National Public Radio)
observed in its coverage of the impending new series shortly before it aired
that, 'From a network perspective, it makes perfect sense. *Prime Suspect* ush-
ered in a wave of successful TV shows starring tough, mature women: *The
Closer. Damages. The Killing.* So why not reboot a known franchise with
Maria Bello occupying Helen Mirren's redoubtable shoes?' (Ulaby, 2011).
Having taken their time over the crucial decision of who would play the new
'Jane Timoney', and 'waiting a year before announcing indie darling Bello had
the role' (Hughes, 2012), NBC had eventually succeeded in casting a highly
regarded actor, twice nominated for Golden Globes in *The Cooler* (Kramer,
2003) and *A History of Violence* (Cronenberg, 2005). Mirren was recurrently recognised in media coverage as a tough act to follow in an iconic role,
and one might have expected this casting to have proved a sticking-point in
the series' failure. But in fact, even among the often lacklustre reviews, there
was a great deal of support for Bello, with Mary McNamara noting in *The
Los Angeles Times*, for example, that '[she] radiates an impatient, soulful
intensity that pulls it all together' (McNamara, 2011a).

However, in the world of television 'perfect sense' is arguably a chimera,
and the 'insurance against failure' that Moran's imagined producers long for
is an impossibility. Looking more closely at these discussions, the variation
or imprecision in language that started to emerge in these earliest accounts
of *Prime Suspect USA* retrospectively seems telling. One might construe that
some of these differences in 'naming' the text point to the creative haziness
that is always at stake in the transnational 'remake' and which was to prove
problematic for the series, as well as distinctions between popular versus
trade discourse. Interestingly, the word 'remake' is absent in Schneider's
Variety article though used in the headline (perhaps being more readily used
by trade journal discourse in relation to feature films). So, prior to the *Prime
Suspect USA* deal, the United Kingdom's new *Law and Order* is instead
described as being a 'version' of the established one, while previous 1990s
series were 'adapted' by Granada America. Of the forthcoming *Prime Suspect,* it notes the NBC series will be a 'new take' on the UK series; while
in the quote attributed to Bromstad, she observes that the intention is 'to
reinvent' the show (my italics), working with the 'original format' ('format'
being an industry term adopted by Moran also). It is also intriguing to note
how Bromstad describes the desire to 'create another *classic*' while simultaneously staking a claim to NBC's '*modern* vision for the show'; an almost
paradoxical ambition which prefigures problems in *Prime Suspect USA*'s
identity, in that it is thereby both tied to an undeniably celebrated, landmark
antecedent it seeks to trade on by association *and* must demonstrate it is
more than a potentially archaic or entirely derivative remake of it.

Further haziness around the new series' status or relationship to the original can be seen too from Neda Ulaby at NPR who refers to it as a 'reboot',

while she goes on to use the industry terminology adopted by Moran also by referring to the series as a 'franchise' (a term which seems fitting too when recalling the variety of writers and directors that worked on the original series). 'Reboot' seems to suggest a more direct relationship with an original – being a text which, to use Carlen Lavigne's definition, 're-envisions a narrative from the beginning but shares its name and copyright with an older property' (2014, p. 2) – while Bromstad's 'reinvention' seemingly implies something a little less imbricated. Indeed, John Doyle's Canadian *Globe and Mail* article declared assertively, 'Prime Suspect is a reboot, not a remake' (Doyle, 2011) – but never explains what he takes the difference to be. Was the series' failure fed in part, then, by a certain obfuscation or misalignment of expectations at work amongst critics, audiences and producers regarding how closely the two series would be allied, or what the exact nature of the relationship between them was?

The 'reboot' debuted in the Thursday 10pm slot on 22 September 2011. London-based Met Police DCI Jane Tennison was now Irish-American New York detective Jane Timoney, recently transferred from midtown to a new squad where her aggressive male colleagues suspect she has wrangled the move by dint of an earlier affair with the bureau chief. The pilot echoes certain aspects of the first season of *Prime Suspect* closely, without being a slave to it; Timoney, like Tennison before her, is excluded from her colleagues' 'boys' club' and unfairly passed over to head up a murder-enquiry, then finds herself belatedly in charge and unravelling the shoddy work of her predecessor after he has a fatal heart attack. She again juggles a hectic work-life balance and lives with a partner anxious to integrate his son from a previous relationship into their shared home. At another level its difference from the original is made very visually evident though, with much foregrounding of the new Manhattan location made by way of recurrent aerial grid-plan shots of the city's endless streets and skyscrapers, sequences which act, too, as interstices aiming to help mask the commercial breaks, accompanied by bursts of rock music.

It was soon evident that NBC's tactic of trying to build audience momentum by scheduling additional repeats had failed to produce the desired results, and media reports very quickly began to speculate that the series' renewal beyond its 13 episode initial commission was doubtful. Curiously, some of this coverage noted that the 'Prime Suspect' name had actually been counterproductive. According to this perspective, the new title was a burden rather than a benefit, implying a continuity that was not really there and a pedigree it couldn't hope to match, where it would have been more strategic for the show to mark its territory as something distinctive with a name of its own. In fact, respected critic Matt Zoller Seitz writing on Salon.com months before the new 'import-adaptation' was broadcast anticipated even then that *Prime Suspect USA* would inevitably be dramatically different (and inferior) to the original due to the institutional differences between ITV/UK commercial terrestrial television versus NBC/US network television; hence, 'it might as well save itself the trouble and call the series something other than *Prime Suspect*' (Zoller Seitz, 2011a). Similarly, June Thomas observed, 'Watching the pilot cemented my sense that NBC had made a terrible mistake by using the famous title' (Thomas, 2011); while Mary McNamara's mid-season review bemoaned the series' imminent cancellation despite its host of 'terrific actors', arguing, 'The only things keeping it from being a solid success are its title and original concept' (McNamara, 2011b). Rather than having managed to exploit the 'Prime Suspect' name as an invaluable commodity in the television marketplace, as a brand preloaded with 'quality TV' connotations, for these critics, the series name had backfired, both failing to deliver expectations of the original contained in the title and diluting the series' already conflictual claim to an identity of its own. How, and why, then, was *Prime Suspect USA* perceived to be 'different' from the original – and very often a pale imitation of it?

'The Problem is the Venue': Remakes and Network Television

Despite years of speculation about a US remake, by 2011 critic Matt Zoller Seitz was predicting months before broadcast that the series was doomed to disappoint, since 'NBC is not the venue for it' (2011a). In familiar terms, he points to how the format of US network TV is fundamentally different to and at odds with the British industrial context that produced the original *Prime Suspect*, and thus how it will be unable to facilitate anything like a comparable series:

> The problem is the venue. The US broadcast TV model – with its 42-minutes-a week, 22 weeks-a-year format, frequent commercial interruptions and still oppressive content restrictions – is the enemy ... They're making product to sell into syndication, where the magic number is 100 episodes ... This get-it-done mentality might have long-term financial rewards, but it's the enemy of quality and consistency ... More important, American TV is averse to letting race, class, politics and other touchy elements drive stories because it might make viewers and sponsors skittish.
>
> (Zoller Seitz, 2011a)

There are clear echoes here of a long-standing tradition in UK versus US television criticism which champions the supremacy of British TV. This might have less mileage today in the light of the latest 'golden age' of US TV and the rich body of work produced in particular in recent years by non-network TV, such as the premium subscription cable channel HBO, which works to less stringent restrictions, not least because they need not worry about keeping sponsors happy. Still, as Lavigne and Marcovitch note, there remains 'a widespread notion of British-made entertainment as inherently superior in terms of complexity and intelligence' (2011, p. ix). Zoller Seitz explicitly lays the blame for this at the door of the US network's industrial practices, which do not allow for series with small numbers of episodes or 'erratic gaps between seasons' as the UK does, a climate which facilitates greater creative freedom and energy. Indeed, Albert Moran points to exactly this pressure having been at work too in the 'cross-border commodity traffic' of the (also short-lived) US remake of British criminal psychologist drama *Cracker*, where reduced screen-time led to 'truncated' storylines (Moran, 2011, pp. 41–51).

The sometimes 'erratic' delivery of UK series that Zoller Seitz speaks of was, as noted, very much the case with *Prime Suspect*'s broadcast history in the United Kingdom. There were hiatuses of several years duration between some 'seasons', and single criminal cases would be pursued typically over two, 2-hour shows rather than solved within 42 minutes. This was a format that also allowed for an unusually reflective and unhurried (if episodic) relationship to evolve between the audience and a rare instance of a woman protagonist leading a prestige drama over the course of an extended period of 15 years. In fact, it is interesting to note the parallels between *The Sunday Times* review of the first *Prime Suspect* back in 1991, and Zoller Steitz's 'preview' of the remake 20 years later. The *Times*' reviewer notes that the series' unparalleled realism 'separated *Prime Suspect* from a thousand US cop shows' (Anon., 1991); while two decades on Zoller Steitz reminds us of the numerous ways the original 'wasn't an American-style network TV show.' Both of them seem at pains, then, to point to how *Prime Suspect* *wasn't* like all those syndicated cop series, hinting there is something fundamentally and profoundly different at work between UK versus US television, where production contexts affect *content* and help produce characteristically different, and perhaps recognisably 'national', sensibilities within crime drama – the latter notion being a particularly problematic one that nevertheless enduringly holds popular weight.

I want to unpack all this now in order to unravel a number of interlinked aesthetic, industrial and socio-historical issues that are at stake here. Some of these predate *Prime Suspect* and operate beyond and outside it, some are specific to the contexts of the series itself; but all point to Zoller Steitz's sense that a US remake of the series that hoped to become a comparable 'classic television show', as NBC Primetime Entertainment President Bromstad put it (cited in Schneider, 2009), was always going to have its work cut out for it.

Tennison's versus Timoney's Temporalities

One of the major themes to emerge across the critical reception of *Prime Suspect USA* was the change in *pace* from the original. A closer consideration of the screen time given over to the entire UK series versus the single US season is instructive here. The original seven season series ran for 15, two-hour broadcasts, which included adverts. The DVD box set reveals a running time of 1488 minutes, then, or just under 25 hours, which were broadcast over a period of 15 years. By contrast, *Prime Suspect USA* ran for 13 episodes of 41–42 minutes duration, or just under 9 hours screen time, over a period of 4 months. The paradox that emerges here is that while *Prime Suspect USA* evidently had considerably *more* screen time in a shorter period to engage audiences and establish interest in the new Jane Timoney, the original series – which had far less screen time over a comparable period – was infinitely more leisurely in pace. Those original 25 hours programmed across 7 seasons comprised just 9 self-contained storylines; *Prime Suspect USA's* 9 hours of screen time comprised 13 storylines. Notwithstanding the fact that different styles and modes of television and of crime drama had come into vogue since 1991, reviewers recurrently commented on the striking shift in the change of pace, which was often seen to have had a detrimental effect on the complexity of the narratives and storytelling, while inevitably entailing (sometimes seemingly irritating) aesthetic modifications.

The Telegraph ran a review from Rachel Ray in Washington, for example, where she observed the original's 'even pace', which had allowed one to 'dwell on the fine performances', had been replaced by a version that 'is fast and furious in quickly solving the crime in one hour' and 'more action-oriented' (Ray, 2011). The acclaim won by recent crime series with an often 'slow' sensibility, from *The Wire* (HBO, 2002–08) to the widely exported *Forbrydelsen* (*The Killing*), seems to suggest that a taste for such an aesthetic is still very much alive and that the genre is broad enough to accommodate a variety of styles at any one time; the more frenetic pace of *Prime Suspect USA*, then, was not merely a case of the remake seeking to abandon a somehow dated style. One might point here to the awkward conceit it introduces to aid exposition, where loud radio 'news bulletins' are used as a kind of narrative voiceover between scenes to provide quick but clumsy updates on the progression of the investigations. According to Sarah Hughes' frank summary, 'Where the original was introspective and clever, as interested in the quiet moments around the edges as the big reveals, the new show bangs us over the head' (2012). Writing for the *National Post*, Nathalie Atkinson notes too how the loss of the 'even pace' and instances of stillness is felt not just at the level of story and character, but the aesthetics of sound: 'The original was quiet, slow and introspective, using music sparingly for atmosphere. In NBC's version, every transition is accompanied by raucous rock guitar' (Atkinson, 2011). Hughes' use of the term 'quiet moments' chimes very keenly with analysis I have made of the show elsewhere, where I have noted that scenes of high drama were counterbalanced with 'occasional, unexpected and quietly observed diversions into the police labs' in scenes of 'dead time' (Jermyn 2010, p. 81); and the import of the pauses that were built into Mirren's performance, where the camera sometimes lingers with/on her in an empathetic process akin to what Richard Dyer has identified in Classical Hollywood as 'the private moment' (cited in Jermyn, 2003, p. 57). Forty-two minute episodes do not allow for such temporal and narrative indulgences. If the original, then, was filmed in 'motion-picture time' (Shoals, 2011), the remake was reimagined as 'New York paced' (Ray, 2011).[3]

From New Scotland Yard to New York City

Ray's notion of the remake having to adopt a 'New York pace' segueways nicely into another issue associated with the change of production context: namely, might one of the 'problems' the project faced from the onset have been the somewhat nebulous matter of whether there is a 'national' difference in UK versus US crime drama traditions and tastes, or what Nelson has posed as, 'a national disposition towards TV fiction, if not quite a national style' (2007, p. 13). This seemingly led to something of a 'crisis of identity' where the 'classic British drama' – a form perceived to be 'too dark, too slow, unattractive, too gritty or socio-political' by some international audiences (Steemers, cited in Nelson, 2007, p. 14) – had to be adapted to meet 'the standard-issue American cop show' expectations of US network drama (Zoller Seitz, 2011b).

Nowhere is the 'problem' of the shift in pace and concomitant crisis in identity embodied more evidently in *Prime Suspect USA* than in the curious decision to overhaul the opening title sequence nearly halfway through the series, a shift presumably instigated as a remedial response to disappointing viewing figures. Early episodes borrowed the stark opening title credit of the original, featuring simply the 'PRIME SUSPECT' title in white-on-black capitals which appeared briefly on-screen before cutting straight to the unfolding drama. This was subsequently dropped for what one might, advisedly, call a more familiarly or recognisably 'Americanized' crime-drama rapid montage credit sequence, featuring scenes of the stars doing their perilous work. There are frantic chases and gun showdowns, punches are thrown and badges are flashed – there is even the promise of hot sex between Jane and her boyfriend – all of which clearly situated the series as being, in Ray's words again, a 'fast and furious ... action oriented' cop show. In fact, the *Los Angeles Times* review went as far as to say:

> [There] is no point in comparing the two shows – they are separated by too much time, space and national personality. *We Americans* like our detectives to size up the situation in a glance, deftly wrest information and aid from witnesses, and fix any mistakes instantly and dramatically.
>
> (McNamara, 2011b) (my italics)

Here, McNamara clearly speaks to a notion of shared cultural taste for a certain mode of storytelling in US network crime drama. Indeed, another recurrent term or discourse that appeared in numerous US newspaper reviews of the remake was that it had been 'Americanized' (see, for example, Atkinson, 2011; Shoals, 2011) – though despite this it evidently still failed to hit the mark with US audiences.

For Weissmann, the concept of being 'Americanized' remains useful in that it 'draws attention to the fact that even in the supposedly 'global' cultural world of US television there is a need for localization, a fact that cultural commentators have highlighted with the development of the phrase 'glocalization' (2012, p. 86). But, of course, one must be wary here of any implication that US television has not facilitated original, innovative crime drama of its own, and of what can appear to be sweeping generalisations about the tastes of an entire (highly diverse) nation. As Jonathan Nichols-Pethick notes, far from the genre being reductive or static in recent years, the competitive environment of 'post-network' television since the 1980s has facilitated the expansion of different stylistic approaches in the US police drama (2012, pp. 30–35). And as Lavigne and Marcovitch observe, '[The] concept of Americanization can be challenging to define – the United States after all, contains many cultural groups, and Americanization may also be conflated with globalization, modernization, or economic imperialism' (2011, pp. xii–xiii). To suggest that American audiences somehow only have a taste for 'Americanized' crime drama also seems at odds with the original series' Primetime Emmy awards and PBS *Masterpiece Theatre* success in the United States, which seemingly pointed to an established audience for the remake readily in place stateside. In fact, these accolades might be said to have constituted something of a deceptive picture, giving the impression of a bigger US audience reach for the original show than had really been the case. As Steemers has observed, 'PBS's low audience share means that British drama is not widely known by US audiences, except among a small Anglophile minority with a high degree of cultural, educational and financial capital' (2011, p. 4). Clearly this was never going to be the demographic that NBC had to woo in order to achieve network success, and neither was there ever any guarantee that this audience would return for an 'Americanized' *Prime Suspect* 2, since it was evidently non-'Americanized' drama they were seeking out on *Masterpiece Theatre* in the first place. Nevertheless, the existence of this audience group, however small, does highlight some of the problems contained in a discourse that claims to speak for '*we* Americans ....'

Feminism and Obsolescence: 20 Years of 'The Daughters of Jane'

These contexts help inform understanding of the remake's failure, bringing cultural and industrial specificities to bear on our grasp of 'what went wrong.' But alongside these one must examine the socio-historical differences at stake between the two; most crucially here, that in the 20 years that had passed between the original and the remake, the work of feminism and the rhetoric of equal opportunities in the workplace – and media representations of these – had undergone something of a transformation. In 2011 in the United States alone, just some of the recent and current crime series with female leads or major female protagonists included not only *The Closer* (TNT, 2005–12), *Damages* (FX Network, 2007–10; Audience Network,

2011–12) and the remake of *The Killing* (AMC, 2011–14) as already noted, but also *Crossing Jordan* (NBC, 2001–07), *In Plain Sight* (USA Network, 2008–12), *Rizzoli & Isles* (TNT, 2010–) and *Homeland* (Showtime, 2011–). In this televisual and cultural landscape, critics of *Prime Suspect USA* repeatedly pointed to how the timeliness of the issues explored in the original series, which was every bit as much about Tennison's survival in a chauvinist profession as it was about solving a serial killer case, was now past. As such, the remake's depiction of sexist bullying in the NYPD was deemed to be 'out-of-date and overdone' (Doyle, 2011) and 'retrograde' (Atkinson, 2011). In 1991, the original's narrative innovation was to have a woman lead a murder enquiry while simultaneously dismantling the institutionalised misogyny of the police, a reconfiguration of TV crime drama that felt bold, fresh and edgy (Jermyn, 2003). Twenty years on, however, and particularly in a postfeminist culture which has undermined recognition of workplace inequalities and misleadingly rendered talk of the 'glass-ceiling' as somehow naively and absurdly out-moded, 'no-one makes the argument that the public just won't accept a female homicide detective. Good news for society, bad news for [*Prime Suspect USA*] which [has] lost the novelty and underlying tension of the [original]' (McNamara, 2011a). As Charlotte Brunsdon has noted, *Prime Suspect* potently 'demonstrated that crime shows with female leads can be extremely successful', and consequently 'the daughters of Jane Tennison' (2012, p. 375) have become protagonists in a plethora of women-led cop shows that now exist on both sides of the Atlantic. In such a changed context, Jane Timoney in and of herself simply did not stand out.

In essence, *Prime Suspect USA* never really found its 'Unique Selling Point'. Its 'workplace sexism' thread seemed passé, and no one raises an intrigued eyebrow at the prospect of a female detective anymore. The adoption of the 'Prime Suspect' moniker spoke to a celebrated classic British series that the remake held only an opaque relationship with, which it was unlikely to ever replicate in terms of innovation or acclaim, so that the shared title and the connotations it invoked arguably worked against the interests of the new series in establishing a 'modern vision' (Bromstad, cited in Schneider, 2011), or identity of its own.

And yet. By way of conclusion, I want to point to two stories encountered in the process of this research, which signal the fact that a wish for still more spiky material from Tennison and 'the daughters of Jane' may not yet be as obsolete a desire as the reports above suggest. The first of these looks ahead a little to the future, and news of an announcement that a *Prime Suspect* prequel is planned for 2016 – to be called simply *Tennison* and adapted for television by La Plante herself from her novel of the same name (Plunkett, 2014). Timed to mark the 25th anniversary of the first season, this anticipated project and its drive to give still greater subjectivity to Tennison, to return to her once more and mine her history in new detail even after the show's demise, seems to underline again a demand for complex, multidimensional women characters at the heart of TV crime drama.

So too, of course, does it speak to a wish to exploit what is evidently Tennison's ongoing commercial potential, as a text which still signals a highpoint in the history of British 'quality TV' and which offers the opportunity to win new audiences for *Prime Suspect* while satisfying the nostalgic desire of original viewers. And finally, an anecdote, tucked away in a news story about the NBC press conference for *Prime Suspect USA*. Executive Producer and writer Alexandra Cunningham, whose first TV screenwriting job was on celebrated US cop show *NYPD Blue* (ABC, 1993–2005), was asked whether the 'brutally overt sexism that Timoney faces' wasn't overdone: '"Sexism isn't gone", Cunningham said. "There are a lot of squads in the NYPD where *there are no female detectives at all*, still, even though it's 2011"' (Doyle, 2011) (my emphasis). It is in the context of this remark that we must be cautious regarding just how much the visibility of contemporary television's postfeminist women cops chimes with the visibility of women in the actual institutions they represent; and remain critically alert to the hegemonic manoeuvring that lies behind any suggestion that *Prime Suspect USA* failed because workplace sexism, or the professional exclusion of women from enduringly 'male' domains, are topics that no longer have traction in the twenty-first century.

Acknowledgements

I am very grateful to Gray Cavender, Andrea Esser, and Ruth McElroy for their helpful comments in the writing of this chapter.

Notes

1. For example, the US version of quirky UK crime drama *Life on Mars* (BBC, 2006–07; ABC, 2008–09) was also cancelled after one season.
2. Indeed, in other recent work, and as touched on here, I particularly examine the failure of *Prime Suspect USA* in the context of postfeminism (see Jermyn, 2016).
3. Weissmann identifies similar shifts at stake in the (short-lived) US adaptation of *Life on Mars*, noting that UK drama's propensity for 'long dialogue pauses' affords its actors '[the] time to develop the complexities of their characters', whilst 'the US (network) adaptations with their shorter running times cannot (or at least not always) grant such insights' (2012, p. 91).

References

Anon., 1991. Review of *Prime Suspect*. *The Sunday Times*, 14 April.
Atkinson, Nathalie, 2011. Prime Suspect remake is defective work. *The National Post*, [online] 5 October. Available at: http://news.nationalpost.com/2011/10/05/prime-suspect-remake-is-defective-work/ [Accessed 23 December 2014].
Brunsdon, Charlotte, 2012. Television crime series, women police, and fuddy-duddy feminism. *Feminist Media Studies*, 13(3), pp. 375–94.
Cavender, Gray and Jurik, Nancy C., 2012. *Justice Provocateur: Jane Tennison and Policing in Prime Suspect*. Urbana, IL: University of Illinois.

Doyle, John, 2011. NBC's reboot of Prime Suspect? A cockamamie idea. *The Globe and Mail*, [online] 4 August. Available at: http://www.theglobeandmail.com/ arts/television/nbcs-reboot-of-prime-suspect-a-cockamamie-idea/article626138/ [Accessed 23 December 2014].

Goldberg, Lesley, 2011. NBC shuts down production on 'Prime Suspect.' *The Hollywood Reporter*, [online] 15 November. Available at: http://www.hollywood reporter.com/live-feed/nbc-shuts-down-production-prime-261837 [Accessed 23 December 2014].

Hughes, Sarah, 2012. Prime Suspect: there's something suspect about this dated detective. *The Independent*, [online] 18 June. Available at: http://www.independent.co.uk/ arts-entertainment/tv/features/prime-suspect-theres-something-suspect-about-this-dated-detective-7857152.html [Accessed 23 December 2014].

Irvine, Chris, 2009. ITV sells Prime Suspect to NBC without Helen Mirren. *The Telegraph*, [online] 3 September. Available at: http://www.telegraph.co.uk/culture/ tvandradio/6129257/ITV-sells-Prime-Suspect-to-NBC-without-Helen-Mirren. html [Accessed 23 December 2014].

Jermyn, Deborah, 2003. Women with a mission: Lynda La Plante, DCI Jane Tennison and the reconfiguration of TV crime drama. *International Journal of Cultural Studies*, 6(1), pp. 46–63.

Jermyn, Deborah, 2010. *Prime Suspect*. London, England: BFI Macmillan.

Jermyn, Deborah, 2016. Silk blouses and fedoras: the female detective, TV crime drama and the predicaments of postfeminism', *Crime, Media, Culture*, DOI: 10.1177/1741659015626578. pp. 1–18.

Lavigne, Carlen and Marcovitch, Heather, 2011. Introduction. In: Lavigne, Carlen and Marcovitch, Heather, eds., 2011. *American Remakes of British Television: Transformations and Mistranslations*. New York, NY: Lexington Books. pp. ix–xvii.

Lavigne, Carlen, ed., 2014. *Remake Television: Reboot, Re-use, Recycle*. New York, NY: Lexington Books.

Lynch, Lorrie, 1993. Who's new. *Boca Raton News*, 4 July. p. 40.

McNamara, Mary, 2011a. TV reviews: 'Charlie's Angels' and 'Prime Suspect.' *Los Angeles Times*, [online] 22 September. Available at: http://articles.latimes. com/2011/sep/22/entertainment/la-et-charlies-angels-prime-suspect-20110922 [Accessed 23 December 2014].

McNamara, Mary, 2011b. Critic's notebook: take the cuffs off 'Prime Suspect.' *Los Angeles Times*, [online] 24 November. Available at: http://articles.latimes. com/2011/nov/24/entertainment/la-et-critics-notebook-20111124 [Accessed 23 December 2014].

Mills, Brett, 2012. 'American Remake – Shudder': online debates about *Life on Mars* and 'British-ness.' In: Stephen Lacey and Ruth McElroy, eds., 2012. *Life on Mars: From Manchester to New York*. Cardiff, Wales: University of Wales Press. pp. 133–44.

Moran, Albert, 2011. Americanization, Hollywoodization, or English language variation? Comparing British and American versions of *Cracker*. In: Carlen Lavigne and Heather Marcovitch, eds., 2011. *American Remakes of British Television: Transformations and Mistranslations*. New York, NY: Lexington Books. pp. 35–54.

Nelson, Robin, 2007. TV fiction exchange: local/regional/national/global. *Critical Studies in Television*, 2(2), pp. 4–17.

Nichols-Pethick, Jonathan, 2012. *TV Cops: The Contemporary American Television Police Drama*. New York, NY: Routledge.

Plunkett, John, 2014. Lynda La Plante writing Prime Suspect prequel. *The Guardian*. [online] Available at: http://www.theguardian.com/media/2014/feb/18/prime-suspect-prequel-lynda-la-plante-tennison [Accessed 23 December 2014].

Ray, Rachel, 2011. Prime Suspect, NBC, US television, review. *The Telegraph*, [online] 26 September. Available at: http://www.telegraph.co.uk/culture/tvandradio/8789008/Prime-Suspect-NBC-US-television-review.html [Accessed 23 December 2014].

Schneider, Michael, 2009. NBC plans 'Prime Suspect' remake. *Variety*, [online] 2 September. Available at: http://variety.com/2009/biz/news/nbc-plans-prime-suspect-remake-1118008061/ [Accessed 12 November 2009].

Shoals, Bethlehem, 2011. Adaptation decay: four more BBC shows you may see stateside. GQ.com, [online] 22 September. Available at: http://www.gq.com/entertainment/movies-and-tv/201109/bbc-remakes-prime-suspect [Accessed 12 November 2009].

Steemers, Jeanette, 2011. British television in the American marketplace. In: Carlen Lavigne and Heather Marcovitch, eds., 2011. *American Remakes of British Television: Transformations and Mistranslations*. New York, NY: Lexington Books. pp. 1–16.

Thomas, June, 2011. NBC's *Prime Suspect* remake is 20 years behind the times. *Slate*, [online] 22 September 2011. Available at: http://www.slate.com/blogs/browbeat/2011/09/22/nbc_s_prime_suspect_remake_is_20_years_behind_the_times.html [Accessed 23 December 2014].

Ulaby, Neda, 2011. NBC's 'Prime Suspect' hopes to fill some very big and very British shoes. National Public Radio recordings archive and blog, [blog] 19 September. Available at: http://www.npr.org/blogs/monkeysee/2011/09/19/140533965/nbcs-prime-suspect-hopes-to-fill-some-very-big-and-very-british-shoes [Accessed 23 December 2014].

Weissmann, Elke, 2012. *Transnational Television Drama: Special Relations and Mutual Influence between the US and UK*. Basingstoke, England: Palgrave Macmillan.

Zoller Seitz, Matt, 2011a. The problem with American remakes of British shows. Salon.com, [online] 9 February. Available at http://www.salon.com/2011/02/09/prime_suspect_remake/ [Accessed 23 December 2014].

Zoller Seitz, Matt, 2011b. Relax, 'Prime Suspect' fans, the remake has promise. Salon.com, [online] 22 September. Available at http://www.salon.com/2011/09/22/prime_suspect_remake_2/ [Accessed 23 December 2014].

Notes on Contributors

Jonathan Bignell is Professor of Television and Film in the Department of Film, Theatre & Television at the University of Reading. His current research is on the technologies and aesthetics of space in TV drama, and he led the AHRC research project 'Spaces of Television: Production, Site and Style' which studied British TV drama from the 1950s to the 1990s. His work on TV drama includes his study 'The Police Series' in *Close Up 03* (edited by Gibbs and Pye, 2009), and two editions of *British Television Drama: Past, Present and Future* (co-edited with Stephen Lacey). He has published a wide range of articles and chapters, and serves on the editorial advisory boards of journals including the *New Review of Film and Television Studies*, *Studies in Documentary Film*, *Critical Studies in Television*, and the *Journal of Science Fiction Film and Television*.

Steve Blandford is Emeritus Professor of Theatre, Film and Television at the University of South Wales' Faculty of Creative Industries. He has written extensively on theatre, film and TV in the United Kingdom including *Theatre and Performance in Small Nations* (Bristol, Intellect, 2013) and *Jimmy McGovern* (Manchester, Manchester University Press 2013). He recently lead a project examining the decentralisation of television drama production in the United Kingdom and its impact on the representational complexity of British television drama.

Mary F. Brewer is Senior Lecturer in the Department of English and Drama at Loughborough University. Her research is located in English and American Studies, addressing drama and literature from the late nineteenth century through the contemporary. Her publications include monographs on gender and theatre (*Race, Sex and Gender in Contemporary Women's Theatre* – Sussex Academic Press), race and theatre (*Staging Whiteness* – Wesleyan UP), edited collections on feminist philosophy (*Problems of Exclusion in Feminist Thought* – Sussex Academic Press), the theatre of Harold Pinter (*Harold Pinter's The Dumbwaiter* – Rodopi) as well as a range of articles on adaptation studies, war writing, and religion and literature.

Charlotte Brunsdon is Professor of Film and Television Studies at the University of Warwick. She is a leading feminist scholar and author of

The Feminist, the Housewife and the Soap Opera (Clarendon Press, 2000) and *Screen Tastes: Soap Opera to Satellite Dishes* (Routledge, 1997). Her most recent book is a study of G.F. Newman's controversial 1978 crime series, *Law and Order* (BFI, 2010).

Ross P. Garner is a Lecturer in Television Studies in the School of Journalism, Media and Cultural Studies at Cardiff University. His research interests include industrial approaches to mediated nostalgia, cult TV forms, branding, and mediated tourism. He has published articles in the journals *Critical Studies in Television* and *Popular Communication* and is currently preparing a monograph, *Nostalgia, Digital Television and Transmediality*, for publication by Bloomsbury in 2017.

Deborah Jermyn is a Reader in Film and Television at University of Roehampton London. Her books include *Crime Watching: Understanding Real Crime TV* (2006) and *Prime Suspect* (2010) for the BFI Macmillan TV Classics series. She has co-edited and edited a number of collections, including *Understanding Reality TV* (2004) and most recently *Back in the Spotlight: Female Celebrity and Ageing* (2012).

Stephen Lacey is Emeritus Professor of Drama, Film and Television at the University of South Wales. He was co-investigator on 'Spaces of Television: Production, Site and Style' an AHRC-funded project that investigated how the material spaces of production (in TV studios and on location) conditioned the aesthetic forms of programmes. He is a founding co-editor of *Critical Studies in Television*, an international, refereed scholarly journal of fictions for the small screen. He is the author of *Cathy Come Home*, BFI/Palgrave (2010) and *Tony Garnett*, Manchester University Press (2007). He is co-editor with Jonathan Bignell of *Popular Television Drama: Critical Perspectives*, Manchester UP (2005) and *Television Drama: Past Present and Future*, Palgrave (2000; 2nd edition 2014).

Janet McCabe is Lecturer in Film, Television and Creative Industries at Birkbeck, University of London. She edits *Critical Studies in Television* and has written widely on feminism, cultural memory and television. She co-edited several collections, including *Quality TV: Contemporary American TV and Beyond* (2007) and *Reading Sex and the City* (2004), and her latest works include *The West Wing* (2012) and *TV's Betty Goes Global: From Telenovela to International Brand* (2012; co-edited with Kim Akass).

Ruth McElroy is a Reader in Media and Cultural Studies at the University of South Wales where she is Director of the Creative Industries Research Institute. She is co-editor (with Stephen Lacey) of *Life on Mars: From Manchester to New York* (UWP, 2012) and has published numerous essays in journals such as *Critical Studies in Television, European Journal of Cultural Studies* and *Television and New Media*. Ruth is currently

Principal Investigator on an AHRC international network examining television production in small nations out of which she has edited a special issue on the subject for the *Journal of Popular Television* (2016).

Manel Jimenez-Morales has a Doctorate in Social Communication from the Universitat Pompeu Fabra. He is a writer, producer and director of film and television projects, as well as cultural programs (Via Digital, Ona Catalana, Barcelona Ràdio/SER). He has contributed to several studies on communication research and cinema. He has also taught at various German universities.

Jonathan Nichols-Pethick teaches film and media studies at DePauw University where he is Associate Professor of Media Studies. He is the author of *TV Cops: The Contemporary American Television Police Drama* (Routledge, 2012).

Rebecca Williams is Senior Lecturer in Communication, Cultural and Media Studies at the University of South Wales. She has published on TV horror in *Critical Studies in Television* (2011), *Gothic Studies* (2013), *Journal of British Cinema and Television* (2015) and *Reading Angel* (I.B. Tauris, 2005) and on television more broadly in *Continuum, Popular Communication, Media History,* and *Television and New Media.* She is the editor of *Torchwood Declassified: Investigating Mainstream Cult Television* (I.B. Tauris, 2013) and author of *Post-Object Fandom* (Bloomsbury, 2015).

Martin Willis is Professor of English at Cardiff University. He also holds an Honorary Senior Lectureship at the Cardiff School of Medicine, where he advises on medical education. His most recent significant publication is *Vision, Science and Literature, 1870–1920: Ocular Horizons* (Pickering & Chatto, 2011), which won the British Society for Literature and Science Book Prize 2011 and the European Society for the Study of English Cultural Studies Book Prize 2011. He is the author of *Mesmerists, Monsters and Machines: Science Fiction and the Cultures of Science in the Nineteenth Century* (Kent State, 2006) and editor of *Jack the Ripper: Media, Culture, History* (Manchester UP, 2008), *The Victorian Literature Handbook* (Continuum, 2008), *Repositioning Victorian Sciences* (Anthem Press, 2006), and *Victorian Literary Mesmerism* (Rodopi, 2006).

Index

For Product Safety Concerns and Information please contact our EU
representative GPSR@taylorandfrancis.com
Taylor & Francis Verlag GmbH, Kaufingerstraße 24, 80331 München, Germany

www.ingramcontent.com/pod-product-compliance
Ingram Content Group UK Ltd.
Pitfield, Milton Keynes, MK11 3LW, UK
UKHW020941180425
457613UK00019B/498

* 9 7 8 0 3 6 7 8 8 1 0 1 6 *